Transforming Asian Socialism

Transforming Asian Socialism

China and Vietnam Compared

ANITA CHAN, BENEDICT J. TRIA KERKVLIET,
AND JONATHAN UNGER

ROWMAN & LITTLEFIELD PUBLISHERS, INC.
Lanham • Boulder • New York

ROWMAN & LITTLEFIELD PUBLISHERS, INC.

Published in the United States of America
by Rowman & Littlefield Publishers, Inc.
4720 Boston Way, Lanham, Maryland 20706
http://www.rowmanlittlefield.com

ISBN 0-8476-9846-7 (cloth)
ISBN 0-8476-9847-5 (paper)

Printed in the United States of America

♾™ The paper used in this publication meets the minimum requirements of American
National Standard for Information Sciences—Permanence of Paper for Printed Library
Materials, ANSI/NISO Z39.48–1992.

Contents

Contributors

Anita Chan is currently an Australian Research Council Senior Research Fellow hosted by The Australian National University, and co-editor of *The China Journal*. Her present research focuses on management styles, worker-management relations in Chinese enterprises, and the Chinese trade union. Her five books include *Children of Mao* and, as co-author, *Chen Village under Mao and Deng*. A forthcoming edited book is *China's Workers Under Assault* (1999).

Adam Fforde is Chairman of ADUKI Pty Ltd, a consultancy company specializing in Vietnam, and concurrently is a Visiting Fellow at the Research School of Pacific and Asian Studies at The Australian National University. His most recent book on Vietnam is *From Plan to Market: the Economic Transition in Vietnam* (1996). He is currently researching the roles played by factor markets in Vietnam's economic growth since 1989.

Benedict J. Tria Kerkvliet, a political scientist, is head of the Department of Political and Social Change at The Australian National University. A specialist in the Philippines and Vietnam, his books include *Everyday Politics in the Philippines: Class and Status Relations in a Central Luzon Village* (1990). He is currently authoring a book on agricultural collectivization in Vietnam.

Hy Van Luong is Chair of the Department of Anthropology at the University of Toronto. He has conducted extensive field research in Vietnam since 1987 on issues of gender, political economy, and social structure in Vietnam. His major publications include *Revolution in the Village: Tradition and Transformation in North Vietnam, 1925-1988* (1992) and *Culture and Economy: The Shaping of Capitalism in Eastern Asia* (co-edited with Timothy Brook, 1997).

Barrett L. McCormick is an associate professor at Marquette University. He is the author of *Political Reform in Post-Mao China* (1990) and co-editor of *China After Socialism: In the Footsteps of Eastern Europe or East Asia?* (1996) and of the forthcoming volume *What if China Doesn't Democratize?* He is currently doing research on the impact of emerging media markets on China's public sphere.

David Marr is professor in the Pacific and Asian History Division at The Australian National University. His most recent book is *Vietnam 1945: The Quest for Power* (1995). He is currently researching Vietnamese political culture in historical perspective.

Irene Nørlund holds a PhD degree in history from the University of Copenhagen. She is now working on a project about Vietnamese trade unions as a senior research fellow at the Nordic Institute of Asian Studies in Copenhagen. She has co-edited the book *Vietnam in a Changing World* (1995).

Stanley Rosen teaches political science at the University of Southern California. He is the author of numerous books and articles concerning Chinese education, youth, political attitudes, and related topics. His current projects include a study of China's political transition (in collaboration with Joseph Fewsmith) and a study of returnees from abroad and their impact on China's modernization and internationalization (in collaboration with David Zweig).

Mark Selden teaches sociology and history at Binghamton University. His recent books include *China in Revolution: The Yenan Way Revisited* (1995), *Chinese Village, Socialist State* (co-author 1991), and *Living With the Bomb: American and Japanese Cultural Conflict in the Nuclear Age* (co-author, 1997). He is the editor of two book series, at Routledge and at M. E. Sharpe.

William S. Turley is a professor of political science at Southern Illinois University. He is the author of numerous articles and monographs on Vietnamese politics and co-author of *The Economics and Politics of Transition to an Open Market Economy: Vietnam* (Paris, OECD, forthcoming).

Jonathan Unger, a sociologist, is head of the Contemporary China Centre at The Australian National University and co-editor of *The China Journal*. His most recent books are *Chinese Nationalism* (1996) as editor and *China After Socialism: In the Footsteps of Eastern Europe or East Asia?* (1996) as co-editor. He is currently writing a book on rural China.

Brantly Womack is a professor in the Department of Government and Foreign Affairs at the University of Virginia. He has published four books about China and is currently conducting research on south and southeast China.

Alexander Woodside is professor of history at the University of British Columbia. A specialist in Chinese and Vietnamese intellectual and social history, his books include *Vietnam and the Chinese Model: A Comparative Study of Vietnamese and Chinese Government in the First Half of the Nineteenth Century*.

Acknowledgements

This book was initially conceived in 1992 by the Transformation of Communist Systems Project at the Australian National University. At that time Anita Chan, Ben Kerkvliet, David Marr, Barrett McCormick and Jonathan Unger, all researchers of either Chinese or Vietnamese socialism, had been involved in comparative studies with scholars specializing in the former Soviet Union and Eastern Europe. The project was premised on the belief that studying the similarities and differences among countries in those regions could provide valuable insights into their momentous transformations. One of the most evident similarities lay in the parallel reform programs that have been under way in Vietnam and China. We concluded that priority should be given to analysing, comparatively, how these programs are being implemented in each country and the economic, political and social consequences in each. Over the years, other scholars from around the world have joined us in this effort to examine the Chinese and Vietnamese reforms as a paired study. The East-West Center in Hawaii graciously hosted a workshop in mid-1994 that was attended by the contributors to this book. A year later in mid-1995, the Transformation of Communist Systems Project hosted a second workshop at the Australian National University. The chapters in this book grew out of these earlier workshops, evolving in the years since then in line with the shifting circumstances in both Vietnam and China. Several chapters were published in July 1998 in *The China Journal*.

As editors, we owe a debt of thanks to Bruce Koppel of the East-West Center, who kindly arranged for the first of the workshops to be held at his Center. Thanks go, too, to Heli Petryk of the ANU's Contemporary China Centre, without whose assistance the second workshop could not have been held, and to Mark Sidel and Tony Saich of the Ford Foundation, who provided financial support to enable several scholars from China and Vietnam to attend the second of the workshops.

Above all, our gratitude as editors again goes to Heli Petryk, who produced the book from typed manuscripts and disks. Heartfelt thanks are also owed to Gary Anson and Anne Gunn, who helped us to copy-edit the book; Beverley Fraser and Claire Smith of the ANU's Department of Political and Social Change, who provided much-needed assistance in preparing some of the chapters for publication; and Robin Ward of the ANU's Department of International Relations, who prepared the book's index and who, alongside John Ravenhill of the same department, helped arrange for its publication.

This is the third edited volume of scholarship that has been sponsored by the Transformation of Communist Systems Project. The first two were Robert Miller, editor, *The Development of Civil Society in Communist Systems* (1992) and Barrett McCormick and Jonathan Unger, editors, *China After Socialism: In the Footsteps of Eastern Europe or East Asia?* (1996).

ONE

Comparing Vietnam and China: An Introduction

Ben Kerkvliet, Anita Chan and Jonathan Unger*

Close to a decade after the collapse of the Communist states in Eastern Europe and almost as many years after the collapse of the Soviet Union, the Communist Parties in China and Vietnam are not only surviving; they are firmly in the saddle and can look with some satisfaction to their recent records of economic performance. While their erstwhile European counterparts have succeeded in establishing new political institutions and systems of electoral politics and are eager to adopt a capitalist economic structure, almost all of them remain mired in economic difficulties: living standards are generally lower than in the 1980s, and the economies of several of them are in a shambles. Paradoxically, China and Vietnam, the two main Asian socialist countries — without undergoing similar political upheavals and without openly admitting that they welcome capitalism (as opposed to welcoming foreign direct investments) — have been enjoying a period of well-publicized economic boom which even the current Asian crisis has not, to date, seriously dented. China, in particular, with an industrial growth rate unrivalled in the world this past decade, has been touted as a successor to the so-called East Asian miracle economies. Vietnam's economy has similarly "taken off", with impressive growth rates since the late 1980s.

In certain significant respects, they can be regarded as a pair. Both countries, after all, have charted broadly parallel paths in their economies — disbanding agricultural collectives in favour of family farming; moving away from the command economy and toward a market economy in their publicly-owned industrial sectors; allowing private enterprises to emerge in almost all areas of the economy; turning vigorously toward the world market and toward export-oriented industrial drives; and successfully opening their doors to investment by foreign firms. Politically, both countries have shifted quietly

---

*   We wish to thank Allison Ley for helping to find some of the publications we refer to in this chapter and David Marr, Mark Selden and Bill Turley for comments and suggestions for improvement.

away from Marxist ideology and rhetoric; have witnessed a progressive retreat in the ambit of what their Parties attempt to control; have shown tolerance for a limited degree of interest-group politics — and yet at the same time, both countries persist in a Leninist structure of party dominance.

It is time to ask, then, whether there exists an Asian socialist reform model. Beyond the broadest of generalities, to what extent and in what specific areas are China and Vietnam indeed following similar paths to modernization and similar reform agendas? Are they carrying out their economic reforms in the same sequence; is there a common logic to their programs? In the political sphere, where political reforms have been announced in tandem with economic reforms, to what extent are the two Party regimes reshaping the political systems and the bases of their political legitimacy in similar ways? And perhaps most importantly, within the broad similarities of what is occurring in China and Vietnam, what are the differences? This last question takes on a special importance in that it may point to new insights about each country's recent experience — insights that would not be evident if a scholar were to focus only on one country.

Any such comparisons between the reform programs in Vietnam and China also raise historical questions. To what extent are any similarities today a consequence of similar historical traditions and mind-sets and predispositions that stretch back into earlier centuries? To what extent do any present-day similarities reflect similar histories of Communist revolution in the two countries in earlier decades?

The contributors to this book variously delve into these diverse questions. In Chapter 2, Alexander Woodside examines the political and administrative legacy of rule by mandarins in both countries and its present-day implications. This mandarinate — today's intellectual managerial elite — has been instrumental in promoting the need for a catch-up mentality in today's global economy, and Woodside looks backward in time to the roots of this mind-set. The next three chapters comparatively examine the processes of reform transition away from the two countries' recent histories of Leninist socialism. Adam Fforde compares the chronologies in China and Vietnam of this shift from planned to market economies and shows how similarities and differences in the two countries' experiences of the socialist period have shaped somewhat different patterns of economic reform. William Turley and Brantly Womack examine this process of transition in two industrializing urban locations, Ho Chi Minh City (formerly Saigon) and Guangzhou (Canton), and they emphasize the effects of local and central government interactions throughout the decades of Party rule. Ben Kerkvliet and Mark Selden focus on the agrarian sector and reveal how the Chinese government's more extensive penetration of China's rural economy and society during the period of collectives is reflected today in greater government influence in the villages even after the return to family farming.

The final four chapters deal mainly with the political and social consequences of the reforms in specific spheres. Hy Van Luong and Jonathan

Unger, turning attention once again to the countryside, analyse the immediate causes and the ramifications of socio-economic differentiation among the peasantry in the wake of the rural reforms. Barrett McCormick considers the impact of the political reforms on political institutions and political legitimacy in both countries. David Marr and Stanley Rosen comparatively examine the new developments in the educational systems and in the attitudes of youth. And Anita Chan and Irene Nørlund explore the impact of the economic reforms on the operations of trade unions and industrial relations in the two countries.

The Limitations of the Extant Literature, and a New Departure

This volume embarks on a new type of comparative research. Although a relatively large corpus of previous writings has compared China and Vietnam, very few of these books and articles examine topics that are in any way directly relevant to the questions posed in this volume.

One earlier genre of comparative writing about the two countries has focused on the fact that China and Vietnam are neighbours with long interwoven histories. This is well demonstrated in the sizeable volume of English-language scholarly literature that pairs them. Books that compare Vietnam and China outnumber by a wide margin the books that compare Vietnam to any of its other Asian neighbours or that compare China to any other Southeast Asian country.[1] But the bulk of this comparative literature on China and Vietnam emphasizes their foreign relations and policies toward each other and their history of periodic conflicts and wars.[2] Some of the literature examines the ethnic Chinese population in Vietnam.[3] Surprisingly few studies have compared the two nations' political, social or economic

---

[1]   Some evidence for this is that a computerized subject search for holdings in the Australian National University's library catalogue turned up 95 titles with both "China" and "Vietnam", but only 36 with both "China" and "Thailand" (the next highest number), 35 for "China" and "Indonesia", 26 for "China" and the "Philippines", and so on downward in number. For "Vietnam" and other Southeast Asian countries, the highest number was 78 with "Cambodia", then down sharply to 31 with "Laos" and 21 with "Thailand". Counts with other Asian countries were seven each with "Korea" and the "Philippines", five with "Japan", four with "Malaysia", and so on down the line.

[2]   They range from relations in the distant past, most notably Keith Taylor's *The Birth of Vietnam: Sino-Vietnamese Relations to the Tenth Century and the Origins of Vietnamese Nationhood* (Berkeley: University of California Press, 1983) to more contemporary interactions, such as William J. Duiker, *China and Vietnam: The Roots of Conflict* (Berkeley: Institute of East Asian Studies, University of California, 1986). Visitors to Vietnam's Museum of History in Hanoi can get a quick sense of the long periods of conflict, particularly in the middle centuries of the second millennium. The museum features memorabilia, maps, and scale models of wars between the two countries.

[3]   For example, Chang Pao-min, *Beijing, Hanoi, and the Overseas Chinese* (Berkeley: Institute of East Asian Studies, University of California, 1982).

processes despite their resemblance. These few can be clustered according to three time periods.

The first period concerns the two countries' pre-modern social and political institutions. An influential example is Alexander Woodside's book on the civil administrations and imperial courts of Vietnam and China in the nineteenth century. He found many similarities, due in large measure to Vietnam's system having been heavily influenced by China's, though he also found striking differences.[4] In the chapter that he has written for this book he develops his thesis further, pondering on how the shared legacy of this pre-modern political tradition is manifested in the present period of reform transition.

The second cluster of existing comparative studies deals with aspects of political upheaval in both countries during the 1920s and 1930s and the revolutionary struggles of the 1940s and 1950s. The perspective taken by most of the scholars who compare these parallel experiences focuses on Vietnam and looks at China for similarities and differences.[5] A few studies, though, give roughly equal weight to both.[6] Edward Moise's book on the land reforms of Vietnam and China is probably the most often cited study in this category.[7] A perspective that has been adopted by some other writers places the two revolutionary movements and Communist regimes in the context of the international revolutionary movement of the twentieth century.[8]

A third cluster of studies examines the broadly similar current overhaul of the economies of the two countries as they relinquish their state-run planned economies and embrace competitive markets. But most of the studies in this cluster focus only on economic issues with an eye to providing guidance to potential investors.[9] The few that have looked at other aspects of the reforms

---

[4] *Vietnam and the Chinese Model: A Comparative Study of Nguyen and Ching Civil Government in the First Half of the Nineteenth Century* (Cambridge, MA: Harvard University Press, 1971).

[5] See, for example, the chapters in William S. Turley (ed.), *Vietnamese Communism in Comparative Perspective* (Boulder: Westview Press, 1980).

[6] Good examples include Brantly Womack, "The Party and the People: Revolutionary and Postrevolutionary Politics in China and Vietnam", *World Politics*, vol.39 (July 1987): pp.479-507; and David Elliott, "Revolutionary Re-integration: A Comparison of the Foundation of Post-Liberation Political Systems in North Vietnam and China", PhD dissertation, Cornell University, 1976.

[7] Edwin Moise, *Land Reform in China and North Vietnam: Consolidating the Revolution at the Village Level* (Chapel Hill: University of North Carolina Press, 1983).

[8] Eric Wolf, *Peasant Wars of the Twentieth Century* (London: Faber and Faber, 1971); John Lewis (ed.), *Peasant Rebellion and Communist Revolution in Asia* (Stanford, California: Stanford University Press, 1974).

[9] Examples include "Emerging Markets: A Legal Guide to Emerging Markets", *International Financial Law Review* (July 1994), 52 page supplement; David L. James, "Can A Socialist Republic Find Happiness Trading in a Capitalist World?", *Business Economics*, vol.30 (April 1995), pp.41-4; Rosario J. Girasa, "Comparative Aspects of

are apt to make sweeping comparisons between the two, and between them and the former socialist states.[10] Very few concentrate on systematically comparing China and Vietnam.

In the face of this dearth of comparative studies, and in light of the significance of the parallel changes sweeping both countries, we considered it important to initiate a comparative set of studies that would move well beyond what has previously been attempted. Yet an obstacle stood in the way: very few scholars around the world who specialize in one of the two countries are equipped linguistically and otherwise to undertake research on the other country. Through discussion, an idea emerged among us that to overcome this deficiency, pairs composed of a China specialist and a Vietnam specialist should collaborate on some of the topics.

Thanks to modern technology, e-mail enabled the paired members to keep in close touch, exchanging ideas, information and readings as they prepared for a workshop in August 1994 sponsored by the East-West Center in Honolulu. Three days of brain-storming sessions there enabled the members of each team, and the contributors of the individually authored chapters, to delineate a framework for their topic. At that workshop it was decided, too, that to understand the present reforms a chapter would need to be added on the historical context, and to this end Alexander Woodside was invited to join the book project as an historian who conducts sophisticated research on both China and Vietnam.

Draft chapters were presented and discussed at a second workshop held at the Australian National University in August 1995. Afterward, the authors redrafted their chapters several times up through mid-1998 in order to help shape a cohesive book that takes account of the fast-moving shifts in the two countries' reform programs.

Commonalities in China and Vietnam's Prior Experience

Vietnam and China both commenced their paths to economic reform from a broadly similar point of departure, in the obvious sense that they had previously adopted from the Soviet Union a common Marxist-Leninist ideology and a Leninist political framework. They were, of course, akin to the socialist countries of Eastern Europe in both this respect and (with the partial exception of Yugoslavia) in the fact that they maintained command economies. So too, in the image of the Soviet Union of the 1930s, both countries had sought to embark on programs of forced industrialization. And again like the countries of Eastern Europe, the two Asian socialist countries had shared in a rhetoric of both nation-building and "class struggle".

Chinese and Vietnamese Trade Law", Working paper no.143, Center for Applied Research, Pace University, 1995.

[10] E.g., Paul Collins (ed.), "Reforming Public Sector Management in Centrally-Planned and Transitional Economies", *Public Administration and Development*, vol.13 (October 1993), pp.323-451.

But at the same time, China and Vietnam stood apart from the European socialist experience. Both countries, as Woodside discusses in these pages, shared long historical traditions of Confucianism, of rulership and bureaucracy that were unlike the historical traditions of the European socialist states. Both countries also shared a somewhat parallel experience of revolution this century that differed from the experience of any part of Europe. And after consolidating power, both of their new Communist governments had adopted organizational patterns in the countryside that differed considerably from what held for Eastern Europe. In all of these important ways, Vietnam and China did hold to a distinctively "Asian socialist experience".

The persisting traditional intellectual and political legacies of both countries were, of course, also overlaid by the Marxist ideology that arrived in Vietnam and China in the second decade of this century. The young intellectuals who were attracted to Marxism had been disturbed by the dominance of Western power, the humiliating "backwardness" that had befallen their own lands, and the poverty of most of their compatriots. The new Marxist-Leninist credo taught them that through revolution and the establishment of socialism, they would be able to leap-frog the capitalist Western imperial states into a more advanced stage of history. This vision of renewed national pride through Communist revolution became a beacon that was not extinguished in many loyalists' minds until the 1970s or 1980s.

Such an ideology could readily be turned to purposes of nation-building, and the Communist Parties of China and Vietnam came to embody a nationalist thrust. They swept to power through long wars of liberation that enabled them to establish effective governments-in-waiting long before they occupied the capital city and could claim nationwide power. In all these respects, their histories were unlike the raft of East and Central European countries that were occupied by the Red Army at the close of World War II. The two Asian Communist Parties came to symbolize national identity and thus enjoyed a status and source of legitimacy that in Europe was comparatively weak. In a country like Poland, it was the Church, not the Party, that became identified with patriotic pride. Even in the Soviet Union, which was more successful in building a nationalist identity for the Party through its leadership in the resistance to German invasion in World War II, the non-Russian nationalities within the USSR continued to hold to their own separate loyalties and historical symbols, and in the longer run these have proven stronger than the bonds that Party rule tried to cement. And among the Russian population, a great many people continued to harbour loyalty to a separate Russian identity that came readily to the fore when the Soviet Union broke apart in 1991. None of this applied to China and Vietnam, countries which, numerically, are overwhelmingly dominated by a single ethnic group and whose Communist Parties could readily wrap themselves in the national flag. This has provided these two Asian Parties with greater staying power: they not only face far weaker potential challenges to Party rule than in a Poland or an ethnically-divided Soviet Union, but also hold a far stronger confidence in their right and capacity to rule than was the case in much of Eastern Europe.

The wars of liberation in China and Vietnam were, notably, rural-based revolutions, again quite unlike Russia, the fount of Communist revolutions, whose Bolshevik Revolution resembled more an urban coup than a protracted revolutionary struggle. The new Bolshevik government nurtured a suspicion of the rural areas and of the farming population, and imposed collectivization almost as a war against the countryside. The regimes that were implanted elsewhere in Eastern and Central Europe after World War II generally followed their mentor's perception. This suspicion of the peasant was entirely lacking in China and Vietnam, where, if anything, the villages were perceived as bastions of support for the revolution. The leadership in both countries believed that they could introduce a far larger degree of administrative decentralization in their countrysides, entrusting local rural Party cadres to loyally pursue the national Party line.

Furthermore, the socialist era arrived in China and Vietnam at a different point of economic development than in most of the Warsaw bloc. Even decades later, at the point of the introduction of reforms in the early 1980s, most of the population in both Asian countries lived in villages and farmed mainly by hand. This contrasted with a country like Russia, where by the 1980s only a relatively small proportion of the work-force remained in the countryside and where the agricultural economy was mechanized and bound almost as tightly into the central "command economy" as industry was. In sharp contrast, Chinese state employees never reached 20 per cent of China's total work-force, whereas in the USSR over 95 per cent of the work-force were essentially employed in the state sector.[11] Almost all were covered by the net of state public services: not so in China and Vietnam, where only the minority who lived in urban areas were covered and where local villages and rural families themselves were responsible for their own welfare. All of these factors affected the prospects for a return to family farming. With a history of local rural economic initiative and of self-reliance in welfare services, and in circumstances where small labour-intensive family farms could be viable, the countrysides of the two Asian socialist states held similar distinct advantages over the former Soviet Union and most of the other East European states.

On the other side of the ledger, both China and Vietnam possessed less fully-developed labour markets in urban areas than was common in Eastern Europe. Whereas employees in the European socialist nations were accustomed to switching jobs in quest of better opportunities (in the USSR during the 1970s and early 1980s, *every year* one industrial worker in five transferred employers),[12] both Asian countries alike have tended to retain

---

[11]   Fan Gang, "Facing the Next Stages of Incremental Reform: Successes and Problems in the Case of China", *Structural Change in Contemporary China* (monograph series), no.5 (Yokohama: Yokohama University International Cultures Department, 1997), p.36.

[12]   Rudra Sil, "The Russian 'Village in the City' and the Stalinist System of Enterprise

To be sure, many of Vietnam's economic difficulties were directly or indirectly due to the fact that the country had been at war virtually non-stop from 1945 to 1975. Enormous amounts of labour power, capital, lives and resources were consumed by the wars, leaving the country considerably poorer than it otherwise would have been. Meanwhile, from 1953 onward, China experienced no major wars and was able to invest more of its resources in social and economic infrastructure. Further, the fact that Vietnam was divided until 1975 meant that, unlike China, the socialist planned economic structure had never taken root in the south. Agricultural collectivization, for example, was never fully implemented throughout the country. In fact, objections to the central leadership's effort to extend socialism southward helped to stimulate the economic reforms.

This point is best illustrated in the comparison that Turley and Womack make between Ho Chi Minh City and Guangzhou. Ho Chi Minh City's economic and political "weight" in Vietnam is much heavier than Guangzhou's in China simply because Vietnam is a tiny country compared to China, with far fewer large cities. Consequently, integrating Ho Chi Minh City into the economy after re-unification in 1975-76 was crucial to the Vietnamese national leaders' project of reunifying the country and expanding the socialist economy. Yet by the late 1970s, those national policies were not in place and economic conditions in the city had deteriorated. When the city's local leaders took measures that deviated from the national model and began to turn the local economy around, central authorities could not afford to squash the city's local initiatives.

Neither country made a wholesale, quick shift from a state-planned economy to a market economy. There was no "big bang" transformation.[15] The process in both has stretched over more than a decade, from about 1979 into the 1990s. The tentative, experimental, drawn-out nature of these transitions to a market economy has been in keeping with the general orientation of policy makers and administrators in both countries. Part of that process involved local initiatives that deviated from the national economic plan and from central directives and policies, some of which were sanctioned by the central authorities, while others were unauthorized. This is discussed and analysed comparatively in the chapters by McCormick, Woodside, Kerkvliet and Selden, Turley and Womack, Luong and Unger, and Fforde.

The economic reform processes in both nations included similar phases but the sequencing and duration of each phase were different. According to Fforde, the initial experimentation phase for national economic reforms in Vietnam was 1979-1980, whereas in China the rural reforms occurred between 1978-1983; and the beginning of the transition toward an urban market economy began earlier in Vietnam (1981) than in China (1984). At the level of

---

[15]   Zuo Xiao Lei comes to a similar conclusion, though several particulars of this author's analysis are at odds with chapters in our book. Zuo Xiao Lei, "Development of an Open-Door Policy: Experiences of China and Vietnam", *Singapore Economic Review*, vol.39, no.1 (1994); pp.17-32.

Ho Chi Minh City and Guangzhou, according to Turley and Womack, the timing was somewhat different. Because the reforms in China initially emphasized agriculture, Chinese farming families were enjoying the early fruits of the reforms by the time national government policies started to push state-owned enterprises toward a market economy. In Vietnam, on the other hand, while experimentation in the countryside continued, this had only limited positive results for rural producers, and Vietnam's initial policy reforms were focused more on the state enterprises. Consequently, as Fforde points out, by the time a concerted national program to decollectivize farming was developed in the late 1980s, market-oriented state enterprises dominated the economic landscape. This account differs from a widely held view that China and Vietnam both started with reforms to the agricultural sector, and that this sequencing was a precondition to the later economic success of the two countries.[16]

China has retained more features of the state planned economy in part because that system was more completely in place at the outset of economic reforms than in Vietnam. Nonetheless, as the market economy has taken hold in both countries, the hand of the central state over an array of economic activities has been relaxed considerably, contributing in turn to an environment that allows, even encourages, a devolution of economic and political initiatives downward into localities. This is not to say that both states now hold little influence over local affairs; they in fact retain a considerable capacity to design and carry out policies. At the same time, though, room for local manoeuvering has expanded markedly.

Having abandoned the command economy, neither China nor Vietnam is likely to return to it.[17] But at the same time, both countries' leaders seem intent on allowing only modest changes in the political system so as to maintain the Communist Party's domination. Yet it remains to be seen how long the *status quo* will last when so much else in each country is changing rapidly. One possible political scenario might be liberal democracy, but this does not seem on the horizon in either country. Another possible scenario would entail authoritarian corporatism, a direction in which both countries do seem to be evolving, whereby the Communist Party-dominated political apparatus manages to control sectoral interest representation.[18] Alternatively,

---

16 For discussions of this argument, see Richard Pomfret, *Asian Economies in Transition: Reforming Centrally Planned Economies* (Cheltenham: Edward Elgar, 1996), p.73; Pradumna B. Rana, "Reforms in the Transitional Economies of Asia", Asian Development Bank, December 1993, pp.9-10.

17 Another analyst has made the same prediction. See Robert A. Scalapino, *The Last Leninists: The Uncertain Future of Asia's Communist States* (Washington, D.C.: The Center for Strategic and International Studies, 1992), p.38. He holds the same expectation for other Communist Party-dominated countries in Asia such as Laos, Cambodia and Mongolia.

18 Jonathan Unger and Anita Chan, "Corporatism in China: A Developmental State in an East Asian Context", in Barrett L. McCormick and Jonathan Unger (eds), *China After*

as some prognosticators have darkly warned, serious turmoil and upheaval could erupt, in which one or both countries get ripped apart by social explosions and/or nationalist extremism. McCormick points to signs of increasing reliance on unilateral arbitrary rule, which could yield serious problems down the track.[19] He believes that of the two countries, China is the more politically volatile.

Both Communist Parties have re-emphasized the imperative to maintain a hold on the political system lest their countries degenerate into chaos like the former USSR and Yugoslavia, that third possible scenario.[20] They hope to rein in what they consider excessive civil-society pressures as economic reforms deepen.[21]

Even though the institutions of the central state have not changed dramatically, each country has experienced considerable political changes as the economic reforms have gained ground. With decollectivization has come a significant shift in power, eroding a state-centric apparatus that used to command agricultural production and the distribution of goods and services. Similarly, in manufacturing and the other non-farming sectors of the economy, workers and entrepreneurs have considerably more freedom of movement, scope to produce, and opportunities to buy and sell their services and wares.

Economic liberalization has also opened up much more freedom in the social, personal and private spheres. As Marr and Rosen observe, a generation of young Vietnamese and Chinese has emerged who are different from their parents. The inroads of a consumer mentality, the opening up to the West, and the spread of mass media, in particular the electronic media, have allowed young people to live a more "modern" and free-wheeling lifestyle. With the termination of the system of assigning jobs to new graduates, authorities have less control over the behaviour of students and young graduates. In both countries, Communist Youth League memberships are in decline and the old-style campaigns launched against "social evils and cultural poison" and "peaceful evolution" seem to yield not positive responses but cynicism. Labour laws governing labour unions and working conditions have given trade unions a greater role in both countries than previously allowed.

But, again, there are noticeable differences. As Chan and Nørlund show, unions in Vietnam are more independent of industrial management than are their counterparts in China. Vietnamese workers have the legal right to strike

---

Socialism: In the Footsteps of Eastern Europe or East Asia? (Armonk: M. E. Sharpe, 1996), pp.95-129.

[19]   Brantly Womack has raised the remote possibility of internal dynamics generating forces that might split south Vietnam from the north. Womack, "Reform in Vietnam", p.186.

[20]   Scalapino, *Last Leninists*, pp.66-7.

[21]   Elsewhere, Brantly Womack has written that the Communist Parties in China and Vietnam have the capacity to survive a Party-led transition to a more democratic political system, but are unlikely to risk the attempt. Instead, he surmises that "indefinite liberalization may be more attractive to reformers". "Asian Communism: Enigma Variations" (Miller Center Occasional Paper, University of Virginia, 1993), pp.59, 63.

and in other respects are less constrained by the central authorities than in China. The cumulative effect of these and other differences is that more room is opening up in Vietnam than in China for labour unions to be advocates for workers' interests and rights.

Despite the expanding private sector and the retreat of the state's commitments to social welfare programs, officially socialism continues to be the ideological goal. Much of the reform policies in both countries have been couched in terms not of dismantling socialism but of protecting and reinforcing it. State-owned enterprises and the rapid expansion of publicly-owned township and village enterprises in China are evidence of the continuing role of the socialist premise. Also indicative is that land is not private in the usual Western sense of the word. Though households privately control the use of fields and their children inherit this control, the land legally belongs not to individuals or even families but to hamlets and village neighbourhoods in China and "the people" in Vietnam.

But how much longer can socialism last as an ideology? Indeed, what, if anything, is left of it? Many defining characteristics such as a class-oriented perspective and appeals to social justice have been watered down; others such as central planning and collectivized production have nearly vanished. Both countries' leaders seem to be searching for a coherent set of beliefs to fill the ideological vacuum created by the withering of the Marxist-Leninist credo. Nationalism may be a viable substitute; developmentalism is another — though both have potentially negative aspects. Developmentalism resonates with Woodside's suggestion that a "latecomer theory" in both countries dramatizes the need for a strong state and a planning intelligentsia to choose the right path to development.

Nationalism and patriotism are corollaries to developmentalism. Having opened up their countries to foreign penetration, both Chinese and Vietnamese leaders are now having second thoughts about the effects on their young people of Western "cultural pollution". Some Chinese youth are receptive to the media campaigns against "foreign" countries, i.e., the developed world, particularly the United States. As Marr and Rosen note, public opinion surveys in China reveal strong anti-Americanism even while visits to McDonald's, the symbol of Americanism, remain unabatedly popular. Despite the long history of wars against foreign domination, Vietnamese patriotism by contrast seems more subdued and less anti-foreign.

The chapters that follow help to identify those areas in which shifts are country-specific, and those that are common to both countries as they attempt to reform their systems. A casual observer might jump to the conclusion that Vietnam is taking its lead from China's experience — this time in terms of how to implement reforms. That may be the case in some policy areas such as Vietnam's "social evils" campaign in the mid-1990s, which Marr and Rosen's chapter refers to. But no author in this volume suggests that Vietnam has followed consciously in China's footsteps except in such minor ways. Turley and Womack conclude from their two-city study that China's experience was governments over the "openness" of their bailiwicks with respect to the control of everything from marketing opportunities to the flow of industrial materials; similar conflict between state enterprises and private ones; and, perhaps most serious of all, conflict between cities and villages over both the unequal terms of exchange between rural and urban products and the unequal concentration of job opportunities in the cities.

Inevitably, the villages are the focal point of the two great planned transitions. And the reforms so far have done little to moderate the tensions in village life between population pressure and dwindling natural resources such as water and farmland. Indeed, the reforms have created new tensions in rural life: between the reformers' promise of greater prosperity for all peasants and the reality of widening regional differences in peasant incomes; between the necessity to enhance the productivity of agriculture and the temptation to invest scarce capital in higher-yield, quicker business enterprises outside agriculture; between the expanding scope of market socialism's markets and the continuing small scale of peasant farming, worsened by the weakness of the intermediary organizations linking peasants to markets; and perhaps most interesting of all, in two countries whose leaders claim knowledge is power, between the need to improve agricultural output through science and technology and the actual slowness of the qualitative improvement of their farming through applied research. (In 1995, for example, China had only 1.2 million agricultural technology "promotion personnel" for 230 million farming households; Japan had 360,000 agricultural technology service personnel for a mere 3.6 million farm households.)[1]

Given these shared complexities, it is remarkable how little the Chinese and Vietnamese reform elites seem to study each other's reforms, at least for public consumption. In China, the Vietnamese reforms are seen in historically disembodied terms. Chinese intellectuals in the 1990s, including some of the most famous of China's Vietnam experts, hailed the existence of a "Han culture circle" (*Han wenhua quan*) that included the Vietnamese as well as the Koreans, the Japanese and the Chinese themselves. This cultural sphere is said to be one of the world's four great civilizations, along with India, the West and Islam. Chen Yulong, an octogenarian scholar who edited the Chinese language anthology of Ho Chi Minh's writings in 1964, has been one of the major promoters of the "Han culture circle" notion. He and other Chinese scholars take inventory of the heritage that pre-modern China shared with Vietnam in law, medicine, poetry and Buddhism, and conclude that Vietnam experienced political self-determination between the tenth and the nineteenth centuries, but never comprehensive "independence" from China.[2]

---

1   See the essay by Wan Baorui, a high Agriculture Ministry official, in *Zhongguo nongcun jingji* [Chinese Rural Economy], no.3, 1995, pp.9-10. For more on contemporary rural problems, see the Chapter in this issue by Hy Van Luong and Jonathan Unger.

2   Chen Yulong et al., *Han wenhua lun gang: Jianshu Zhong-Chao, Zhong-Ri, Zhong-Yue wenhua jiaoliu* [An Outline Discussion of Han Culture: A Concurrent Account of

In Chinese eyes, however, the contemporary reform process in Vietnam is not part of the history of the "Han culture circle". One of the best recent Chinese studies of the Vietnamese reforms even argues that these reforms — in terms of the suddenness of Vietnam's decontrol of prices and foreign exchange and foreign trade mechanisms, and its abandonment of state subsidies — resembled far more the "shock therapy" applied to the Russian economy after 1991 than the more gradual Chinese reform process (though it is conceded that the Russians privatized far more of their economic life than the Vietnamese). Chinese researchers argue, dismissively, that the Vietnamese had to choose Russian-style shock therapy rather than Chinese gradualism because of the Vietnamese economic crisis of the 1980s; this was allegedly more acute than the Russian one, let alone the Chinese, even to the point of the disintegration of the state-owned enterprises' system of subsidies.[3]

In Vietnam, it is said, young Vietnamese prefer to study the West rather than China. The director of the recently formed Institute of Chinese Studies at the Hanoi National Centre for the Social Sciences and Humanities has even complained that research work on China done in Hanoi is inferior to that done in Singapore or Leiden. Vietnamese researchers associated with the State Planning Committee who wish to study the Chinese economy apparently need financial assistance from the Ford Foundation in order to undertake visits to China.[4] As visitors to Vietnam in the 1990s can attest, Chinese romance and "knight errant" novels (and even Chinese novels banned in China itself) are sold by sidewalk vendors in Vietnamese cities; but Chinese books in the sciences and humanities are very scarce indeed. When China-watching economic reform specialists in Vietnam do write cogent public analyses of the Chinese reforms, they not surprisingly seem to link them to their own thwarted interests in Vietnam itself. A recent Vietnamese analysis of the Pudong economic zone in Shanghai, for instance, argued that what Pudong's success must teach the Vietnamese is the importance of emphasizing "the role of intellectuals", and teams of research advisers, in planning and development.[5]

Chinese-Korean, Chinese-Japanese, and Chinese-Vietnamese Cultural Exchanges] (Beijing: Beijing daxue chubanshe, 1993), p.365.

3   Wang Jincun, "Yuenan yu Eluosi guoyou qiye gaige bijiao" [A Comparison of State-Owned Enterprise Reform in Vietnam and Russia], *Shijie jingji* [World Economy], Beijing, no.223 (March 1997), pp.5-9.

4   I rely here on the excellent summary by Mark Sidel, "The Re-emergence of China Studies in Vietnam", *The China Quarterly*, no.142 (June 1995), pp.521-40.

5   Do Tien Sam, "Mo cua va khai phat Pho Dong-Thuong Hai, mot trong diem cua chien luoc mo cua doi ngoai cua Trung Quoc" [Opening and Developing Pudong-Shanghai, a Strong Point of the External Open Door Strategy of China], *Nghien cuu Trung Quoc* [Chinese Studies Review], Hanoi, no.3, 1995, pp.38-44. By Vietnamese calculations, Chinese investment in "research and development" at the end of the 1980s was low (1.66 per cent of GNP), but Vietnam's was much lower (0.33 per cent of GNP). Vien Khoa hoc Viet-Nam (Vietnam Sciences Institute), comp., *Ban ve chien luoc phat trien khoa hoc va cong nghe Viet-Nam den nam 2000* [On the Science and Technology

claimed in 1902 that modern civilization was the product of two intellectuals, Descartes and Francis Bacon, he was making one of the great neo-mandarinal statements of the twentieth-century.[11] After all, Bacon epitomized the doctrine that knowledge is power. At a Vietnamese social scientists' conference on "Social and Cultural Development in Asia" held in Hanoi in December 1994, the Vietnamese intellectual who summarized the work of the conference returned to one of twentieth-century Asia's favourite mandarinal inspirations, this time hailing Francis Bacon as an inspiration to Asians in learning how to combine economic growth with ecological planning.[12] As for the "statecraft" thinkers' formula "ordering the world", it is embedded in abbreviated form in the contemporary Chinese and Vietnamese term for "economics".

Furthermore, reform thought in contemporary China and Vietnam has been accompanied in the 1990s, in both countries, by a significant revival of interest in the "statecraft" thinkers of the late imperial world, and the ways in which such thinkers tried to constitute knowledge as power in the design of a more ideal polity. It is not clear how much the key reformers have been connected to the revival; but the revival itself, invisible in much Western writing about present-day China and Vietnam, is incontestable, and themes in the thought being revived can be shown to echo in the arguments of the reformers. In 1989 China published a three-volume anthology of the "solid learning" (a synonym for "statecraft") achievements of 56 major statesmen of the Ming and Qing dynasties. The work proved to be so popular that an abridged version of it, this time a mere single volume of 600,000 words, was brought out in Beijing in 1994.[13]

Recently in Vietnam, where one famous colonial-era reformer once complained that every Vietnamese was pregnant with a mandarin,[14] Hanoi reissued, in fifteen volumes, a modern romanized edition of the encyclopedic guidebook to administration originally compiled in the 1840s for Vietnamese emperors and their mandarins: the "Imperially Authorized Compendium of Institutions and Institutional Cases of the Imperial South" *(Kham dinh Dai Nam hoi dien su le)*. The point was made when it was reissued that every Vietnamese library, school and cultural agency should have a copy of this work during the reform period.[15] At about the same time, articles in the main Vietnamese Communist Party journal praised the "geo-humanist" territorial administration theories of Phan Huy Chu (1782-1840), one of the major precolonial "world-ordering" theoreticians in Vietnam. His major work

---

11   Yu Lichang, *Peigen ji qi zhexue* [Bacon and His Philosophy] (Beijing: Renmin chubanshe, 1987), p.453.

12   Hoang Trinh, as quoted in *Nhan dan chu Nhat*, Hanoi, 4 December 1994, p.6.

13   Chen Guying et al., *Ming-Qing shixue jianshi* [A Simplified History of the Solid Learning of the Ming and Qing] (Beijing: Shehui kexue wenxian chubanshe, 1994).

14   Hoang Dao, *Muoi dieu tam niem* [Ten Articles of Faith] (Saigon: Khai Tri, 1964), p.53.

15   See the article on this work by Nguyen Q. Thang in *Nhan dan*, Hanoi, 28 July 1993, p.3.

(written between 1809 and 1819) was also reissued in the 1990s in multiple volumes. It was claimed that theories such as Phan Huy Chu's could be used to help remedy the weaknesses in the Leninist conception of government, thereby allowing Vietnam to escape the fate of the European Leninist states that had already disappeared.[16]

More people in China and Vietnam undoubtedly read John Naisbitt than seriously immerse themselves in pre-modern statecraft books. Chinese and Vietnamese reform thinkers are not imprisoned in any kind of Confucian strait-jacket. But lack of attention to the neo-traditional elements in their style does decontextualize at least some of them, particularly the ones to whom the Western term "technocrat" is most misleadingly applied. In 1986, an economic thinker who was then pioneering the introduction of "macro-economics" into post-Mao China demanded the exploration of a third value system in China. Li Yining asserted that in the long run reforms would probably work in China, only through the creation of new "value concepts" that lay outside both the familism and small producer egalitarianism of "traditional Oriental culture" and the individualism and endless conflict of "modern Western culture".[17] Whatever one thinks of these stereotypes, a summons to the creation of new values is not usually the mission of a technocrat. Bonnin and Chevrier are right to argue that one cannot divide Chinese (or Vietnamese) intellectual elites into two separate categories, technocratic intellectuals serving the state on the one hand and, on the other, intellectuals with an autonomous base in society serving society's interests. The two kinds are present "mostly as a mix".[18] And that was also true before the revolutions.

The Two Revolutions' Incomplete Assault Upon Mandarinism

In theory, if not always in practice, pre-modern China and Vietnam were both mandarinates, without hereditary nobilities of any significance and whose elites were recruited through civil service examinations. Western observers

---

16   Van Tao, "Ket hop truyen thong va hien dai trong xay dung va quan ly chinh quyen" [Combining the Traditional and the Modern in the Construction and Management of Administrative Power], *Tap chi Cong san* [The Communist Journal], Hanoi, no.4, 1992, pp.43-5. See also Alexander Woodside, "The Struggle to Rethink the Vietnamese State in the Era of Market Economics", in Timothy Brook and Hy V. Luong (eds), *Culture and Economy: The Shaping of Capitalism in Eastern Asia* (Ann Arbor: University of Michigan Press, 1997), pp.61-78.

17   Li Yining, *Zhongguo jingji gaige de silu* [The Train of Thought of Chinese Economic Reforms] (Beijing: Zhongguo juzhong chubanshe, 1989), p.11. For a good discussion of Li's ideas, see, inter alia, Joseph Fewsmith, *Dilemmas of Reform in China: Political Conflict and Economic Debate* (Armonk: M. E. Sharpe, 1994), pp.185-92.

18   Michel Bonnin and Yves Chevrier, "The Intellectual and the State: Social Dynamics of Intellectual Autonomy During the Post-Mao Era", *The China Quarterly*, no.127 (September 1991), pp.569-3, 579.

who encountered these mandarinates for the first time were often amazed by them. One French writer, in a book about "Annam and Cambodia" published in Paris in 1874, even argued confusedly that pre-modern Vietnamese society was "an academic democracy" though one with a "hereditary Caesar" at its head.[19] Pre-modern China and Vietnam were in fact absolute monarchies. But, in theory at least, the elites who served these monarchies needed to merit their power through academic success. They did not have the formally hereditary ascriptive social power of the Thai nobility or the Malay aristocracy, let alone of the eastern European nobility like the Potockis or Esterhazys who controlled tens of thousands of serfs in Poland, Hungary and Russia as recently as two centuries ago.

The Chinese and Vietnamese scholar-gentry therefore had to defend their positions by other means than through the possession of serfs and the manorial courts of pre-modern eastern European elites. They had to defend it by their claim to exemplify Confucian virtue. But as China and Vietnam expanded, they had to claim in addition that they exemplified a theoretical all-knowingness, as in the eighteenth-century Vietnamese scholar-official Le Quy Don's claim in 1776 that he could write a book — the *Phu bien tap luc* — that would explain all of central and south Vietnam to rulers who remained in their courtyards in Hanoi.[20] In both China and Vietnam in the 1800s, the most important local official, the county magistrate, was known literally as the mandarin who "knows the county" (*zhi xian* in Chinese, *tri huyen* in Vietnamese). The stress here was on his empirical knowledge of local administration, as contrasted with the "eating" of local jurisdictions as income-producing feudal appanages, as local power-holders were said to do in Southeast Asian countries west of Vietnam.

The sanction for all this could be found in Book Five of Mencius, the classical text which dominated pre-modern Chinese and Vietnamese civil service examinations. Confucian teacher-officials, it was written in Mencius, were "first knowers" and "first apprehenders of principles", who had the duty to instruct those who were slower to know or to apprehend. The Chinese and Vietnamese Communist states superimposed a Marxist-Leninist central planning apparatus, with the compulsion to draw up recurrent five-year economic development plans, on top of this older mandarinal tradition. But it would be an error to assume that Soviet-style central planning commissions, with their specialized sections and esoteric planning tables, completely effaced the older Chinese and Vietnamese tradition of state intellectuals as clairvoyant, age-reforming "first knowers". Giving a practical demonstration of how a mandarin "first knower" could plan reforms for his society, the seventeenth-century Chinese philosopher Gu Yanwu (1613-1682) wrote, in

---

[19]   Nguyen Van Phong, *La société vietnamienne de 1882 à 1902* (Paris: Presses Universitaires de France, 1971), p.109.

[20]   Le Quy Don, *Phu bien tap luc* [Miscellaneous Chronicles of the Pacified Frontiers], (Hanoi: Nha xuat ban Khoa hoc xa hoi, 1977), p.29.

the sixth part of a very famous essay on prefectures and counties, that poverty was the Chinese empire's greatest problem; but that he had a strategy to cure poverty which could create a condition of relative prosperity or "small tranquillity" (*xiao kang*) for China in five years, and a condition of "great wealth" in ten years.[21] It was this tradition of futurology of pre-modern mandarins like Gu Yanwu which Deng Xiaoping mimicked three hundred years later at the end of the 1970s, when he proposed the achievement of a "small tranquillity" of relative prosperity in China by the year 2000.

If one aspect of the political tradition which China and Vietnam shared was state intellectuals who claimed to be able to plan better futures based on proper timing, another aspect of that tradition was the belief in centralized power. In both countries, the myth of a centralized kingdom was more potent than the reality. Of the two thousand years between 221 BC and 1800 AD, one could calculate that China had a roughly effective centralized government for less than half the time, once one subtracts such periods as the Six Dynasties, the An Lushan turmoil, the Song-Liao-Jin-Xi Xia era, and the disorder at the end of Mongol rule in the fourteenth century. In Vietnam, the great centralizing emperors like Le Thanh-tong (1460-97) and Minh-mang in the early 1800s were less representative of royalty than the failure of any dynastic house to impose a politically satisfying unity upon the country between 1528 and 1802. But the ideal of a centralized, continuous emperorship as an expression of political unity nonetheless had an enormous influence. It encouraged expressions of a national will-power at the very top, such as would have seemed alien in the world of the Indian or Malay principalities — or even in the world of most southern European principalities before the 1800s. The first Ming emperor's attempt to create community schools in villages all over China in 1376 is just one such example of the projection of a national will-power by pre-modern emperors; the effort by the first two Nguyen emperors of Vietnam to prepare land registers for some 15,000 to 18,000 villages and hamlets (of which more than 10,000 registers have survived) is another.

In both China and Vietnam, the elite belief in the centralization of power reflected a more general notion of the state as a monistic agency which conflated political power and religious or moral indoctrination: "government" and "teaching" (*zheng jiao* in Chinese, *chinh giao* in Vietnamese), a classical formula more than two thousand years old. The problem with this long tradition of the monistic state is that it made it difficult to develop theories of the legitimate separation and subdivision of powers. Yet to the extent that the tradition was effective, it blocked organized religions from fracturing the unity of China or Vietnam in the manner that religions caused civil wars in sixteenth-century Europe or threaten today to cause disunity in the modern Malay-Indonesian world. Even today, the difference in size between the

---

[21]   Gu Yanwu, *Gu Tinglin yishu shi zhong* [Ten Bequeathed Works of Gu Yanwu], vol.2, (Taibei: Jinxue shuju, 1969), pp.786-7.

Mahayana Buddhist church in Vietnam and the Theravada Buddhist church in Thailand points to startlingly different levels of formal religious mobilization: about 20,000 monks and nuns at 4,000 Buddhist temples in Vietnam, as contrasted with 200,000 monks, 100,000 novices and 30,000 Buddhist temples in Thailand.[22] Of course the smaller size of the Vietnamese church is due in part to the Communist government's repression of it. But behind that government lurks a political tradition in which Buddhist monks were licensed and their numbers controlled by pre-modern Vietnamese courts, following the pattern of China's "Caesaropapist" rulers. In short, both China and Vietnam in the 1800s were national variations of post-feudal mandarinates, with traditions of national political leadership which were — however weakly institutionalized by twentieth-century standards — less challenged by organized religions or by hereditary nobilities than most of the political leaderships elsewhere in the region.

It is equally important to state that traditional China and Vietnam, however much they shared, were probably more different from each other than we know, or, at present, can know, given the primitiveness of our knowledge, even if they were closer to each other typologically than either was to another Asian civilization such as India. The formal Vietnamese political system itself embraced a significant difference. Its rulers were both communal chiefs (*vua*) and Chinese-style emperors (*hoang de*), with a split personality, rather like the German or Frankish chiefs of early medieval Europe who called themselves Holy Roman emperors, or the medieval princes of Serbia who called themselves tsars. Given the more dualistic imperial-communal nature of the Vietnamese system, Vietnamese Confucian literati were more interested than the Chinese in the representation of communal village traditions. They were less interested than the Chinese in grand metaphysical speculations.

China and Vietnam also share a tradition of twentieth-century revolutions that were responses, in part, to the general crisis of the Confucian mandarinates. Chinese and Vietnamese revolutionaries perceived their revolutions as antidotes to the mandarinates, even if they also eventually came to embody some of those mandarinates' forgotten dreams and gave these dreams a mass basis. The Chinese and Vietnamese Communist Parties, drawing upon peasant discontent, exhibited a comprehensive hostility to intellectuals who were isolated from this peasant constituency. The Chinese revolution led by Mao Zedong, and the more primitive Cambodian revolution of Pol Pot that Mao partly inspired, attacked the virtue and the legitimacy of educated elites more than any other revolution in history. By contrast, the French revolution, which similarly occurred in circumstances where more than 80 per cent of the population were peasants, led to the creation of the *grandes écoles* that still shape French higher education. In the Soviet revolution, Stalin did not attack intellectuals as a group; and the expansion of higher education

---

[22]   *Nhan dan*, Hanoi, 14 June 1993, p.4; *Far Eastern Economic Review*, 4 July 1991, p.21.

that Stalin initiated eventually allowed the Soviet Union to claim as many as a quarter of all the world's research scientists by 1984.[23]

No doubt Mao Zedong's raging personal insecurities, as a largely self-taught provincial trying to be a political leader in a civilization which had uniquely revered book learning, partly explain the antipathy to intellectuals which runs through the Chinese revolution. Yet opposition to intellectuals, as members of a would-be national mandarinate detached from peasants and their problems, extends beyond Mao in twentieth-century China. It is found even among foreign-educated reformers of the most unimpeachable scholarly quality, such as Tao Xingzhi, the village educator before World War II, who called for "living teachers", based forever in the countryside, to replace the ineffectual "scholar ghosts" of the traditional town-based educated class. Beyond Mao's peculiarities, the failure of the traditional "scholar ghosts" to preserve China against scientific backwardness and foreign imperialism, or to show even minimally adequate solicitude for the fate of China's poor, has worked against the notion of a modern intellectual meritocracy in a civilization which otherwise ought to have been absolutely ripe for it. The very civilization which pioneered mandarinate politics inevitably pioneered some of the pathologies of mandarinism, to which Maoism was a belated, brutal and eccentric antidote.

The result is that one of the major social forces that demanded political change in the Soviet Union before 1991 — a large white-collar intelligentsia of doctors, lawyers, scientists, engineers and teachers such as the Gorbachovs themselves — is much thinner on the ground in China. Chinese statistics show that as late as 1987, only 2 per cent of all Chinese in the university student age cohort were actually at a university, as contrasted with 9 per cent in India and 11 per cent in Pakistan. In 1995, Li Ruihuan conceded that in the early 1990s China was spending only 2.7 per cent of its GNP on basic education, as contrasted with what he thought was the "average" rate of expenditure on basic education for "developing" countries of 4.1 per cent.[24] All of this is a Maoist hangover, even with full allowance made for other contributing factors. Similarly in Vietnam, at the beginning of the 1990s, the ratio of university students to the general population was far lower than it was in neighbouring Thailand.

What, then, is the extent of the Maoist influence in Vietnam? It is difficult to think of a more sensitive question in contemporary Vietnam studies. Courteous (or ignorant) foreign researchers rarely raise the issue; the Vietnamese themselves prefer not to discuss it except obliquely. Professor Dao Xuan Sam significantly begins a recent book about the transition to market economics in Vietnam by proposing the benign exceptionalism of Ho

---

[23]   Martin Walker, *The Waking Giant: Gorbachev's Russia* (New York: Pantheon Books, 1988), p.xxi.

[24]   *Xinhua yuebao* [New China Monthly Report], Beijing, no.1, 1989, p.53; and no.2, 1995, p.47.

Chi Minh as a socialist leader. He argues that, compared to other countries (read China), the errors of Ho Chi Minh's Vietnam (land reform, collectivization, bureaucratic corruption) were corrected "earlier" and occurred "at the least disastrous level"; the demons of "immature leftist tendencies" and "state socialism" existed, but were curbed by Ho's personal qualities and "democratic aspirations" before he died in 1969, after which problems worsened.[25]

The implication that Ho Chi Minh's legacy is better than Mao Zedong's is not entirely erroneous. Chinese critics of Mao have noted how much of his behaviour resembled that of the traditional emperors: the near-deification of the ruler and of his power at the initiative of the ruler himself; the capricious slaughter of meritorious ministers such as Liu Shaoqi; the manipulation of court factions and the arbitrary personal selection of one's own successor, such as Lin Biao or Wang Hongwen; and the seizure of power by the ruler's wives or relatives.[26] Not one of these emperor-like activities could plausibly be associated with Ho Chi Minh.

Nor did Ho scream publicly at eminent intellectuals the way Mao screamed abuse at Liang Shuming in 1953; he was not as personally hostile as Mao was to the traditional mandarinate. Through his father, indeed, he stood in direct descent from it. The history of Confucianism in twentieth-century Vietnam is, when compared to China, more simple in intellectual terms but more complex sociologically. There was a more dramatic moral and imaginative split in Vietnam than in China between the office-holding courtier and the more aloof village scholar who might serve rulers or rebel against them, like Cao Ba Quat, depending on what he thought of them. How much of this was due to differences in social structure, how much to differences in national "mentality", is impossible to say. The Vietnamese literary tradition did not accommodate the sort of mockery of village schoolteachers as could be found in the fiction of Ming-Qing China, where greater urbanization had socially isolated the more successful part of the scholar class in walled towns, leaving rural China to a struggling academic underclass.

The French Indochina colonial regime co-opted Vietnamese Confucianism at the court level, but never gained complete control of its crucial rural component, to make use of the classical distinction of "court and countryside" (*trieu da*) the Vietnamese themselves used. In 1939 the pro-Communist intellectual Dao Duy Anh wrote a book asserting that Confucianism, though now out of date, had consolidated Vietnam's national

---

25   Dao Xuan Sam, *Chuyen sang nen kinh te thi truong: dinh huong va giai phap* [The Transition to Market Economics: Directions and Solutions] (Ho Chi Minh City: NXB Thanh pho Ho Chi Minh, 1992), pp.10-12.

26   On this, see, for example, the memoirs of Mao's doctor in Li Zhisui, *The Private Life of Chairman Mao: The Inside Story of the Man Who Made Modern China* (London: Chatto & Windus, 1994).

spirit and facilitated resistance to foreign invaders.[27] In 1962 another eminent pro-Communist intellectual, Nguyen Khac Vien, publicly claimed that Vietnam's first Marxist militants came from the ranks of Confucian village teachers, and that there was an "affinity in the domain of thought" between Communism and "authentic" Confucianism.[28] No Chinese intellectual would have dared to write anything remotely like this in Mao's China.

Even so, none of this immunized the Vietnamese revolution against Maoism. Modern Vietnam has never had an opposition to Chinese revolutionary influences comparable to — for example — the extensive opposition that Polish intellectuals once offered to practices and institutions in the unreformed Soviet Union. Yet Vietnamese anxieties about the Chinese as potential oppressors and colonizers of their country seem to mirror Polish fears of the Russians. The historical differences are more important than the similarities, however. Poles could remember a Russian occupation of a large part of their country in the 1800s, and the linguistic Russification of their schools during that occupation; the last major Chinese effort to occupy and colonize Vietnam had occurred in the early 1400s. Poles could remember a Bolshevik invasion of their country in 1920 and liquidations of Polish Communists by Stalin in the 1930s, both of which made established Soviet Communism look like a threat to Polish independence. In contrast, during the formative years of Vietnamese Communism, the Chinese Communists were in opposition to the established government in China, not themselves the government. Poles saw themselves as standing separate from the pre-modern Russian political tradition of absolute power, to which some of them linked the "Red Tsars", Lenin and Stalin; the Vietnamese were more willing, within limits, to identify themselves with much of the Chinese political heritage. (Even today Vietnamese newspapers occasionally call Hanoi Trang An, that is Changan, the name of the medieval capital of Tang dynasty China.)[29]

From the 1940s, Ho Chi Minh shared power with Party general secretary Truong Chinh, whose name, a pseudonym, referred to Mao's Long March. Truong Chinh was arguably the most dedicated Maoist outside China in the 1940s and 1950s, a period long before his improbable and "unexpected" trans-mogrification into a reformer in the years immediately before Vietnam's sixth Party congress in 1986.[30] Truong Chinh's lectures on "Marxism and Vietnamese Culture" in 1948, during the guerrilla phase of the First Indochina

---

[27] Dao Duy Anh, *Khong Giao phe binh tieu luan* [A Small Essay of Criticism of Confucianism].

[28] Nguyen Khac Vien, "Confucianisme et marxisme", in J. Chesneaux, G. Boudarel and D. Hemery (eds), *Tradition et révolution au Vietnam* (Paris: Editions Anthropos, 1971), pp. 21-57.

[29] Jakub Karpinski, "Polish Intellectuals in Opposition", *Problems of Communism*, vol.XXXVI, no.4 (July-August 1987), pp.44-57; for Hanoi as Changan, see *Nhan dan*, 3 October 1994, p.3.

[30] Dao Xuan Sam, *Chuyen sang nen kinh te thi truong*, p.12.

War, called in the Maoist fashion for a "new democratic culture" in Vietnam that would be based upon the masses, that would eliminate "sicknesses" in Vietnamese literature such as "individualism", and that would use the "experiences of the labouring masses" to criticize intellectuals and offset the inadequacies of Vietnamese science and technology.[31] Later, Ho Chi Minh himself praised Mao Zedong's disastrous Great Leap Forward, with its populist notion of bypassing even "technocrats" in favour of peasant-built iron foundries in every backyard.[32]

Ironically, Maoism may have taken root in Vietnamese soil for peculiarly Vietnamese reasons as well. The French Indochina government deliberately preserved the old mandarinate examinations in Vietnam until 1919, more than a decade after the Chinese examination system had been abolished. Enough Vietnamese intellectuals in the early twentieth century took the examinations and then became paid servants of the colonial power to discredit the very notion of patriotic office-holding scholars, if not the broader Confucian tradition. Maoism in Vietnam could therefore provide the theoretical basis for a revulsion against a stratum of "state officials" (*cong chuc*) whom many nationalists now regarded as "lettered slaves" to foreigners. (China was never fully colonized, so China knew no equivalent *nationalist* opposition to the idea of mandarins.)

Subsequently, both the Chinese and Vietnamese socialist states seriously constricted the old examination-based meritocracy that was part of their common traditional culture; their revolutions from below were more explicitly aimed against examination-taking mandarins, as opposed to the hereditary nobilities targeted by the first Communist revolutionaries in Russia and eastern Europe. Only recently (1987 in China, 1991 in Vietnam) have these two states begun to resurrect national civil service systems as a check on the Party "cadres" who — because they were supposed to be the tribunes of a mass revolution — were subject to fewer checks than pre-modern mandarins, as well as to less strict professional surveillance.

Reform intellectuals in contemporary China and Vietnam are undoubtedly bent upon a genuine restoration of their historic position in the life of their societies. Their position remains insecure. Theory-making embodies a claim to privilege that is potentially anti-populist and anti-democratic. They must live down decades of Maoist scepticism of their functions in poor peasant societies, or of their disguised "revisionism".[33] Nearly half of the Vietnamese

---

31   Truong Chinh, *Chu nghia Mac va van hoa Viet-Nam* [Marxism and Vietnamese Culture] (Hanoi: NXB Su that, 1974 ed.), pp.71-2, 69-71.

32   Bui Tin, translated by Judy Stowe and Do Van, *Following Ho Chi Minh: Memoirs of a North Vietnamese Colonel* (Honolulu: University of Hawaii Press, 1995), pp.43-4.

33   See Sun Yefang's comment in 1961, in Nina Halpern, "Economists and Economic Policy-making in the Early 1960s", in Merle Goldman (ed.), *China's Intellectuals and the State: In Search of a New Relationship* (Cambridge, Mass.: Harvard University Council on East Asian Studies, 1987), pp.45-63.

intellectuals surveyed by the Hanoi Sociological Institute in 1990 complained that state economic agencies did not see the practical value of brain power.[34]

Even the reform intellectuals with the strongest-seeming kinship to the mandarin past may be ambivalent about that past. Liu Guoguang, a Moscow-trained economist who was close to Chen Yun, observed in 1988 that China's economic reforms were a huge venture in "systems engineering", requiring much research and planning. But he acknowledged that he himself was afraid of the danger that "strategic" theory-making might become so excessively idealized in China that it would lapse into utopianism. The presumption that only a short distance may lie between "systems engineering" and utopianism resonates not just with memories of Maoist turmoil, but with the fears of pre-modern state intellectuals that high-flying theoreticians, whether of "well-field" equality or of ancient phonetics, could destabilize the polity.[35]

On the other hand, Liu Guoguang criticized Chinese state intellectuals who still resisted total plans, and who held that the famous reform metaphor of the 1980s of "crossing the river by groping for stones" could be regarded as an end in itself, not as a means to an end. Economic reforms in socialist countries required theoretical breakthroughs, such as Oskar Lange's market socialism model in the 1930s or Yugoslavia's economic experiments in the early cold war. Theory-making strengthened consciousness itself, and faith in the very process of reform.[36] Here Liu's defence of theory preserved the traditional close association between the achievement ethic of a non-hereditary educated elite and a state power thought to be based in part on forms of elite "consciousness".

The Latecomer Notion in Chinese and Vietnamese Reform Ideology

The British geographer David Harvey has argued that command of time, and command of the definition of time, are as significant a part of the development of political power as the command of space or money. But he sees this as an important attribute of power largely in "post-modern" capitalist societies, with their struggle to accelerate the turnover time of capital and their search for discipline *vis-à-vis* time that can synchronize divisions of labour.[37]

---

34   The results of the survey are reported by Pham Lien Ket in *Xa hoi hoc* [Sociology], Hanoi, no.3, 1991, pp.79-81.

35   Liu Guoguang, *Zhongguo jingji tizhi gaige de moshi yanjiu* [The Study of Models of the Chinese Economic System Reforms] (Beijing: Zhongguo shehui kexue chubanshe, 1988), pp.52-7. On Liu and Chen Yun, see, among others, Richard Baum, *Burying Mao: Chinese Politics in the Age of Mao* (Princeton: Princeton University Press, 1994), p.320.

36   Liu Guogang, *Zhongguo jingji tizhi gaige de moshi yanjiu*, pp.52-7.

37   In fact, there is little that is exclusively "post-modern" about it. One good earlier example of how command of the meanings given to time, including planned future time, translates into political power could be found in Europe's military mobilization

Elite claims to manage time productively and prophetically are part of the quest for willed economic progress which both China and Vietnam today find enticing. For Chinese and Vietnamese elites time is not a destroyer, as it is in great Western novelists like Thackeray or Proust, but a creator of self-legitimizing opportunities. Deng Xiaoping's echo of the pre-modern mandarin Gu Yanwu in proposing the achievement of a "small tranquillity" of relative prosperity in China in less than two decades is one of the more modest examples.

By no coincidence the situation is similar in Vietnam. Hanoi theoreticians in the mid 1990s were proposing that Vietnam industrialize in three stages whose growth rates they would prescribe *in advance*: there would be a stage from 1995 to 2000 with annual industrial growth rates of 15 to 18 per cent, a stage from 2000 to 2010 AD with growth rates of 12 to 15 per cent, and a stage from 2010 to 2020 with growth rates of 10 to 12 per cent.[38] Also claiming to know how to take command of time, a Vietnamese industrial strategist has theorized that economic growth is the competitive response of national economic "nervous systems" (*he than kinh*) to the sheer speed of the rate of capital and information movements, and the speed of the marketplace's application of technical discoveries. This means that for underdeveloped countries, time itself has become a factor of competition; and as time periods become "golden" the traditional components of production like labour and raw materials become less and less valuable.[39] He defended this political mystification of time as a weapon designed to attack the "long established" concept in Vietnam that industrialization was "purely" the process of development of various industrial branches; but it is obvious that this new philosophy of industrialization has political and social consequences as well. In the "nervous system" of the polity, mandarins manage time. Miners and construction workers manage raw materials and labour.

In other words, the political absolutization of time, whatever its objective validity, can be made to substitute for the former political absolutization in China and Vietnam of class struggle and class solidarity. It also becomes part of a new agrarian managerialism based on global models, in which space is increasingly separated from place, sometimes with genuinely liberating results in theory if not in practice. As one example, the brilliant Vietnamese agricultural scientist Dao The Tuan proposed in 1988 that the poverty of the high population-density agriculture of northern Vietnam was not objectively

---

schedules of 1914, which army generals manipulated in order to usurp civilian politicians' decision-making privileges at the outbreak of World War I. David Harvey, *The Condition of Postmodernity* (Oxford: Blackwell Publishers, 1990), pp.226 on; Norbert Elias, translated by E. Jephcott, *Time: An Essay* (Oxford: Blackwell Publishers, 1993).

38   Article by Nguyen Dinh Phan and Nguyen Van Phuc of Hanoi National Economics University in *Nghien cuu kinh te*, vol.208, no.9 (1995), pp.19-25.

39   See the essay by Nguyen Thanh Bang in *Tap chi Cong san*, Hanoi, no.8, 1994, pp.17-20.

preordained, but reflected conceptual failures. Were the Red River delta landscape to be reimagined along the lines of Dutch high-density agriculture, the conceptual impasse would end.[40]

Crucial to the political absolutization of time over both place and class in Chinese and Vietnamese reform thought is the theme that China and Vietnam are "latecomers" on a common road to industrialization, and that the position of the latecomer state legitimizes certain forms of elite power. Obviously, the theme that industrial latecomers, and the elites which govern them, possess creative powers to skip historical stages and to avoid the difficulties of countries which modernized earlier, rather like the power of heroes in literary quest myths, is not at all new.

Before the Revolution of 1911, Kang Youwei claimed that a guide to Japanese-language books about modern law and economics that he had sponsored would allow China to analyse the Japanese reforms of 1868-98 so closely that China itself could duplicate them in just three years: one text could accelerate developmental time.[41] Sun Yat-sen argued that Europe and America were condemned to undergo second revolutions because their earlier first revolutions had been too early and too narrowly political to solve the problems of industrial society; China, in contrast, could learn from their troubles and (under the right leaders) could carry out its political and social revolutions simultaneously and less painfully.

Some contemporary state intellectuals, even the most cautious ones, echo Sun Yat-sen's optimism. In 1986 the octogenarian Chinese reform thinker Xue Muqiao discussed the "economics of shortage" theories of the famous Hungarian economist Janos Kornai. Repeating Kornai's critique of the discipline-avoiding "soft" budget administrations of socialist states, in which the bureaucratic investors do not own the capital they invest and therefore invest it rashly for short-term results, thus causing a "capital starvation disease", Xue then asserted that he was more optimistic than Kornai about the capacity of Chinese elite reformers to use their deep cognitive recognition of the dangers of this disease, and their "conscious" macroeconomic control skills, to rationally lengthen investment time horizons.[42] During the reform period there have been many different Chinese and Vietnamese ways of

---

[40]   See Dao The Tuan's essay in *Nhan dan*, Hanoi, 21 October 1988, p.3. One could cite similar examples of Chinese researchers trying to reimagine Chinese peasants as efficient Dutch polder farmers — for example, the essay by Liu Jingjiang of Shandong Agricultural College in *Nongye jingji wenti* [Problems of Agricultural Economy], no.3, 1993, pp.14-18.

[41]   Chen Yaosheng, "Lun Kang Youwei muluxue sixiang" [On the Bibliographical Thought of Kang Youwei], *Jindai shi yanjiu* [Modern History Research], no.3, 1995, pp.179-94, 188-9.

[42]   Xue Muqiao, *Gaige yu lilun shang de tupo* [Reform and Theoretical Breakthroughs] (Beijing: Renmin chubanshe, 1988), pp.125-6. On Xue and reform, see Fewsmith, *Dilemmas of Reform*, pp.68-70.

reading a writer like Kornai; they would merit a study in themselves. But Xue Muqiao's way of digesting Kornai on this occasion was a little like a conventional American liberal sociologist's digesting of Max Weber: the pessimism of the original became less pessimistic when it was transferred. Jiang Zemin, as promoter of the fledgeling Chinese electronics industry in 1984, proposed a variation on the theme that elite administrative consciousness could avoid the danger of impatient, quick-results investment behaviour (vis-à-vis colour television sets, in this case): state managers should think of China as a single chessboard, in which boundaries between departments and regions were downplayed.[43] Jiang, with his automobile plant background, may have been a technocrat, but chess is the game of mandarins.

The fact that the latecomer notion takes a Eurocentric view of the development of modernity does not disturb the people who invoke it. Historically, China and Vietnam had civil service examinations, paper, and even paper money before the West did (albeit the medieval Vietnamese experiment with paper money in 1396 AD was short-lived). The irony of calling these two countries latecomers, with no qualification, is obvious. When Bertrand Russell wrote patronizingly in 1922 that China had to modernize rather than merely "remain an interesting survival of a bygone age, like Oxford or the Yellowstone Park", his England still had a hereditary House of Lords and an aristocratic principle that would have seemed outdated in China one thousand years before he was born.[44] Most Western economic historians would probably agree with Dwight Perkins' claim that China in 1949 was superior to other "under-developed" countries in terms of education and literacy, the size and sophistication of its cities if not of its business organizations, and its familiarity with bureaucratic organization and market behaviour.[45]

But the latecomer notion has too many uses to permit qualifying it much. Its changing functions in the elite search for post-revolutionary rationality and social discipline are revealed in the arbitrariness of its statistics and time frames. The use of latecomer time as a sort of national instrumental consciousness is prominent in Vietnamese thought. If one looks at the value of industrial output in Vietnam's GDP, one scholar at Hanoi's National Economics University recently wrote, Vietnam was less industrialized in the mid-1990s than Taiwan was in 1960, Thailand in 1970, or China in 1980.[46] His buried concession that Vietnam was not nearly so inferior to its neighbours in such categories as adult literacy was not allowed to disturb the

---

[43]   *Xinhua yuebao*, no.10, 1984, pp.85-8.

[44]   Bertrand Russell, *The Problem of China* (London: Allen and Unwin, 1922), p.214.

[45]   Dwight Perkins (ed.), *China's Modern Economy in Historical Perspective* (Stanford: Stanford University Press, 1975), pp.4-5.

[46]   Phan Thanh Pho, "Chuyen giao cong nghe trong qua trinh cong nghiep hoa, hien dai hoa o Viet-Nam" [The Transfer of Industrial Technology in the Industrialization and Modernization Process in Vietnam], *Tap chi Cong san*, no.7, 1994, pp.11-14.

general thrust of his essay: the representation of a national crisis in temporal terms, more than in the old social terms of class struggle.

In its classical Western form, as found in economic philosophers from Thorstein Veblen to Alexander Gerschenkron, the latecomer notion was optimistic. It was intended to make a limited departure from Marx's argument in *Das Kapital* that the industrially advanced countries presented to less developed countries a picture of their own future, both in end result and in process. The notion did not go so far as to advertise a pluralist vision that there were as many different modes of industrialization as there are developing countries. But it supposed that borrowed technology would enable latecomers to skip stages in economic development that the early industrializers could not skip. "Industrialization always seemed the more promising the greater the backlog of technological innovations which the backward country could take over from the advanced country", Gerschenkron wrote in 1952.[47] What Gerschenkron and other economists like him could not foresee in the early 1950s was that the concept of industrial latecomers could be expanded, decades after they wrote, to comprise a post-revolutionary political world view and made to serve the interests of state and elite formation in those parts of Asia conditioned to mandarinism.

In part this happened because globally influential Western futurologists, such as Alvin Toffler in his 1980 book *The Third Wave*, glamourized the concept. They suggested that a new technological revolution — involving such things as genetic engineering, electronics and computers, information theory, and aquaculture — had enabled Asian and African countries to bypass the stages of industrialization of the old, resources-gobbling "Second Wave" civilizations. In the 1980s there was a Toffler boom in both China and Vietnam, qualified by bursts of pessimism such as that exemplified by the Chinese television series "River Elegy" (*He shang*). Toffler's prophecies in his subsequent books were quickly translated into both Chinese and Vietnamese; and some Chinese students even publicly told their elders that Toffler had replaced Marx.[48]

Veteran Russian-trained Chinese economists like Luo Yuanzheng argued against Tofflerian utopianism in the early 1980s. Luo suggested in 1984 that the new technologies would actually increase the gap between developed and underdeveloped countries: the latecomer countries, because of the inadequacy of their existing technical and capital resources, would find it more difficult to

---

47   Alexander Gerschenkron, *Economic Backwardness in Historical Perspective* (Cambridge, Mass.: Harvard University Press, 1962), p.8.

48   For Toffler in China, see Alexander Woodside, "The Asia Pacific Idea as a Mobilization Myth", in Arif Dirlik (ed.), *What is in a Rim? Critical Perspectives on the Pacific Region Idea* (Boulder: Westview Press, 1993), pp.13-28; for a characteristic Vietnamese discussion of Toffler, see Vo Thu Phuong, "Thang tram quyen luc" [Power Shift], *Tap chi Cong san*, no.4, 1992, pp.63-4.

assimilate the new technologies.[49] But the continuing East and Southeast Asian economic boom after 1984 weakened the effect of such doubts about the capacity of latecomers to succeed rapidly through technological transfers from other countries. Indeed, the demonstration effect of Asian countries as diverse as Japan and Singapore not only seemed to validate Toffler, but to supply Asia-affirming versions of economic development theories which had originally been profoundly Eurocentric.

To understand some of the Chinese reform theories since the 1980s, it is useful to show how the influence of prophets like Toffler interacts with shifts in the explanatory legends of Japanese success which are also integral to that theory. In 1906, the Chinese imperial court's Rescript on Education attributed Japan's success to its primary school textbooks. These were said to inculcate patriotism, Confucianism and Francis Bacon's association of knowledge with power through practical scientific experimentation.

In the aftermath of Maoism's assault on educated elites, in the reform era of the early 1980s, Chinese interpretations of Japanese success inevitably renewed the emphasis upon Confucianism and education. Chinese planners turned to Japanese works like Michio Morishima's *Why Has Japan "Succeeded"? Western Technology and the Japanese Ethos*, translated into Chinese in 1986, along with Chinese translations of the medieval Japanese anthologies of poetry that figured heavily in Morishima's arguments. From reading Morishima, they learned that if Japanese Confucianism was responsible for Japan's modern economic growth it was because it had deviated from Chinese Confucianism, much as European Protestantism had deviated from Catholicism. Japanese Confucians allegedly stressed loyalty and strict indebtedness for favours, whereas Chinese Confucians had been more interested in shallower, less politically catalytic principles like "benevolence" which did not provide the same national discipline. But the conclusions drawn by Chinese disciples of Morishima still generally echoed the Rescript of 1906. Confucian influences had brought Japan economic success through education, particularly the world's finest post-war middle schools, which China should imitate.[50] The importation of Morishima's writings into Vietnam has just begun, with roughly similar results but with an added Vietnamese anxiety about the Japanese being masters of acculturation and the Vietnamese merely being intuitive "mimics" (*nguoi bat chuoc*).[51]

---

[49]   Luo Yuanzheng, *Shijie jingji yu Zhongguo* [The World Economy and China], (Changsha: Hunan renmin chubanshe, 1985), pp.46-7.

[50]   Li Suping, *Shengren yu wushi: Zhong-Ri chuantong wenhua yu xiandaihua zhi bijiao* [Sages and Warriors: A Comparison of Chinese and Japanese Traditional Cultures and Modernization), (Beijing: Zhongguo renmin daxue chubanshe, 1992), pp.264-5.

[51]   As in Nguyen Thi Kim Phuong, "Thu so sanh tinh cach nguoi Viet-Nam va nguoi Nhat trong kinh doanh" [A Tentative Comparison of Vietnamese and Japanese Personalities in Business], *Nghien cuu kinh te*, vol.198, no.4 (1994), pp.65-8.

Japan's capture of the secrets of the American electronics industry since 1960 has superimposed new legends about Japanese success upon the older ones, validating Toffler more directly. Some Chinese reformers now hail Japan not as a paragon of Confucianism, but as an industrial latecomer whose historically unparalleled conversion of borrowed technology has been so brilliant as to make this a "productive force" in its own right. By spending about one quarter of its entire investment in technology between 1960 and 1979 on the transfer to Japan of thousands of advanced foreign industrial techniques, Japan, the greatest importer of high technology in world history, soon became the century's greatest exporter of high technology products. In this picture, other features of Japan's success — not just Confucianism, but low population growth since World War I, the capacity to supply its own capital rather than rely on outside investors, the benefits of serving as an American base area in the Cold War — get reduced in importance or ignored.[52] In their place, the notion of the industrial latecomer, whose elites have the capacity to make omniscient choices among rapidly unfolding global technologies, escapes beyond the academic cloisters where it originated with Veblen and Gerschenkron. For the belief in a Japanese model of managed technology transfers presupposes a stronger state just as much as improved education does, with the 1957 Japanese Electronics Industry Development Law becoming the state-strengthening text that managerial Chinese elites can use for inspiration.[53]

All of this is true of Vietnam as well, but with an added poignancy. In Vietnam, the triumph of an Asia-centred latecomer economic ideology serves also as an antidote to memories of captivity in the autarkic Soviet bloc, when the Vietnamese government officially saw its task as replicating the transition to elementary industrialism which the Communist states of eastern Europe had theoretically accomplished by the early 1960s.

This more rigid and more Eurocentric latecomer narrative was so unreal as to generate some of the critical intellectual ferment that informed the early years of *doi moi*. The economist Vu Tuan Anh, for example, pointed out in 1985 that Vietnam was an utterly different society from Poland or Bulgaria — that Poland in 1960 had eleven times the average *per capita* income of Vietnam in 1980, and that Bulgaria in 1960 had produced twenty-seven times the quantity of steel on a *per capita* basis that Vietnam produced in 1980; that orthodox Marxist-Leninist theory had never been able to take full account of rural poverty outside Europe — and that Soviet-bloc foreign aid had disguised such theoretical inadequacies temporarily and made the Vietnamese economy

---

52   Pan Yiyong, *Yanhai jingjixue* [Coastal Economics], (Beijing: Renmin chubanshe, 1993), pp.188-9.

53   See especially the article on the legal theory of high technology development, by Huang Guomin of the Beijing University Law Faculty, in *Weilai yu fazhan*, vol.82, no.3 (1995), pp.24-8.

seem more like those of eastern Europe than it in fact was.[54] The desire to escape from the tyrannical premises of a Soviet-bloc latecomer narrative whose image of industrialization was out of date has a great deal to do with the current Vietnamese interest in a more Asia-centred picture of industrial progress. When the intellectual history of postwar Vietnam has been better explored we will probably find important premonitions of this changeover even during the Second Indochina War. Just one such example was Dao The Tuan's proposal in 1974 that Vietnam should show more interest in Indian agriculture, no doubt the only politically safe Asian example he could cite at that time, and in 1975 his warning, Toffler-like, that the "industrialized" agriculture of Soviet-bloc collectivization was not properly conscious of "ecosystems".[55]

Altogether, one may hypothesize that the political absolutization of the notions of time associated with latecomer theory in China and Vietnam functions as a partial substitute for the wholesale reconstruction of the political order itself. It stimulates a sense of timebound duty outside of any particular constitutional structure; indeed latecomer time serves as a sort of sublimated contractualism, replacing the inner call of Calvinism or Confucianism with the external call of an imagined great international chain of competitive industrialization schedules. It dramatizes the necessity for a strong state, in which is vested the power to choose the right latecomer options at the right moment and thus avoid "detours". Equally important, it dramatizes the necessity for a strong state-planning intelligentsia. But will the formula actually make China an economic superpower and Vietnam a worthy partner of the economically strongest Asian states?

The Vulnerability of the Theory Makers

China and Vietnam *are* latecomers in one respect. They are latecomers to the ranks of high-productivity economies whose effectiveness derives from their progressive qualitative improvement rather than from the extensive annexation of resources and outside capital. One Chinese sociologist calculated in 1991 that between 1953 and 1989, increases in capital investment accounted for almost all of the growth rate in the Chinese national income; by contrast, increases in labour productivity rates made minimal contributions.[56] Pursuing

---

54   Vu Tuan Anh, "Thu phan tich nen tai san xuat xa hoi nuoc ta duoi goc do co cau nganh kinh te" [An Attempted Analysis of the Basis of the Social Reproduction of our Country from the Angle of Economic Sector Structures], *Nghien cuu kinh te*, vol.144, no.4 (1985), pp.31-45.

55   See the articles by Dao The Tuan in *Tap chi hoat dong khoa hoc* [Journal of Scientific Activities], Hanoi, no.5, 1974, pp.14-21; and in *Hoc tap* [Study and Practice], Hanoi, no.8, 1975, pp.70-8; both under the circumstances at least mildly subversive.

56   Wu Zhongmin, "Lun Zhongguo fazhan shichu jieduanzhong de ernan xianxian" [On the Dilemmas in China's First Stage of Development], *Shehui kexue* [Social Sciences],

this point, in 1995 a Chinese demographer claimed that Chinese industry's efficiency was still so low that it had to consume 450 tons of water to produce one ton of paper, two to eight times the amount of water required in "developed" countries, and 90 tons of water to produce one ton of steel, or two to four times the water consumption rates for steel production in more modern economies.[57] Vietnamese statistics are unlikely to be very different.

Failure to make the transition to greater efficiency will bring with it not only disastrous pollution, but also a dangerous dependency upon large and uninterrupted capital investment flows, most of which will remain fatally diverted away from agriculture. But success in making the transition is inhibited in both countries by big "surplus" labour forces, a relatively high disguised unemployment rate among workers who do have jobs, and the general need to preserve the existing "extensive" rather than "intensive" pattern of growth for reasons of political stability. Elites in China and Vietnam have yet to figure a way out of this impasse, and it may not be possible without a transformation of systems of government, as some Chinese critics concede.[58]

The fondness of the latecomer ideology for theories of unbalanced or uneven development, both within nations and among them, has reintroduced, through the back door, a topic which fascinated the great pre-industrial philosophers of political economy: that is, the effect of differences in size upon the development of nation-states. Chinese critics have recently argued that there are both advantages and disadvantages in China's great size. The advantages lay in the sheer scale of the human and natural resources China commands, which make it "easy" for China to establish a position in the global community, and in the latent capacities of China's huge domestic market, which give China "room for manoeuvre". The disadvantages lay in the psychologies of complacency big countries have usually generated, making it more difficult for them to sustain a high level of exertion over a long term; the greater likelihood of big countries suffering breakdowns in their "control systems" because their size necessitated more "links" between the different parts of such systems; and the greater likelihood in big countries of domestic conflicts of interest, whether between social strata or between regions.[59]

Generally speaking, the list of supposed advantages reflects the arguments of a long line of economists, from Adam Smith to the American Hollis Chenery (also popular in China now), about big countries' capacity to use their domestic markets to carry out economies of scale and thereby to launch

---

Shanghai, no.12, 1991, pp.36-7.

[57]   Dai Xingyi, "Zhongguo de chixu fazhan wenti" [The Problem of China's Sustained Development], *Renkou yu jingji* [Population and Economics], Beijing, no.5, 1995, pp.10-19.

[58]   Wu Jiapei et al., *Zhongguo hongguan jingji fenxi daolun* [An Introductory Discussion of Chinese Macro-economic Analysis], (Beijing: Zhongguo jihua chubanshe, 1993), p.324.

[59]   Wu Zhongmin, "Lun Zhongguo fazhan", p.26.

multifaceted industrialization programs, even while the incomes of individual members of their population remain low. The list of supposed disadvantages, on the other hand, is a mechanistic and authoritarian echo of what a contemporary of Adam Smith, Rousseau, argued in Book Two of his *Social Contract*. Rousseau proposed that the more that geography stretched a state's social bonds, the slacker they became; small states were relatively stronger for their sizes than large ones.

Comparisons of China and Vietnam can hardly avoid the size issue. Vietnam is after all about the same size as a Chinese province, even if there is no one specific Chinese province to which Vietnam could be readily likened. To whom should we accord the greater importance, Adam Smith or Rousseau? Pre-modern history favours the ghost of Adam Smith. The unification of China into a single political system starting in 221 BC undoubtedly helped, despite recurrent breakdowns, to nourish the emergence of a bigger, richer, more specialized Chinese economy than any that could be found in smaller Southeast Asian polities. This encouraged the partial annexation by ethnic Chinese of various sectors of Southeast Asian economic life, including Vietnam, from mining to retail trade, beginning about two and a half centuries ago. Even so, the Vietnamese remained important economic players in the region and even transferred important economic gifts to China (for example, early ripening Cham rice in the medieval period).

The effects of Vietnam's relative disadvantage in market size, historically, were worsened by French colonialism. The France of the Third Republic which ruled Vietnam between the 1880s and 1954 was itself backward industrially by the European standards of that era. It failed even to begin to industrialize Vietnam, and was denounced for this even by Vietnamese colonial politicians who were friendly to France, like the conservative landowner Bui Quang Chieu.[60] In China at the same time, whatever one thinks of the Kuomintang government's economic policies, the Japanese created an industrial base in Manchuria which is still useful, and they and other colonial powers initiated the modern factory age in treaty-port cities like Shanghai and Tianjin. In China and North Korea at the end of the 1940s, the eminent Vietnamese social scientist Pham Xuan Nam once asserted, "modern" industry accounted for 17 per cent and 42 per cent respectively of the value of economic output; but it accounted only for 1.5 per cent of the economic output value of north Vietnam in 1954.[61] His statistics were rhetorical, but the general comparative impression they convey is not wrong. The devastation of the Second Indochina War did not improve matters.

---

60   Alexander Woodside, *Community and Revolution in Modern Vietnam* (Boston: Houghton Mifflin, 1976), p.124.

61   Pham Xuan Nam, "Thu nhin lai nhung buoc chuyen bien lich su cua quan chung nong dan lao dong nuoc ta tren con duong tien len chu nghia xa hoi" [Reviewing the Historic Changes of the Labouring Peasant Masses of our Country on the Road of Advancing to Socialism], *Nghien cuu lich su* [Historical Researches], Hanoi, no.1, 1977, pp.5-23, 10.

Consequently, local governments in the previously most collectivized parts of rural north Vietnam so far have not been able to supply new town-village enterprises with capital funds and credit on the scale that local governments in coastal China could in the 1980s.

For all of Vietnam's greater poverty at present, the ghost of Rousseau may still have the last laugh. Vietnam, a coastal country, has no equivalent of the six huge poor inland provinces of China (Sichuan, Anhui, Jiangxi, Hubei, Hunan, and Henan) which in 1994 supplied almost half of the sixty million or more migrating rural workers who annually filled Chinese coastal cities' railway stations and worried Chinese planners.[62] Current economic reform theory in China, particularly if it is written by Cantonese reformers, celebrates the multiplication of the world's special economic zones from 68 before World War II to more than 800 at the end of the 1980s. Cantonese theorists affirm the long-term hegemony of coastal regions. They propose that the interior regions of China should serve the Cantonese and other coastal peoples as they continue to modernize by relieving them of their more out-of-date, labour-intensive industries.[63] These latecomer theoreticians, who presuppose that economic modernization is a single highway along which different parts of the world move at different paces, tend to tolerate a worsening of regional disparities.

In the past, foreign students of Vietnam may have exaggerated Vietnam's admittedly very real regional differences, while foreign students of China under-estimated Chinese ones. That will not be possible in the future. Edward Friedman has recently cogently differentiated what he calls the "authoritarian, militarist, Confucian nationalist project" of north China from a south China which is "successfully and fearlessly open to the world".[64] Beyond the north-south split, however, it is now becoming a practice within the ranks of Chinese reform thinkers to conceptualize the country as five or more different rural development zones not because of different popular cultures that should be respected but entirely in terms of their relative positions on the path to the elite economists' Judgement Day. There may be the rural "Middle-level Industrialized High-level Development" region (the village hinterlands of Beijing, Tianjin and Shanghai, dominated by villagers who no longer work in agriculture); the rural "First Stage Industrialization Developed Areas" (Liaoning, Shandong, Jiangsu, Zhejiang, Fujian and Guangdong, all with thriving village industries); the rural "Beginning Industrialization

---

62   Luo Yousheng et al., "Nongcun laodongli kua quyu zhuanyi" [Inter-regional Transfers of the Village Labor Force], *Zhongguo nongcun jingji*, no.8, 1994, p.3.

63   For example, see the recent work of the Cantonese economist Pan Yiyong, *Yanhai jingjixue*, pp.166, 176, 190-2.

64   Edward Friedman, *National Identity and Democratic Prospects in Socialist China* (Armonk: M. E. Sharpe, 1995), p.79. See also Diana Lary, "The Tomb of the King of Nanyue", *Modern China*, vol.22, no.1 (January 1996), for a brilliant account of the "ambivalence" of Beijing's relations with south China.

Underdeveloped Areas" (Shaanxi, Sichuan, Anhui, Gansu, Hunan, Jiangxi, Guangxi, Hubei, Hainan, Hebei and Shanxi, with small but discernible village industrial work forces); the rural "Pre-industrial Middle-level Developing Areas" (Heilongjiang, Jilin, Xinjiang and Hainan, with no rural industries to speak of but peasants with good farming incomes); and the rural "Pre-industrial Underdeveloped Areas" (Qinghai, Tibet, Ningxia, Inner Mongolia, Yunnan and Guizhou, with the poorest and most non-industrialized villages in China).[65]

This imaginative reconstitution of the Chinese state through the metaphorization of its regions as different developmental stages marks a significant displacement of older forms of political theory which lent more weight to the urban exploitation of rural areas. The strategy is to replace class resentment with a belief in the law of comparative advantage. Obviously, the provocation of such a strategy is greater in a continental empire like China than in a smaller coastal state like Vietnam. Hence, too, the fears among China's leaders that political experiments which diverge from straitjacketed Leninist dictatorship will cause this whole precarious gigantic state to fly apart. If Vietnam's smaller size ultimately makes political escape from Leninist dictatorship less psychologically threatening to its leaders, Rousseau will be vindicated. At least the greater opportunity is there. Taiwan, which has begun to make this escape, is admired by some Vietnamese for combining economic growth with the avoidance of stability-threatening income differentials between the richest and the poorest parts of its population as extreme as those elsewhere in Asia.[66]

Any future comparative studies of Chinese and Vietnamese reforms must pay particular attention to the effects of their difference in size. Yet the danger of latecomer theory in both China and Vietnam is that it objectifies most of the ordinary people of both countries as occupying something revealingly still called "the peasant problem". Moreover, it sees this "problem" more in terms of anthropologically outdated binary oppositions between tradition and modernity, urban and rural, the elite and the popular, than in terms of the peasantry's own economic strategies.

Such habits give the reform theoreticians who have them a continuing self-legitimization problem, and one that has less and less to do with residual Maoist influences. Theory-making, moreover, had relatively little to do with the early successes of reforms in Chinese and Vietnamese villages. The successes are more explainable in terms of peasant emancipation from

---

65   Qin Zhihao et al., "Woguo nongcun jingji fazhan de quyu chayi, yuanyin qi duice" [The Regional Differences in our Country's Villages' Economic Development: Causes and Counter-measures], *Nongye jingji wenti*, no.12, 1994, pp.27-30.

66   See, for example, Do Duc Dinh, "Kinh nghiem cong nghiep hoa, hien dai hoa cua mot so nuoc va kha nang van dung sang tao o Viet-Nam" [The Industrialization and Modernization Experiences of Some Countries and the Capabilities of Creative Application of them in Vietnam), *Tap chi Cong san*, no.6, 1994, p.37.

previous generations of urban theoreticians — with the restoration of household-based farming. In China, for example, the contracting of agricultural production to peasant households, a seemingly small change imagined at first in the theoretically narrow terms of Lenin's New Economic Policy, touched off an explosion of economic growth such as Lenin's Soviet Union never saw. This release of the peasants from the controls of centralized theory (up to a point) saw huge increases in the production of grain and other crops, the appearance of many tens of thousands of village enterprises, and the formation of village markets and even a national market just to deal with the surplus crops and the textiles, toys and household electrical appliances produced by the new enterprises. This transformation occurred before the Party elite itself had decided it wanted to make a transition to a "market economy". In the elite debate about the direction of the reforms, the Twelfth Party Congress in 1982 remained committed to a planned economy; the Thirteenth Party Congress in 1987 wanted to blend planning and the market; and only the Fourteenth Party Congress in 1992 could accept that what China was really trying to establish was a "socialist market economy".

Hence when the head of the Chinese Soft Sciences Research Society, a former State Council development research adviser, argued in 1997 that the historical successes and failures of world communism were linked to the rightness or wrongness of its "intelligentsia policies", the claim was by no means self-evident. (Aware of it, he then played the ethnic destiny card, asserting that a great national people like the Chinese could not be detached from theoretical thinking.)[67] Tu Wei-ming is right to argue that in premodern China, mandarinism was part of a state in which "symbolic communication and a shared value orientation" were more important than bureaucratic control.[68] The present techno-mandarinism — a curious blend of the present and the past, manipulating time consciousness in ways inspired both by premodern "world-ordering" thought and by the theories of Western business schools — does not appear to share nearly as much "value orientation" with the villagers. The more astute Tofflerian reform thinkers have made some efforts to develop one. Tong Dalin, for example, argued in the mid-1980s that China was entering a new age of "thinking agriculture" in which all peasants could work with their minds, not just intellectuals.[69] But this scientistic substitute for the old Neo-Confucian ideal that all people were potential sages is simply not strong enough to satisfy the needs of an industrializing society.

In recognition of this, a distinguished Vietnamese economist warned that

---

[67]   Ma Bin, "Lun xinxi chanye geming" [On the Information Industry Revolution], *Weilai yu fazhan*, no.4, 1997, pp.4-9.

[68]   Tu Wei-ming, "Intellectual Effervescence in China", *Daedalus*, Spring 1992, pp.251-92.

[69]   Guowuyuan Nongcun fazhan yanjiu zhongxin [State Council Village Development Research Center], comp., *Zhongguo nongcun fazhan zhanlue wenti* [Strategic Problems of Chinese Village Development] (Beijing: Zhongguo nongye keji chubanshe, 1985), pp.38-44. For Tong Dalin and Toffler, see, among others, Baum, *Burying Mao*, p.166.

if Vietnamese reformers did not learn to strike a balance between elite theory and unwritten popular investment strategies, they would never be able to mobilize Vietnam's hidden domestic capital (which he estimated in 1991 as being at least three times the size of the national budget): ordinary Vietnamese possessed "orally transmitted" economic strategies that were outside elite control.[70] Much of the planned use of time in Chinese and Vietnamese reform theory is, indeed, anti-populist. In a 1988 essay on the "total design" of economic reform, Li Yining even argued that the reform of state-owned enterprises, between 1988 and 1995, would have to be conceptualized in terms of three different time periods in order to avoid, not just price instability, but "social resistance".[71] But such neoclassical conversions of political problems into administrative ones, through timing stratagems, may become more and more weightless without a shared value orientation at least as strong as the ones in the societies the Chinese and Vietnamese revolutions overthrew.

---

[70]   Hoang Kim Giao, "Chien luoc phat trien kinh te ngoai quoc doanh" [Economic Development Strategy Outside the State Enterprise Sector], *Nghien cuu kinh te*, vol.180, no.4 (1991), pp.27-30.

[71]   Li Yining, *Zhongguo jingji gaige de silu*, p.36.

THREE

From Plan to Market: The Economic Transitions in Vietnam and China Compared

Adam Fforde*

I argue in this chapter that the transition from plan to market was significantly different in China and Vietnam. The transition in both countries involved a shift away from an economic system in which the state controlled or attempted to control the distribution of physical inputs and outputs for production, and into a system in which those inputs and ouputs are distributed instead through markets. In short, the transition entailed a shift from a state-centred economy to a market economy. Such a transition does not necessarily involve privatization of land, labour and capital. By the mid-1990s both China and Vietnam had market economies, even though they were conditioned and constrained by their experiences with central planning, including a continued resort to state-owned enterprises (SOEs) and carryovers from earlier periods in the handling of land, labour and property.

Underlying factors

Before comparing how the shifts in China and Vietnam occurred, I must draw attention to two important factors underlying the process. I have employed these and other features in an analytical framework to study in detail the transition in Vietnam.[1] From the literature on China, I conclude that these are

* I owe thanks to many colleagues, in particular Anita Chan, Ben Kerkvliet and Jonathan Unger, for editing as well as ideas, and Xiao Liu, Borje Ljunggren, Xin Meng, Mark Selden, Christine Wong, James Kung, Stefan de Vylder, Regina Abrami and Denise Hare for comments and suggestions. I have also benefitted from discussions about contemporary Vietnam with David Marr, Melanie Beresford, Dau Xuan Sam, Tran Viet Phuong, Nguyen Quang Ngoc, Tran The Duong, Dang Ngoc Dinh, Nguyen Manh Huan, Dang Phong, Tran Phuong and others. The chapter draws upon research accomplished under a number of research programs and funding sources. Thanks are owed to the UK ESRC for its PhD Studentship and Post-Doctoral Fellowship schemes. For Visiting Fellowships, thanks to the National Centre for Development Studies, and the Depart-

features of the transition in China as well.[2] One concerns the impetus for change. In both countries, "bottom up" pressures were as important, if not more so, than "top down" policies for the shift toward a market economy. For this reason, I use the word "transition" rather than "reform" to summarize how the process evolved. "Reform" suggests changes occurring largely as a consequence of policy decisions by national leaders. "Transition" can include such policy decisions but also draws attention to important additional factors that lie outside the policy-making circles.

Second, one major source of pressure on the state-centred economic system was the long-term impact of "economic rents". That term refers to resources acquired at well below their actual costs. The state-centred economies in both countries were riddled with opportunities for well-placed organizations, including agencies of the state itself, to secure such resources. The state in both countries tried to keep this in check. But eventually, economic rents got out of control, squeezing and undermining the state's attempts to plan and control production and distribution. Increasingly, in both China and Vietnam even prior to any transition, units of the state-centred economy became more responsive to local incentives and less subject to the plan. Efforts by central authorities to rein in this dynamic sometimes were effective, but increasingly were not.

My chapter first discusses basic similarities between the two countries' transitions. It then divides the processes of economic change into several stages and, in examining each stage, points out important differences between China and Vietnam in their transition to the market.

Similarities in the Transition Process

The first similarity is that the process of change in both countries did not involve implementation of an economic reform blueprint. This is immediately obvious from a comparison of the main policy documents of the period in both countries (see the 'Comparative Chronology of Events' at the end of this chapter). Given the two Communist Parties' longstanding official definitions of socialism, it was politically impossible for reformers to advocate any policy

ments of Economics and of Political and Social Change, Research School of Pacific and Asian Studies (all at the ANU); and to the Stockholm School of Economics. Thanks are also owed to the Australian Research Council for a Large Research Grant.

1   See Stefan de Vylder and Adam Fforde, *From Plan To Market: The Economic Transition in Vietnam* (Boulder: Westview Press, 1996).

2   I am not a China expert and have had to rely upon the abundant literature in modern China studies. Many Vietnamese, it should be noted, pay close attention to developments in China. See, for instance, Do Tien Sam, *Xi Nghiep Huong Tran o Nong Thon Trung Quoc, Qua Trinh Hinh Thanh va Phat Trien* (TVEs in Rural China: The Process of their Formation and Emergence), Hanoi: NXB Khoa hoc Xa hoi, 1994).

measures that overtly attacked the core premises of socialism.[3] Prior to the transition, both Communist Parties were, in the main, doctrinaire in their attitudes to the dogmatically correct nature of "socialism" — traditionally understood in terms of centrally-planned state-owned enterprises and collectivized agriculture. Today, they have attained economic and political success by shifting toward a market economy but have no clear idea of what new ideological premises are appropriate. Above all, though, in the initial stages of transition both Parties were concerned to avoid too radical a political discontinuity. The obvious point of contrast here is central Europe after 1989.

Second, both countries have posed analytical problems for foreign scholars, especially economists. China and Vietnam's extremely fast economic growth during the transition from planned to market economies has lacked what is often considered to be the crucial prerequisite for it — a market economy marked by clear private property rights and backed up by a relatively autonomous legal system.

A third similarity involves political and economic decentralization. Unlike many other countries that have attempted central planning, both countries prior to transition possessed relatively decentralized administrative institutions that placed restraints on the state's central administrative apparatus. In both countries, this distinction between central and local state institutions appears to have been important.[4]

Fourth, in both countries the economic transition has involved the gradual shift of SOEs out of the centrally-planned socialist economy and into the market. A key element common to both countries has entailed the increasing involvement of officials in market activities through such economic enterprises.[5]

Fifth, the socialist economic system had a history of significant reform in both countries prior to the adoption of clear market-oriented policies. Yet this earlier "conservative" reform had its limits. The dogmatic socialist position hobbled overt policy changes to create a market-oriented system. It is possible to argue that the socialist project was based on two sets of principles — one

---

3   For reasons of space, no mention can be made here of the policy debates in the 1950s and 1960s and the effects of "revisionism" and other ideological issues upon the position of market-oriented reformers. For a rare but penetrating Vietnamese analysis see Phan Van Tiem, *Chang Duong 10 Nam Cai Cach Gia 1981-1991 Quoc Doanh* [Ten Years in the Reform of State Prices, 1981-1991] (Hanoi: NXB Thong Tin, 1990).

4   See Gabriella Montinola, Qian Yingyi and Barry R. Weingast, "Federalism, Chinese Style: The Political Basis for Economic Success in China", *World Politics*, vol.48, no.1 (October 1995).

5   Barry Naughton's work comes close to my own conclusions from Vietnam, especially his *Growing Out of the Plan: Chinese Economic Reform, 1978-1993* (New York: Cambridge University Press, 1994). His work, however, appears in some areas to view the final outcome as more predetermined.

definitional, the other operational.[6] The first and more fundamental set defined socialism in terms of public ownership of the means of production, central planning, and distribution according to labour. The second set, which was of secondary importance, included such operational principles as a central mono- poly of foreign trade, a state monopoly over the domestic circulation of goods, cooperative production in agriculture and the handicraft industry, planning of industrial production, state control of finance and credit, state determination of virtually all prices (including state-sector wages) and planned allocation of labour. Early "partial" reforms — such as China's rural reforms of the late 1970s and Vietnam's reforms of 1980-81 — attempted to tackle the operational rather than the definitional principles: that is, they attempted to strengthen socialism by modifying the operation of the system. This could happen most easily in three areas: freeing up domestic and foreign trade from administrative controls; permitting greater participation in markets by SOEs; and allowing a return to family-based farming.

Finally, in both countries the changes in the organization of economic activity have entailed somewhat similar alterations to power relations and shifts in the nature of politics. Be it China or Vietnam, the shift to a market economy could not have taken place without major political change. The fact that the two Communist Parties remain in power and that there has been no shift to what much of Western political ideology would view as a normal democratic polity should not blind us to the changed power relations in these societies. To say to farmers who were once members of collectives and are now more or less independent producers that there has been no political reform is surely to mis-state the meaning of politics.[7]

---

6   Melanie Beresford and I use this dual perspective to examine the evolution of interests in the Vietnamese transition in "A Methodology for Analysing the Process of Economic Reform in Viet Nam: The Case of Domestic Trade", *Journal of Communist Studies and Transition Politics*, vol.13, no.4 (December 1997), pp.99-128.

7   While not wishing to belabour the point, many discussions about political reform in China — as in Vietnam — appear to ignore analysis of real change in power and politics in favour of a somewhat narrow definition of political reform. Thus Steven Goldstein ("China in Transition: The Political Foundations of Incremental Reform", *The China Quarterly*, no.144 [December 1995], p.1108), claims that "Deng ... had learned from Gorbachev's fate, resisting any reforms that would weaken China's Leninist political system". Francesca Bray's work on the political rationale of agricultural collectivization stresses the application, by Lenin and others, of arguments regarding economies of scale in European agriculture, and their implications for the emergence of a rural class of landlords that would be opposed to Party rule. She also argues that this does not apply to wet rice cultivation. See Francesca Bray, "Patterns of Evolution in Rice-growing Societies", *Journal of Peasant Studies*, vol.11, no.1 (October 1983). Does decollec- tivization thus not imply, for Communists, an important political change? Such issues are the meat and drink of the strategizing of a Communist Party wishing to stay in power in a country possessing a market economy.

The Importance of the Sequence of Changes

The sequencing of policy shifts in the transition processes of China and Vietnam was quite different. In Vietnam the transition started with SOEs and was subsequently strongly influenced by the limited availability of state resources combined with powerful processes of *de facto* privatization.[8] Although the initial partial reforms in the early 1980s commenced simultaneously in both collective agriculture and state industry, only the SOEs enjoyed any sustained process of capital accumulation. Rural income growth did not accelerate significantly until the start of the 1990s.

This pattern is different from China's.[9] There, domestic savings, partly from the growth of agrarian incomes, but mainly from the relative success of central planning, were already high when state and quasi-state enterprises began in the first half of the 1980s to engage extensively in market-oriented commercial activities, and provided them with a large consumer market. Yet the common notion that China was successful because agriculture was reformed first is incorrect. Vietnam was, by the mid-1990s, also successful, yet agricultural reform there came much later. As the comparative chronology at the end of this chapter shows, Vietnam's farmers emerged from their cooperatives during a *de facto* decollectivization in 1988-89 to an economic landscape dominated by commercialized SOEs. In 1978-79, when Chinese farming families first started to enjoy the fruits of reform, China's SOEs still had some half a decade to wait before their access to the market economy was legalized. In short, China began with agriculture, Vietnam with SOEs, and *the sequencing is therefore fundamentally different.* This in turn is related to the different conditions in the two countries prior to their periods of transition, as will be observed below.

---

[8]   The term is used here in the wider sense of the tendency for economic resources and processes to become subject to methods of control more outside official structures than within them.

[9]   There is considerable discussion in the scholarly literature on China about sequencing. Of particular value when comparing the two countries are Susan Shirk, *The Political Logic of Economic Reform in China* (Berkeley: University of California Press, 1993); Christine Wong, "Fiscal Reform and Local Industrialization: The Problematic Sequencing of Reform in Post-Mao China", *Modern China*, vol.18, no.2 (April 1992); and "China's Economy: The Limits of Gradual Reform", in William Joseph (ed.), *China Briefing 1994* (Boulder: Westview, 1994); Barry Naughton, "Chinese Institutional Innovation and Privatization from Below", AEA Papers and Proceedings 1994, pp.266-70, and "China's Macroeconomy in Transition", *The China Quarterly*, no.144 (December 1995); John McMillan, "China's Non-conformist Reforms", *Policy Paper No.11*, December 1994, Institute on Global Conflicts and Cooperation; Jean Oi, "The Role of the Local State in China's Transitional Economy", *The China Quarterly*, no.144 (December 1995).

Pre-Transition China and Vietnam

Under central planning, state power appropriated and then channelled investment into priority areas. In many of the socialist countries, this strategy created large investments in heavy industry and a particular pattern of urbanization and proletarianization. The process relied heavily upon state control over SOEs and agricultural cooperatives, using them as mechanisms for appropriating their output and then delivering these to the plan at "low" fixed state prices. The plan had two aspects to it: a plan for production and a plan for distribution. SOEs and agricultural cooperatives were under pressure to meet or exceed a planned output level using inputs delivered by the state. The state's ability to control distribution of products was therefore crucial, since this permitted it to influence the terms of trade facing various producers, and through this to create and then utilize the economic surpluses. A typical example of this would be the delivery to state trading companies of agricultural products at low prices that could then be used to provide cheap rations to state industrial workers, thus keeping down industrial costs.

The plan, for all that it was intended to control production, was less enforceable inside the SOEs and agricultural collectives. Planners found that they had to negotiate and compromise on the production quotas for the SOEs and collectives. It was far easier to enforce the procurement of foodstuffs at low cost from the collectivized peasantry and to keep the prices of inputs low. The "terms of trade" between the various sectors of the economy of these centrally planned economies were intended to ensure that SOEs made large profits. These were delivered to the state and became investable surpluses similar to what Stalin had used in the Soviet Union to finance forced industrialization. The coercive arm of the state was vigorously employed against evasions through the black market and against those who wished to avoid joining socialist institutions.

In both Vietnam and China, the cadres and industrial workers were at the "top of the food chain", receiving considerable social prestige and material privileges. Yet (and this is a crucial point for the analysis of transition used here) surpluses could also be captured by local interests and used to finance other activities — for instance, in enlarging various local economic enterprises or enhancing working families' living conditions. Naturally, during and after the transition to a market economy, these surpluses could become the seed capital for relatively independent business activities. In China, locally controlled rural collective enterprises (TVEs) and county SOEs appear often to have benefitted from this diversion of capital; and in Vietnam (as in China) some of the private-sector limited liability companies that emerged in the 1990s were shells, acting as covers to obtain various resources accumulated within SOEs.[10]

10   Adam Fforde, "The Level Playing Field Problem and Rural Development in Vietnam", paper presented at the Conference for Exchanging Vietnamese and Chinese Rural Development Experiences, February 1995, Hanoi.

While discussions of the background to the economic transition in China focus upon the legacy of Mao, for Vietnam they frequently refer to the end of the armed struggle and national reunification in 1975-76. The economic performances and the realities of socialism in each country during the two decades that preceded these two watersheds were quite different. In a nutshell, China had expanded the productive capacity of a centrally planned economy; Vietnam had not. The low levels of economic efficiency in command-economy systems typically require high levels of savings to attain rapid growth. The Chinese economy had been able to produce levels of domestic savings adequate to finance high investment rates, while Vietnam remained dependent upon foreign aid which, even when combined with low levels of domestic savings, was far too little to finance high levels of investment and growth. Between 1960 and 1981, China's average annual growth of per capita GNP was around 5 per cent. This growth relied on domestic economic resources once Soviet aid to China had been terminated. The rate of growth had declined by the mid-1970s but had then recovered prior to the reforms. Gradually, too, agriculture's contribution to growth dropped, barely keeping up with demographic increases. Heavy industry was generating a rising share of total output.

The policy measures that China initially adopted in 1976-78 after Mao's death did not attack the basic institutional framework of socialism. This was to come in the early 1980s with rural decollectivization and a return to family farming. In 1976-78, policy measures involved little more than cuts in basic construction and general fiscal retrenchment. These did, however, assist in a significant improvement in state finances — entailing a rapid rise in state revenues and a sizeable budget surplus. In 1977-78 the economy was growing fast and well, although the policy changes had not addressed systemic issues. The limited shift in attitudes implied by the early reforms can be summarized as follows:

> ... the fundamental ideas of the reformers at the end of the 1970s were simple. They arose logically from their perception of the shortcomings of the inherited economy. Premised on the fundamental need for political stability, policy pronouncements extended no further than advocacy of a greater (but supplementary) role for the market mechanism, less emphasis on egalitarianism, the pursuit of proportionate and balanced growth, the decentralization of economic decision-making, and the closer integration of China in the world economy.[11]

Why, granted the weak commitment to a shift towards a market economy, did these early partial reforms lead to rapid output gains? One answer is that the inefficient allocation mechanisms of the centrally-planned economic system provided a potential for improved productivity that a system in transi-

---

[11]   Peter Nolan and Robert F. Ash, "China's Economy on the Eve of Reform", *The China Quarterly*, no.144 (December 1995), p.986.

tion could use to increase output rapidly. Economic resources did not just vanish as markets emerged, but were harnessed to the social and economic reorganization needed to shift to a market-oriented system.

As noted, ideological constraints existed in both China and Vietnam. For example, agrarian change in China, similar to Vietnam, had to emerge from below in the face of continuing doctrinaire opposition to market-oriented ideas. The new efforts to free up the farmers could potentially have been little more than a replay of the experiments with partial decollectivization in the 1950s, which had run foul of political opposition. This had parallels with the attempts, which were also eventually condemned, to introduce family contracts into Vietnamese cooperatives under wartime conditions in Vinh Phu province. But China's 3rd Party Plenum in 1979 made it possible to explore effective means for rural reform. This eventuated in the introduction of the household responsibility system, along with a very gradual reform of the systems of state purchases of agricultural products and a liberalization of agricultural prices and markets. The new Chinese system of providing land to households — who were under contract to supply a certain volume of output to the state, to pay agricultural taxes and to contribute to collective services — was far more liberal than the reforms envisaged by the Vietnamese Communist Party in its January 1981 edict (see below).

The north of Vietnam — the Democratic Republic of Vietnam, an area burdened with over-population and minimal agrarian surpluses — had attempted relatively traditional socialist development prior to the onset of the US air war in 1964-65. By then, most farming families had joined agricultural producer cooperatives, large-scale industry was subject to central planning, petty producers had either been closed down or brought into cooperatives, and so forth. But the economy was stalling, unable to increase the supply of goods and services required for "expanded reproduction" as laid down in the orthodox economic planning textbooks. By 1964 the share of consumer goods in the aid program was rising; and the economy was failing to generate the increasing domestic supplies needed for investment.[12] Meanwhile, pressure for growth rose.

In this environment a free market emerged; a large percentage of the agricultural producer cooperatives did not function as Party policy stipulated; and the SOE sector became heavily dependent upon aid from other socialist nations both for its inputs and for wage goods for its workers. These unofficial modifications reduced the effects of the central planning system's inefficiencies. The difficulties of returning the north to something close to the socialist program while wrestling to institute socialism in the south was at the root of the late 1970s crisis, out of which was to emerge the process of transition in Vietnam.

---

[12]   See Adam Fforde and Suzanne H. Paine, *The Limits of National Liberation* (London: Croom Helm, 1987).

This had been preceded by limited, conservative, but nevertheless important policy reforms in the late 1960s and early 1970s. Agricultural policy attempted to place the farming families in collectivized agriculture under strong control, with strict limits to family-plot activities. Cooperatives were supposed to increase in size and be brought under the district planning level. Rural policy goals on the eve of national reunification were actively anti-market and opposed to family farms. The underlying aim was to reverse the consequences of wartime *laissez-faire*. In the area of SOEs and central planning, conservative reforms tried to improve incentive structures (the "three funds" system) and to establish closer and more effective planning procedures and enhance discipline. Small-scale industrial cooperatives were permitted to procure resources in a direct quasi-market manner — but subject to obligations to supply goods at state prices to the state planning system.

In short, the overall development program after reunification in 1975-76 had two parts: to implement established but frequently violated norms in the north; and to apply the existing northern system to the south.

The size of savings and investment as a share of total output illustrates the different economic situations on the eve of transition in the two countries: China had a rate of accumulation as a share of total output of around 33-35 per cent in 1978-79, compared with Vietnam's 12-13 per cent, largely financed through aid from the socialist bloc (see Graph 1). This comparison highlights the fact that the Chinese economy, unlike the Vietnamese, was already generating large investable surpluses before the transition started. Since this was occurring in a socialist system, it follows that the state was to a great extent in control of these flows — the basic goal of the traditional socialist program, to redistribute resources controlled by the state for investment in the state sector, was therefore realized. By comparison, the Vietnamese state controlled far lower levels of economic resources. Not only had it been far less successful, both before and during wartime, in generating high levels of domestic savings, but also whatever investment was occurring was highly dependent upon external assistance. This deeply affected the process of transition that began in 1978-79, during an economic crisis sparked by cuts in aid from OECD countries and China. It also determined the way in which Vietnam ended its period of transition to market pricing, for the emergence of a "one-price" system in Vietnam during 1989 coincided with the loss of Soviet aid and occurred at a time when, despite widespread commercialization of SOEs, domestic savings were still very low.

The crucial difference between China and Vietnam on the eve of transition, then, was China's relative economic success in traditional socialist terms, and Vietnam's relative failure. Both countries had been tinkering with the norms of the traditional socialist system, but for rather different reasons. In China, these took the form of attempts to ease the pressure from high levels of investment through fiscal retrenchment, whereas Vietnam sought to confront a more general failure to attain sustainable economic growth based upon domestic resources.

Graph 1

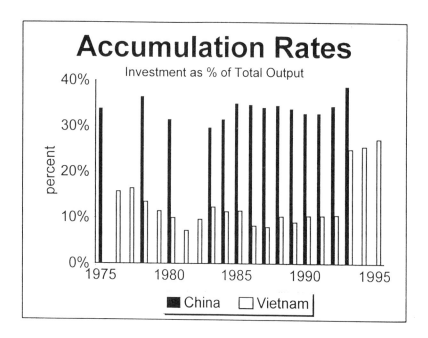

Accumulation Rates
Investment as % of Total Output

■ China   □ Vietnam

Sources: For Vietnam, Stefan De Vylder and Adam Fforde, *From Plan to Market: The Economic Transition in Vietnam* (Boulder: Westview Press, 1996). For China, *China Between Plan and Market* (Washington, D.C.: World Bank, 1990); supplemented by *Zhongguo tongji nianjian 1995* [Statistical Yearbook of China 1995] (Beijing: Zhongguo Tongji Chubanshe, 1996).

The Periods of Transition in China and Vietnam

In both countries, we can identify three stages: a period of experimentation; a period of transition during which elements of central planning and the market coexisted; and the present post-transition period where little remains of the old command economy.[13] The key indicator here is the continued existence of the essential element of central planning — administrative resource allocation.

---

[13]   The chronology of events for China is based upon Martin W. Bell, Khor Hoe Ee and Kalpana Kochhar, *China at the Threshold of a Market Economy*, IMF Occasional Paper 107 (September 1993), which I have updated partly based on *The China Quarterly* and *China News Analysis*. For Vietnam, I am drawing on de Vylder and Fforde, *From Plan to Market*, updated from the journal *Vietnam: Economic Commentary and Analysis* (Canberra: ADUKI Pty. Ltd.).

This gave rise to the twin-track pricing system common to both countries during their transition, under which one track continued to depend upon administrative measures rather than markets.[14] The term "twin-track pricing" is somewhat misleading, as the key distinction is between the methods used for allocating resources, rather than the existence of different prices: goods allocated at the "low" fixed state prices were distributed according to the administrative instructions of the plan, while those subject to "high" prices saw prices established by supply and demand in the market. Vietnam entered a post-transition period with the abolition of two-tier pricing in 1989, and by the mid-1990s so had China.[15]

In both countries, the transition period can be further divided into two sub-stages, the first being a time when doctrinaire socialist views were still pronounced, and the second after these views had retreated and arguments favouring market economics prevailed. In China, this change was incremental, with most observers agreeing, for example, that official policy in China by the early 1990s more whole-heartedly supported a market system than had been the case in the mid-1980s. The shift is more precisely demarcated in Vietnam, given the emergence of "Renovation" (*Doi Moi*) as an overall goal at the 6th Party Congress in 1986. Vietnam emphatically marked the emergence of a market economy in 1989, aided by a successful anti-inflationary stabilization policy.[16] These events, incidentally, encouraged some analysts to erroneously view Vietnam's policy measures that year as being "big bang" in character.[17] They are similar, however, to the period of "rectification" and macroeconomic stabilization in China during 1989-90.[18]

The Experimental Stage

Both China and Vietnam had periods of experimentation associated with "grassroots" pressures. Such experimentation occurred in Vietnam from the

---

[14]   Anjali Kumar, *China — Internal Market Development and Regulation* (Washington, DC: World Bank, 1994), ch.3.

[15]   From 1989, Vietnam — unlike China — no longer had multiple exchange rates, state procurement prices for agricultural products, or twin-track prices for key industrial inputs that were allocated according to administrative targets. By the mid-1990s, very little of these transitional forms remained in the Chinese economy.

[16]   See the interesting short book by Nguyen Manh Hung and Cao Ngoc Thang, *Viet Nam co mot Nam Nhu The!* [Vietnam — What a Year!] (Hanoi: NXB Su That, 1990).

[17]   Jeffrey Sachs and Wing Thye Woo, "Experiences in the Transition to a Market Economy", *Journal of Comparative Economics*, no.18 (1994). The characterization is based upon no cited empirical evidence.

[18]   For an interesting schematization of the process of interaction between policy changes and other elements of the transition process, see Thomas G. Rawski, "Implications of China's Reform Experience", *The China Quarterly*, no.144 (December 1995), pp.1151-56.

August 1979 6th Plenum to the December 1980 9th Plenum, and in China from the December 1978 3rd Plenum to the 1984 3rd Plenum. Both countries' leaders were attempting to generate economic growth by altering the institutions of traditional socialism without threatening traditional socialism's definitional principles.

The experimental stage in China is marked by the rise to power of Deng whereas Vietnam had no similar key personnel change, for Le Duan remained General Secretary until his death in 1986. China's experiments seemed more in the order of trials in policy implementation, whereas in Vietnam they were more an attempt to label grassroots innovations in a politically acceptable manner. The Chinese period of experimentation officially approved agricultural decollectivization, which did not come until much later in Vietnam.

In both countries, the experimental period ends with the legalization of the SOEs' market participation. Clear formal policy shifts in this direction can be seen at the 1984 3rd Plenum of the CCP and the various policy measures of early 1981 in Vietnam. In China, experimentation was also marked by economic success in the rural areas, based upon which the SOEs were granted greater freedoms. In Vietnam, however, this experimental period was much shorter and the spontaneous "private" forces pushing for liberalization were more clearly threatening systemic breakdown.

The comparative chronology at the end of this chapter indicates that policy changes in both countries addressed operational rather than definitional principles of socialism. For example, pricing policy reform in China took the form of selected experiments by SOEs in selling part of their output at negotiated prices, rather than widespread liberalization. Vietnam allowed more latitude in market participation, but then imposed restrictions once again in the second half of 1982.

The Transition

Reforms in both countries (again, see the Chronology) continued to involve an incremental easing of the operational principles of socialism. This is clearly seen in pricing policy, for example.

In Vietnam the agrarian reform edict of January 1981 was not followed by any sustained improvement in rural incomes. The edict did not in principle permit decollectivization, and Vietnam's rural work point system was to last until 1988, although there are suspicions that, from the beginning, the extent of family-based farming in Vietnam's ostensibly collectivized system was far higher than was officially reported. Agricultural output did rise around 35 per cent between 1981 and 1988, crucially, but staples output *per capita* stagnated from around 1982 (see Graph 2). Rural income only grew from around 1988-89, after a more sweeping reform was decreed in 1988 by the Politburo, accompanied by a liberalization of exports.[19] In 1988, urban incomes were

---

[19]   See the Chronology for details.

Graphs 2 and 3

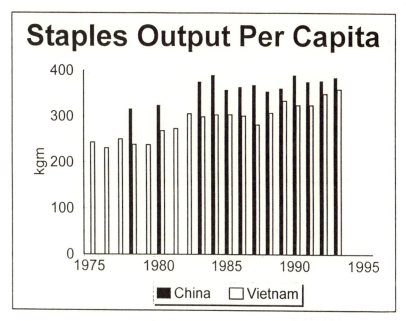

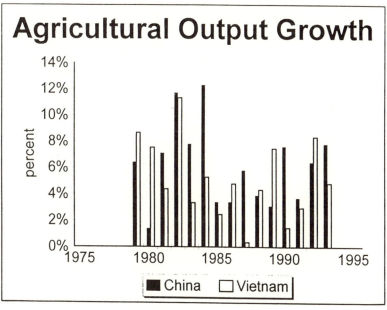

Sources: as in Graph 1.

also starting to grow rapidly, and farmers benefitted from access to better markets.[20]

In China, purposive state action in reducing state exactions on agriculture played a far more important role in the early stages of reform, along with far more thoroughgoing shifts toward family farming. These early agricultural reforms greatly encouraged rural growth. This began accelerating in 1979 and amounted to some 55 per cent between 1978 and 1984, at which point pro-market industrial reforms began in earnest.[21] Staples output per capita rose by nearly a quarter. The different patterns of agricultural output growth can be seen in Graph 3. The Chinese agricultural spurt in the early 1980s is clear; so is Vietnamese stagnation after the short-term effects of Hanoi's 1981 measures. Yet Vietnam, although slow off the mark, eventually moved even more decisively to free up agricultural prices. At the start of economic transition the gap between the state price and free market prices was far higher in Vietnam than in China (10 times compared with 2.5 times),[22] yet in China

---

[20]   Adam Fforde, *The Agrarian Question in North Vietnam, 1974-79* (Armonk: M.E. Sharpe, 1989). Here it is important to add the caveat that by the mid-1990s there was gathering but still largely uncollated evidence for the systematic erection of entry barriers to agricultural product markets, shifting the locus of capital accumulation away from farming families. These structures involved SOEs, whose share of agricultural processing had been rising. Further research is badly needed here.

[21]   *China Between Plan and Market* (Washington, D.C.: World Bank, 1990), p.108, quoting *China Statistical Yearbook 1988* and *Statistical Abstract 1989.*

[22]   See Chris Bramall, "The Role of Decollectivization in China's Agricultural Miracle, 1978-90", *Journal of Peasant Studies,* vol.20, no.2 (January 1993), pp.271-95; Bramall, "Origins of the Agricultural 'Miracle': Some Evidence from Sichuan", *The China Quarterly,* no.143 (September 1995); and Yuming Sheng, *Intersectoral Resource Flows and China's Economic Development* (London: St Martin's Press, 1993). For the data referred to in the text, see Yuming Sheng, p.151; and de Vylder and Fforde, *From Plan to Market,* p.172. Note that whereas the Vietnamese state's procurement prices for staples expressed as a percentage of free market prices rose from 10 per cent in 1979 to around 40 per cent in 1981, then deteriorated to near 20 per cent in 1984-85 as inflation pushed up free market prices, in China over the equivalent period (1979-83) the ratio was reportedly constant at around 40 per cent (idem). Sheng argues that "in the period 1979-83, the returned resources [to agriculture] may compensate for a large part of the extracted resources" (Sheng, p.170). This suggests that Bramall's observation that "an increase in farm procurement prices of over 20 per cent across China sharply reduced (but did not eliminate) the pro-industrial pattern of intersectoral resource flows" (Bramall, "The Role of Decollectivization", p.732) perhaps confuses cause and effect — Sheng's work argues that, on balance, increased financial transfers to agriculture in 1979-83 comprised the main way in which state-farmer relations were changing in a way favourable to farmers. Note, however, that in comparison to Vietnam it is the far better fiscal capacity of the Chinese state that is striking — first, in not starting off with a very unfavourable state-free market price ratio, and second, in being able to maintain, after increases in state procurement prices, a more favourable (to farmers) state to free-market price ratio without its being eroded, as in Vietnam, by inflationary free market prices,

the state remained a major player in the procurement of agricultural produce for longer, exerting significant monopsonistic power well into the 1990s.

In SOE reform, Vietnam preceded China. SOE policy went through two distinct phases in Vietnam. The initial 1979-85 market-oriented concessions in Vietnam were brought in as tactical responses to contain spontaneous marketization. These reforms supported a substantial but purposely constrained development of autonomous SOE activity. Crucially, Vietnam legalized "two-track" pricing for all SOEs in a decree of January 1981, aiming to restrain spontaneous commercialization by setting limits to it, as well as encourage those who had not yet reached those limits to move towards them. State industry grew rapidly between 1978 and 1984, with most of the output growth occurring *after* the liberalizing decree of 1981. During the second phase (1986-89), government policy granted steadily increasing autonomy to SOEs, ending in the abolition of "hard" price planning in 1989. With this, the residual element of central planning came to an end. In China, by contrast, "two-track" pricing was not even introduced until 1984.[23]

During 1989-95 rapidly increasing foreign direct investment in Vietnam was accompanied by rising domestic savings, so that even though domestic savings throughout the 1980s were extremely low, by the mid-1990s they reportedly comprised some two-thirds of the investment rate in China, and nearing 25 per cent of GDP. This pattern can be seen in accumulation rates (Graph 1).

The relative weakness of the state's position within the Vietnamese economy throughout the period of Communist rule has meant that attempts to support SOEs through tax breaks or cheap credit have often been inflationary. During 1989-92, the state set negative real interest rates for credits to SOEs, which led to fiscal deficits, exacerbated by the SOEs' failure to return adequate tax revenues. This resulted in a resurgence of inflation that greatly worried politicians. Macro-economic stabilization mechanisms were put in place in 1992 as visible domestic savings started to emerge, coinciding with the start of a period of macro-economic stability and rapid economic growth, mainly in the state and service sectors. In China, by comparison, the favoured areas of the economy — SOEs and TVEs — could rely upon high levels of reallocated economic surpluses as they came into contact with the market.

The data on accumulation rates confirm that China started its period of economic transition with the very high rates of investment typical of a successful centrally-planned economy — around 35 per cent. Vietnam, which had never managed to create a viable central-planning system, simply did not have such funds available in the years immediately after reunification, and this shows up clearly in the aggregate data. Given the premises of party-led

---

and third in being able to find the financial resources to channel into agriculture so as to reduce the "pro-industrial pattern of resource flows".

[23]   Bell et al., 1993, p.77.

socialism, the state's access to the Mekong Delta rice bowl should have created high levels of resource flows for investment; yet it did not.[24]

The decline in accumulation rates in China during the early 1980s reflected an economic shift in priorities as heavy industry obtained fewer resources at the expense of agriculture, which was receiving better prices. In Vietnam, however, the reverse was the case, and the erosion of state control over economic resources during the period of transition provoked recourse to the desperate policy option of inflationary state finance.[25] Without more radical systemic change to alter the resource base of the regime, China's pattern of support to industry could not occur in Vietnam: the resources were not there. While China set off on a pattern of rapid growth, Vietnam had only managed to generate the resources needed to finance rapid growth by 1994-95, by which time the systematic subsidies of the transitional system, based upon administrative resource allocation, were long gone. Vietnam's subsequent slowdown in growth during 1995-96 showed the possible weaknesses of this project.[26] The two economies were thus quite different. China had far higher levels of state-controlled economic surpluses to play with; Vietnam's surpluses were far smaller and largely derived from foreign aid. China never experienced the hyper-inflation that befell Vietnam in 1986-88 (Graph 4), and Vietnamese inflation rates even in the early 1980s were far faster. The large inflationary fiscal deficits run up in Vietnam revealed a state that lacked the resources to meet the conflicting demands placed upon it.

The pattern of industrial output growth (Graph 5) also differs between the two countries. The acceleration of output in the early 1980s in Vietnam is striking, as is the stagnation in the late 1980s. The sharp fluctuations seen in the graph reflect the effects of the foreign aid cuts in the late 1970s, and their restoration as Soviet assistance rose in the early 1980s. Most interestingly, though, the structure of industrial growth towards the end of this period diverges. Vietnamese state industry had far better growth rates than the non-state sectors, while in China the non-state sectors grew faster than the state sector. There was an explosion of rural collective industry in China, which in Vietnam has been lacking. The Chinese experience poses the question as to why the spurt in agricultural output of the very early 1980s in Vietnam did *not* result in significant local rural industrial growth of this type. One answer would be that the preconditions were not there: the state was favouring central industry, local market demand was too weak, and the increase in rural incomes and accumulation that kicked in during the 1980s was far less than that

---

[24]   See Melanie Beresford, *National Unification and Economic Development in Vietnam* (London: Macmillan, 1989).

[25]   de Vylder and Fforde, *From Plan to Market,* p.36.

[26]   See Adam Fforde (ed.), *Doi Moi: Ten Years After the 1986 Party Congress* (Canberra: Political and Social Change Monograph No.24, Australian National University, 1997).

Graphs 4 and 5

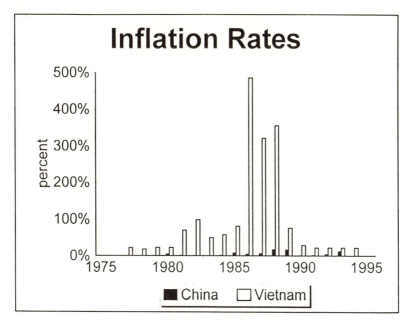

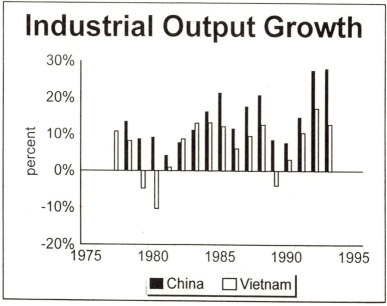

Sources: as in Graph 1.

produced by the Chinese agricultural reform measures.[27] The Vietnamese did not have the economic resources to push into local rural industrial growth.

Even so, there were striking growth surges in both countries in the early and mid-1980s (Graph 6), at a period when their urban industrial economies were still largely unreformed. The Vietnamese economy then stagnated in the second half of the 1980s.

The Post-Price Transition Period

This period in Vietnam commences in 1989, and is helped by rapidly increasing foreign investment and related external forces pushing the state away from supporting SOEs via "twin-track" pricing. Vietnam arguably shows what happens when a redistributionist socialist state can no longer rely upon existing resources. The Vietnamese state had to find the revenues to fund state

Graph 6

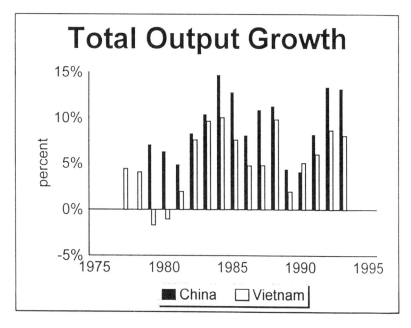

Sources: as in Graph 1.

---

27   An intriguing alternative explanation for the weakness of the response of the Vietnamese collectivized rural economy to the micro liberalizations may be that spontaneous decollectivization prior to that date had in fact been rather extensive. Adam Fforde, *The Agrarian Question in North Vietnam 1974-1979.*

programs. By the mid-1990s this had been rather successful thanks to various "technical" reforms in the tax system, banks and state organization. Tax revenues, bank credits and state investment grew considerably (see Table 1). Yet during 1989-92 the Vietnamese state had seen its power greatly eroded, for the resources at its disposal were still very limited. In 1990-91 fundamental questions of regime survival therefore came to the fore at a time when the state had at its disposal neither extensive price controls nor large budgetary subsidies to slow the contraction of a SOE sector now exposed to severe competition.

Table 1: Vietnam: Opportunities for State Influence and Intervention (US$ billion)

	1990	1995
Real tax revenues	1.1	5.0
Foreign trade taxes	0.1	1.7
Bank credit outstanding	1.0	4.1
Foreign investment disbursements	0.1	1.8
State investment	0.2	1.2

Source: Adam Fforde, *Vietnam: Economic Commentary and Analysis,* no.8 (November 1996) (Canberra: ADUKI Pty. Ltd.).

Yet by the mid-1990s the Vietnamese state was again controlling important resource flows, and the heightened prioritization of the state sector in 1995-96, confirmed at the 8th Party Congress in 1996, revealed a bias against the non-state sectors.[28] The rapid increase of investment in SOEs in the mid-1990s was also related to their access to foreign investments, almost all of which went to joint ventures with SOEs.

Even though in the mid-1990s the state sector remained the Vietnamese reform's priority sector, it was far from certain that this thrust could be maintained. After all, there were internal conflicts within the socialist sectors as they interacted with the privatizing drift in the rest of the economy. This drift has enhanced economic performance, both nationally and locally, and helped spark the rapid GDP growth of the 1990s. State priorities may not be able to stand against these trends.

[28]   Ari Kokko and Mario Zejan, "Vietnam — At the Next Stage of Reforms" (Stockholm School of Economics, April 1996), unpublished.

With no historical event similar to Vietnam's loss of Soviet bloc aid, the end of the transition period is far less clearly marked in China. Throughout most of the 1990s, familiar forms from the past, such as output quotas on key agricultural produce, were present.[29] The relative value of such forms to the Chinese state had led to their being maintained; the state had retained its ability to levy "economic rents" in this way. The Vietnamese state did not.

A reading of the economic and political reporting from the period shows that the main concern of Chinese policy-makers was to cope with the consequences of China's rapid growth and the tensions created by a progressive decline in the profitability and viability of the state sector.[30] By the 15th Party Congress in September 1997 this had led to a decision to convert a great many of the SOEs into share-holding corporations, essentially privatizing many of the smaller ones, a program that is currently underway. At the same time, policy was focusing upon the need to ensure the continued development of markets for capital, labour and technology.[31] The impression gained is that in the post-transition Chinese economy (defined in the terms used in this chapter) the existing levels of savings, combined with a dynamic efficiency in the economy high enough to offset the lack of efficient factor markets, precluded the serious issue of investment capital faced in Vietnam. Once again, the high levels of resource mobilization and domestic savings of the Chinese economy permitted it to move forward at high rates and with a momentum that was not available to the Vietnamese. Economic growth appeared more robust. However, with political tensions far greater than in Vietnam, as witnessed in the Chinese bloodletting of 1989, it is hard to say whether this greater economic robustness was underpinned by similarly solid political foundations. For many political analysts, including traditional Communists, there were deep social implications to the idea that factor markets — especially for capital — should emerge, especially when the role of the state sector was, *de facto*, being reformulated.

---

[29]   A striking example is the deregulation of the selling price of cabbage and an end to the imposition of production quotas for farmers near Beijing, which occurred as late as October 1997 (*China News Analysis*, 1 May 1998). I can recall watching a discussion between a group of visiting Chinese experts and members of a Vietnamese reformist institute in the mid-1990s, which dealt with proposed reforms to state housing. Animated Chinese discussion of changes in housing subsidy rates for particular categories of Chinese officials was viewed by the Vietnamese as something far from their own recent experience and reminiscent instead of the 1980s.

[30]   This is clear from key policy pronouncements, such as the speeches at the 1995 9th Plenum and the speech by Li Peng at the 4th Session of the National People's Congress just after the death of Deng Xiaoping.

[31]   *The China Quarterly*, no.152 (December 1997), pp.909-10, reporting on Jiang Zemin's speech to the Congress.

Conclusion

Some have argued that the relative success of Vietnam and China in achieving rapid economic growth has been due to their "gradualist" policies and an initial focus upon agrarian reforms.[32] These supposedly created ideological support for the reforms as well as a basis for increased domestic savings. Yet what is often ignored is that in both countries the economic growth has been deeply associated with the role played by state redistribution of resources in various forms, and the response to this of various semi-autonomous forces. "Reform" cannot be easily understood, nor the constraints upon reform programs appreciated, in isolation from the growth of commerce and the material interests that support or oppose further change. This in turn is related to the sequence of change. The two countries are quite different in this regard. Rather than agriculture, as in China, the key focus of change in Vietnam during the early 1980s was the SOE sector, supported by foreign aid from the Soviet bloc. A second factor is that even though the reforms in both China and Vietnam have involved extensive official intervention in commerce as the market has "emerged from the plan", the relationship between state and market has evolved differently, partly resulting from different starting points but also because of the different sequencing. Moving away faster from the 'rents' typical of transition, Vietnam abandoned twin-track pricing in 1989, and redistributions of resources through allocative central planning no longer exist. China continued twin-track pricing up through the early 1990s, and although by the late 1990s it too had essentially passed through that transitional phase, some energy-resource inputs preserved two-track pricing to the advantage of state-owned enterprises.

Comparing the sequence of events reveals that approximately two decades were needed for both countries to shift from their own particular version of socialism into the market economies that emerged in the middle of the 1990s. The Chinese took longer to pass through their period of experimentation; but the Vietnamese ended theirs with a period of reaction, in

---

[32] It is worth stressing here that the notion of "success" is *relative to the goals of crucial actors*, mainly the ruling Communist Parties; it also refers to various comments by foreign commentators, such as economists, for whom economic growth is valued highly compared with other goals. The jerry-built housing thrown up in hundreds of cities in the service of China's industrialization, for example, appears to the author as likely to be one of the great mistakes of the coming century, creating with the one-child family policies social tensions that will take generations to resolve, much as the brutal circumstances of Britain's Industrial Revolution still haunt that country's social fabric. Similarly, the Tay Ho urban development in Hanoi, and the pattern of corruption and unregulated urban growth that it represents, point to major social issues that Vietnam's 1996-97 campaigns against "social evils" failed to address in any fundamental way. Economic growth and economic development are, as any course in development studies will teach, very different things.

contrast to the Chinese acceleration of reforms. The Chinese process also appears somewhat more top-down than the Vietnamese. This conforms to a picture where the Chinese state controls resources and has more room for manoeuvre than the Vietnamese.

The Chinese sequence can be characterized as, first, reforms to agriculture, then to industry, then stabilization, followed by rapid growth with ongoing massive redistribution of resources and subsidies. The Vietnamese sequence was breakdown, concessions and conservative reaction that opened a wider door to SOEs than to farmers, a U-turn and rapid shift to a market economy amidst loss of aid. In Vietnam this led (in its early days at least) to less extensive state activity in relation to capital, labour and product markets, with decreasing macro-economic "distortions" and low subsidies.

Comparative Chronology of Transition, Focusing upon Policy Changes

Sources: For China, mainly Bell et al., 1993; also Wanda Tseng, Hoe Ee Khor, Kalpana Kochhar, Dubravko Mihaljek and David Burton, *Economic Reform in China: A New Phase* (Washington, D.C.: IMF Occasional Paper No.114, November 1994); and *The China Quarterly's*, Quarterly Chronicle and Documentation (passim). For Vietnam, de Vylder and Fforde, 1996; Fforde, *Vietnam: Economic Commentary and Analysis* (1996), especially section 4, *Economic Legislation*.

Experimental Period

China: 1978-83	Vietnam: 1979-80
3rd Plenum, December 1978. **Main ideological thrust:** Shift from class struggle to economic development.	6th Plenum, August 1979. **Main ideological thrust:** Atmosphere shift encouraging acceptance of anything that would lead to "explosion" of output (*bungra*).
Dominant political context initiating period: Rise to predominance of reformists led by Deng Xiaoping.	**Dominant political context initiating period:** Economic problems resulting from loss of Chinese and Western aid, failure to establish traditional model and powerful spontaneous pressures from below supported from above in various ways.
External Sector Much experimentation with foreign exchange sharing as central monopoly was broken down; multiple exchange rates continue. Foreign trade gradually decentralized within the state framework.	**External Sector** Concessions made to local authorities, mainly in the south; removal of barriers by certain state units finding ways to access foreign exchange. Crisis measures designed to stimulate exports through liberalization (1980).
Agriculture Experiments with responsibility system start in 1978, with household responsibility system dominant by 1982-83. State price controls continue but procurement prices increase as scope of price controls falls. State subsidies increase sharply. Private inter-provincial trade permitted.	**Agriculture** Spontaneous breakdown of co-operatives in north Vietnam; failure to establish collectivization movement in Mekong as basis for procurement of food. Various measures to support improved output by effectively liberalizing the collective system. Spontaneous experiments with household contracting recognized and ways found to grant them ideological approval.

Pricing Policy
Selected experiments by SOEs with selling part of output at negotiated prices. Most retail prices and input prices remain under state control.

Pricing Policy
No significant change. Informal loosening up. Decision to stabilize the economy prior to price reform (1980). U-turn in attitude to free market, liberal then controlling, seen in sequence of decrees through 1979 and 1980. Domestic markets remain divided along administrative lines.

Enterprises
Minor experiments — pricing of output; replacement of direct profit levies with income taxation. No real change to ownership structure which remains dominated by the state. Experiments with permitting SOEs greater autonomy in investment decisions.TVEs expand, benefiting from rising agricultural incomes, cheap labour supply and state support. Retail sector remains dominated by socialist sector, but private traders start to emerge.

Enterprises
Substantial informal removal of barriers as SOEs seek out direct suppliers and free disposal of output. Private sector emerges, cautiously.

Labour
Little change. Bonuses reintroduced in 1978, but largely unrelated to performance. Housing supplied to state employees by municipalities or unit, with heavy subsidy. Social security covered similarly, but not extended, for example, to TVEs.

Labour
No significant changes. Experiments with piece-work systems in SOEs.

Fiscal and Monetary Policy
Revenue sharing between levels of the state, state revenue largely derived from SOEs, whose capital spending treated as part of the state budget. No change to monobank system.

Fiscal and Monetary Policy
Entrenched revenue sharing continues, largely based upon allocation of foreign aid. District level (below province) remains a budgetary level.

Early Transitional Period
China: 1984 to 1988

Vietnam: 1981 to 1986

Initiating political event:
3rd Plenum of Central Committee summing up positive results of previous period, expanding reforms.

Initiating political event:
9th Plenum of December 1980 — political compromise granting concessions but aiming to preserve neo-Stalinist core, with return to collectivization of the Mekong and continued hostility to private sector.

Main ideological thrust:
Establishment of a "socialist planned commodity economy".

Main ideological thrust:
"Strengthening of socialist transformation in the south, plus reinforcement and reform of socialist production relations in the North". (*Nhan Dan* 12/3/82).

Dominant political context initiating period:
Success of previous period of experimentation.

Dominant political context initiating period:
Entrenchment of conservatives in wake of 1979-80 crisis.

External sector
Failed attempt to unify exchange rate leading to institutionalised "twin-track" system based upon trade in foreign exchange retention rights. Continuation of complex system of foreign exchange retention right system, with eventual extension to all domestic enterprises with foreign earnings or retention quotas (1988).
Expansion of numbers of SOEs permitted to carry out foreign trade.
Trade remains controlled through licences and tariffs used to rein in imports when trade balance threatened.

External sector
1981 Decree tightens up on exporters' autonomy.
Provincial foreign trade companies closed down by teams from Hanoi, prison sentences imposed (ca 1982-83). Further attempt to restrain grass-roots pressures in 1985.
Allocated quotas to localities, based upon foreign exchange allocations from central government; above-quota output of export goods could be exported and the resulting foreign exchange "owned" by the SOE concerned.

Agriculture
Procurement obligations replaced in 1985, in name only, by contracts at negotiated prices. State still dominant in staples wholesale trade. Reduction in retail price controls; by 1987 grain and oil to urban areas still subsidized — state subsidies increase rapidly.
Stagnant grain output met by increased intervention.

Agriculture
Limited improvements in procurement conditions. Output gains from easing of collectives' pressures upon farming families increasingly taxed away by the state. State remains dominant in staples trade. Inter-provincial trade barriers still strong. Partial decollectivization only in 1981 leaves workpoint system intact.

Pricing Policy
Introduction of "twin-track" pricing — planned goods still allocated at "low" fixed state prices; state purchasing agencies operating at "guided prices"; market prices used for other sales. Spread of negotiated prices parallels penetration of private sector into retail trade — 53% in 1987.

Pricing Policy
Some limited reduction in scope of retail goods rationing, but private retail trade still subject to police pressure and confiscations. 1982 Decree follows the trend to seek to control the free market. SOEs increasingly involved in sales at free or negotiated prices, sold to state traders or under the counter. Increasingly distributional tensions lead to 1985's "price-wage-money" reforms, leading to hyperinflation from early 1986.

Enterprises
Spread of inter-SOE investments under
various forms, from 1986.
Use of "contract responsibility system" to
manage relations between SOEs and higher
levels, specifying performance targets, supply
quotas and tax obligations.
Investment responsibility largely shifted from
budget to SOEs, supported by bank credit
and greater access to retained earnings.
Bankruptcy Law formulated in 1986.
TVEs granted tax concessions and favourable
access to credit (1984). Around three-quarters
of small commercial SOEs contracted or
leased to collectives or individuals.

Labour
Introduction of labour contracts for recruits
to SOEs, many exceptions. Cap on bonuses
replaced by tax on excessive bonuses.
Attempts to monetize wages through raising
rents and granting wage supplements.

Fiscal and Monetary Policy
Revenue sharing between central and local
governments continues. Rapid growth of extra-
budgetary funds, based upon enterprises'
retained earnings and government unit.
Commercial banking activities removed from
People's Bank of China, heading for two-tier
system (1984); provincial banks established
(1986); state commercial banks unspecialized
by sector set up (1987). Rapid growth of
financial institutions — Trust and Investment
Companies — aimed at financing domestic
business, reined in during 1988. Some SOEs
issue shares starting from 1985. Credit controls
remain key monetary policy instrument,
with loss of central control over provincial
banks when in confrontation with provincial
authorities. Interest rates free to move
within frame set by authorities.

Enterprises
1981 Decree generalizes so-called "3
Plan system" to SOEs, subject to
constraint that planned output should
have priority. This supported by later
legislation in 1982 and 1984. The latter
permitted SOEs to have foreign
exchange accounts loans, but sought to
remove most SOE authority in price
fixing. By the 6th Congress interests of
SOEs already powerful, leading to
U-turn with Decree in 1986 which
argued for greatly increased autonomy.

Labour
Introduction of piece-work systems.

Fiscal and Monetary Policy
Revenue sharing continues. Increasing
inflationary pressures.
Growing provincial and city
independence

Late Transition Period
China: 1989 to early 1990s

Initiating political event:
Late 1988 crisis measures.

Vietnam: 1986 to 1989

Initiating political event:
Death of Party General Secretary
Le Duan followed by 6th Party
Congress (Decmber 1986).

Main ideological thrust:
Revival of slogans abour danger of "peaceful evolution".

Main ideological thrust:
"Doi moi" and the need for a multi-sectoral market economy with macroeconomic regulation by the state.

Dominant political context initiating period:
Macroeconomic instability and political unrest met by repressive measures.

Dominant political context initiating period:
Political conflicts to garner credit for market-oriented reform in the face of the evident failure of the political compromise marked by the early 1981 measures.

External sector
Continuation of multiple exchange rate system. Gradual extension of access to foreign exchange and foreign trade (through the licensing system). Individuals allowed to buy and sell at foreign exchange adjustment centre rates from 1991. Export subsidies abolished in 1991.
SOEs increasingly allowed to trade directly. Mandatory export planning abolished in 1991.

External sector
Continued conflict between central pressure to preserve central monopolies and increasingly strong and successful "fence breaking" by local authorities.

Agriculture
Continued state intervention through various mechanisms: household responsibility system, centralized organizations providing services to farmers, extensive and expensive use of support-pricing.
Rationing abandoned by 1993.
Use of inter-provincial trade barriers during the macroeconomic "rectification" of 1988-89.

Agriculture
1988 Decree in practice decollectivizes northern and central agriculture.
Rapid growth in rice output and exports from 1988.

Pricing Policy
Trend to reduce the number of goods subject to dual track pricing, with many prices unified. Producer goods included in this trend, but with around two-thirds of goods still subject to fixed or guided prices by 1991. During stabilization of 1988-89, price control tightened, control over market prices eliminated by 1991, with prices regulated largely through use of buffer stocks where possible. By early 1993 "90%" of prices are market determined.
Establishment of national exchanges for metals and wholesale nonferrous metals.

Pricing Policy
Number of goods subject to rationing reduced. State prices brought closer to those on the free market.
Extent of "self-balancing" by SOEs increases as both inputs and outputs increasing traded directly. Major steps to establish a national staples market during 1987-88 are successful.

Enterprises
Emergence of embryonic formal capital markets with securities exchanges in Shanghai (1991) and Shenzhen (1991);

Enterprises
Decree grants greatly increased autonomy for SOEs, preventing planners from issuing targets for which

6,000 share-issuing companies listed by end
1991 — most without listing on stock markets.
Continuation of system of contracts for SOEs,
but with shorter periods.
Attempts to improve taxation of SOEs.
Key SOEs protected from effects of "rectification"
by use of direct administative measures involving
preferential resource allocation in return for
guaranteed low-price deliveries to the state.
Retrenchment in 1988-89 leads to closures,
falls in investment and (after 1991) mergers
of inefficient SOEs with others.

Labour
End of state system of wage controls within
SOEs (1991).
Continued attempts to monetize wages —
shift to cheap sales of state housing and
further rent increases. SOE workers remain
linked to their units through housing.
Experimental pension and unemployment
schemes.

Fiscal and Monetary Policy
Attempts to strengthen central control with
limited success. System of tax contracting
with SOEs continues, with attempts to introduce reforms towards a normal tax system.
Temporary slowdown in growth of formal
financial institutions in 1988-89. SOEs allowed
to work with more than one bank. Secondary
markets for treasury bonds opened in major cities.

they do not supply adequate resources.
Plans laid to reduce numbers of plan
indicators. Depreciation retention rates
increased. Many SOEs shift to single
target — budgetary contributions.
Rapid emergence of inter-SOE joint
ventures, informally.
Private sector now encouraged
officially, but occasional statements
about "leading role" of the state prompt
caution.

Labour
Beginnings of use of labour contracts.
De facto lay-offs from some SOEs.
SOE wages increasingly determined by
profitability rather than the official
structure.

Fiscal and Monetary Policy
Rapid inflation.

Post-transition Period
China: ca. 1993 onwards

Vietnam: 1989 onwards

Initiating political event:
Deng Xiaoping goes south, 1992.
14th Congress accepts Deng's position
that the market mechanism "is merely an
instrument of economic development".

Initiating political event:
None

Main ideological thrust:
"socialist market economy"

Main ideological thrust:
Implementation of 6th Congress slogan,
"Doi moi".

**Dominant political context initiating
period:**
Relative stability in wake of rectification
and violent supression of unrest, rapid
growth apparently institutionalized, with
highly materialistic character.

**Dominant political context initiating
period:**
Loss of Soviet aid; anti-inflationary
measures; effects of overturn of
Communist Party rule in Central
Europe.

External Sector
Unified exchange-rate system introduced in January 1994. Foreign exchange access remained segmented, with certain businesses allowed access to the swap market. Obligatory trade planning eliminated, starting in 1994.

External Sector
Single exchange rate introduced 1989; *dong* essentially convertible. Borders in essence "opened", exposing SOEs to great competitive pressures and allowing economy access to both south Chinese as well as world markets. Liberalization of foreign trade greatly accelerated, starting with Decree in 1989 followed by further measures in 1990s. Private sector granted access. Rapid increase in exports. Massive acceleration of FDI, almost entirely in joint ventures with SOEs. Private sector starts to emerge rapidly from around 1992-93.

Agriculture
No major changes.
Problems with "white slips" (IOUs) used to pay farmers for state purchases.

Agriculture
Old co-operative structures, and district management structures, fade away. Rapid growth in rural incomes.

Pricing Policy
Further reductions in extent of twin-track pricing, tending to be retained in certain producer goods. By 1993 5% of retail goods, 15% of producer goods and 10% of agricultural products subject to price control.

Pricing Policy
Abolition of "two-price" system (1989). Rapid penetration and replacement of state trade by the private sector.

Enterprises
Policy attempting to unravel large numbers of loss-making SOEs; reluctance to introduce rapid "top-down" equitization.

halving

Enterprises
SOEs no longer subject to mandatory targets; basic obligation is to meet budgetary contributions. Major rationalisation of SOEs — of numbers by 1994-95.

Labour
Trend to further monetization of wages and expansion of experiments with pensions, health insurance and unemployment schemes.

Labour
With removal of rationing, strong efforts to monetize wages, dispose of state housing and restore real state wages.

Fiscal and Monetary Policy
Realization of realities of liberalization — investment projects still largely subject to state approval at various levels. Little sign of progress. Major tax reforms implemented January 1994. Attempts to clarify and regularize relations between centre and localities (new system introduced from 1994). National Tax Service established 1 January 1994. Treasury remains part of People's

Fiscal and Monetary Policy
Two-tier banking system set up (1990). Interest reforms in 1989 and 1992 make interest rates positive in real terms and allow banks a positive lending margin. Rapid development of formal financial institutions — commercial banks, housing banks, treasure bills. Fiscal control tightened through exercise of tax reforms and through

Bank of China, state expenditure control system unreformed. Major efforts to improve payments system and strengthen central bank. Credit plan remains main basis for monetary policy.

establishment of normal centralized departments responsible for taxes and for Treasury activities under the Ministry of Finance.

Late Post-transition Period, 1997 onwards

By 1997/98 China's economic development was characterized by a focus upon macro-economic rather than institutional issues, although the decisive moves to close or corporatize most SOEs taken at the 15th Party Congress in September 1997 pointed to a maturing system that was starting to develop formal structures of a more normal market economy.

The political economy was such that pro-market reformers could act against SOEs and, to maintain macroeconomic stability, push for the creation of state structures with great potential power, such as the central bank.

China's freedom to manoeuvre in the face of the 1997 Asian financial crisis, which coincided with the push against loss-making SOEs, revealed a broad political support for this trend.

By 1997/98 Vietnamese economic development was slowing, with clear signs of a lack of political support for measures to deal with loss-making SOEs. There was no push to encourage the private sector, despite the formal opportunity offered by the change of the top leadership and the accession of Le Kha Phieu to the Party Secretaryship.

As the Asian financial crisis developed, the Vietnamese seemed increasingly vulnerable, and through 1997-98 there were no major policy initiatives that had real impact.

FOUR

Asian Socialism's Open Doors:
Guangzhou and Ho Chi Minh City

William S. Turley and Brantly Womack*

No country is more similar to China than Vietnam in terms of traditional society, revolutionary experience and post-revolutionary government. Yet it is equally obvious that China is not only much larger in population and territory; it is considerably more advanced economically today, and its state structure has had more time to develop organizational complexity and managerial capability. China also started the move toward a more open, competitive market economy earlier and from a stronger base, and it has experienced the most rapid economic growth in the world during the past fifteen years. All of these differences together create a contextual disparity in which similar policies in the two countries can have different effects, intermediate units have different capacities, and national-local governmental relationships have different dynamics.

This Chapter will explore this disparity and the dimensions of regional reform in China and Vietnam by comparing the national roles of Guangzhou and Ho Chi Minh City, the two most prominent municipal leaders in economic reform in their respective countries. Most particularly, the paper will examine how the differences in historical context and in the relative importance of the

* We thank the participants of the Workshop on Transforming Asian Socialisms and discussant Peter Rimmer for their comments on earlier drafts of this chapter. Special thanks are due to Anita Chan, Adam Fforde, Ben Kerkvliet and Stanley Rosen for providing written critiques. We gratefully acknowledge the financial support of the Social Science Research Council for research trips by Womack to China and Turley to Vietnam in autumn 1995, and the help we received in those countries from Peter Lee of the Chinese University of Hong Kong, the Guangzhou Social Science Institute, the China Institute of Contemporary International Relations, and the Vietnam National Centre for Social Sciences and Humanities in Hanoi and Ho Chi Minh City.

two cities to their respective countries have differently shaped their experiences of socialism and reform.

The Cities' Significance and Roles in a National Context

Guangzhou and Ho Chi Minh City have been selected for comparison because both cities serve as gateways through which technology, capital, management skills and ideas flow into China and Vietnam. They are both entrepôts, facilitating contact between national hinterlands and world markets. Both of them are financial and service centres for their respective domestic regions. And both are major domestic centres of manufacturing and of multinational firms. In these respects the two cities are quite similar, with Guangzhou performing these functions in greater volume than Ho Chi Minh City, although the Vietnamese city's contribution is much larger in the context of Vietnam's smaller size. Both cities are alike, too, in that their significance to their countries depends in large measure on the freedom provided to them to perform the roles in which historically they have had a comparative advantage. When national policy has encouraged interaction with the world economy, these cities have gained relative to other urban centres; when their national governments have restricted that interaction, they have experienced relative decline.

Scale is of the utmost importance in understanding the economic and political impact of each city relative to its own country. Even though Guangzhou is one of China's largest, most wealthy and most economically progressive cities, its contribution to the Chinese political economy is inevitably less significant than that of Ho Chi Minh City within Vietnam. As Table 1 shows, Ho Chi Minh City's percentage of Vietnam's population is twelve times as large as Guangzhou's share of the population of China. Similarly, Ho Chi Minh City's share is twenty times that of Guangzhou in industrial employment and nearly six times in foreign investment.

Ho Chi Minh City all but dominates Vietnamese industry; it produces fully 35 per cent of all of Vietnam's industrial output. It thus goes without saying that Ho Chi Minh City overshadows its nearest domestic rival, Hanoi, by a wide margin. In the early 1990s it accounted for six to seven times as much industrial output value as Hanoi, seven times as much foreign trade, and had more foreign capital investment than the entire northern region.

In some respects Ho Chi Minh City is more important within Vietnam than Guangzhou is within the province of Guangdong, of which it is the capital (this comparison is shown in Table 1). Another way of looking at this is that Ho Chi Minh City's relative importance to all of Vietnam is more than the significance within China of the entire province of Guangdong (again see Table 1).

Table 1: Percentages of National Totals, 1996

	Guangzhou	Guangdong	Guangzhou as % of Guangdong	Ho Chi Minh City
Population	0.54	5.64	9.51	6.48
Employment				
Total	0.57	5.29	10.79	5.04*
Industrial	0.84	7.53	11.20	16.91*
GDP	2.11	9.50	22.16	18.26
GDP by sector				
1 Agriculture	0.58	6.78	8.62	1.76
2 Industry	2.01	9.73	20.66	25.15
3 Other	3.26	10.94	29.83	23.92
Retail sales	2.77	10.41	26.63	28.71
Foreign economic relations				
Imports	2.86	36.45	7.84	34.57
Exports	4.31	39.29	10.98	52.76
Foreign investment	4.74	25.36	18.71	28.30
Governmentt revenue				
Income	1.15	6.47	17.77	31.10**
Expenditure	1.54	7.57	20.28	6.67**
Hospital beds	1.04	4.94	21.93	7.31**

* 1994
** 1995

Sources: *Guangdong tongji nianjian* [Guangdong statistical yearbook], 1997; *Guangzhou tongji nianjian* [Guangzhou statistical yearbook], 1997; *Nien Giam Thong Ke* [Statistical yearbook (of Vietnam)], 1995, 1996; *Nien Giam Thong Ke Thanh Po Ho Chi Minh* [Ho Chi Minh City statistical yearbook], 1996.

In light of this, in the pages that follow it will become more appropriate at times to make reference to Guangdong rather than to Guangzhou in our comparative discussions. This will particularly be so when discussing regional political leadership. Administratively, Ho Chi Minh City is a province of Vietnam, without any intermediary level standing between it and the national government. In China, as we will detail below, Guangdong, because of its province-level status, similarly bears the weight of centre-region relations, with the municipal leadership of Guangzhou playing only an important subordinate role.

Table 2:   Ho Chi Minh City and Guangzhou, Basic Data, 1996

	Ho Chi Minh City	Guangzhou	Ratio GZ:HCMC	Per cap: HCMC	Per cap: GZ
Population (mil)	4.88	6.56	1.34		
Non-agricultural	4.4	4.03	0.92		
Urban districts	3.51	3.9	1.11		
Area (sq.k)	1,093.7	7,434.4	6.80		
Population density	2,383	882	0.37		
Urban district area	140.3	1,443.6	10.29		
District density	25,239	2,703	0.11		
Workforce (mil)	2.83	3.93	1.39		
Employed persons	1.85	2.03	1.10		
GDP (mil US$)	4,227.6	17,379.18	4.11	866	2,649
Agriculture	111.9	976.16	8.72	23	149
Manufacturing & construction	1,810.1	8,123.33	4.49	371	1,283
Services, transport, etc.	2,355.6	8,279.69	3.51	438	1,262
Fixed investment	1,688.2	7,684.92	4.55	346	1,171
Housing	191.6	2,071.16	10.81	39	316
Retail trade	3,742.9	8,256.24	2.21	767	1,259
Foreign trade and investment (mil $)					
Imports	3,852	3,971	1.03	789	605
Exports	3,828	6,514	1.70	784	993
Total utilized foreign investment	3,302*	11,100	3.36	677	1,692
Average annual wage ($)	800**	1,421			
Education					
No. of college-level institutions	17	25	1.47		
College-level students ('000)	41	99	2.41		
Secondary school students ('000)	397	523	1.32		
No. of primary schools	598	1,612	2.70		
Primary students ('000)	421	705	1.67		
Health ('000)					
Hospital beds ('000)	14.3	29.7	2.08		
Medical personnel ('000)	10.5	52.5	4.61		
Doctors ('000)	3.3	22.4	6.79		

*   Cumulative since 1988 in Ho Chi Minh City and since 1979 in Guangzhou.

** Estimated.

Sources: *Guangzhou tongji nianjian* 1997; *Nien Giam Thong Ke* 1996; *Nien Giam Thong Ke Thanh Po Ho Chi Minh* 1997.

Certain differences at the city level must be borne in mind as well. Ho Chi Minh City and Guangzhou are about as carefully matched cases of Vietnamese and Chinese cities to compare cross-nationally as one can find, making them suitable candidates for "controlled comparison". But our units are not perfectly homogeneous, and differences that are inherent in the intrinsic character of each city do bear on our effort to interpret the way similar processes of change have been played out within each context.

One of the major differences has to do with internal structure. As is typical for large Chinese cities, Guangzhou city controls the surrounding rural areas. It includes eight urban districts and four counties,[1] which vary enormously in population density. Ho Chi Minh City's twelve urban prefectures and six rural districts cover a total area just over a quarter the size of Guangzhou.[2] Administrative boundaries determine that the proportion of agricultural population and of rural area is about three times as large in Guangzhou as in Ho Chi Minh City. It is thus not surprising to find differences in the extent to which politics in the two cities have been entwined with land reform and agricultural issues.

The other major difference involves the level of economic development. With a population 36 per cent larger than Ho Chi Minh City, Guangzhou produces over four times the latter's GDP, possesses nearly five times the fixed investment, conducts over two times as much retail trade, has nearly twice the exports and over three times the foreign investment. So, too, in line with Guangzhou's greater prosperity, the average wages there are considerably higher, and even in the provision of education and health care, the disparities between the two cities are higher than the population ratio of 1.34. Thus Ho Chi Minh City has the greater significance in a national context but Guangzhou has the greater complexity and wealth.

Four Stages in Centre-Region Relations

With some simplification, it can be said that Guangzhou and Ho Chi Minh City have passed through similar phases of historical development. We identify four phases and label them incorporation, consolidation, exceptionalism and reform vanguard. Table 3 shows the years of each stage for each city. Incorporation refers to the initial establishment of urban governance under the Communist Party, during which the new Communist regimes adopted inclusive tactics to smooth the transition from the old

---

[1] Confusingly enough, most counties (*xian*) have been renamed "cities" (*shi*) in Guangdong. Guangzhou includes Conghua county, Beiwan city, Huadu city and Zengcheng City.

[2] Ho Chi Minh City prefectures (*quan*) "within the walls" (*noi thanh*) are divided into a total of 182 neighbourhoods (*phuong*); districts (*huyen*) "outside the walls" (*ngoai thanh*) are divided into a total of 100 villages (*xa*).

regimes and to restore normal functioning. The primary thrust of the second stage, consolidation, was to redirect policy toward an internally-oriented

Table 3: Stages of Centre-Region Relations

Stage	Guangzhou	Ho Chi Minh City
1. Incorporation	1949-51 (3 years)	1975-77 (3 years)
2. Consolidation	1952-78 (27 years)	1978-79 (2 years)
3. Exceptionalism	1979-85 (7 years)	1980-85 (6 years)
4. Reform vanguard	1986-	1986-

pattern of socialist development, in other words, to revalue existing urban resources in terms of new national goals and to transform them accordingly. In the third stage, exceptionalism, the cities deviated from national norms on an exceptional experimental basis, either as a result of national policies granting privileges to certain localities (in China) or of localities' adapting to the situation at hand (in Vietnam). Finally, in the reform vanguard stage, the localities took major roles, in alliance with reformists at the centre, to push for a broadening and deepening of reform. For each phase we identify a characteristic composition of local elites and their role in national politics, and for each phase we identify a transitional dynamic linking one phase to the next. The framework helps us to highlight the basic similarities and differences of the two cities' development.

1.   Incorporation

Guangzhou was an important port city of China for centuries before the French transformed Saigon from a fishing village into the centre of trade and commerce for Indochina in the late nineteenth century. From then until the Second World War, both cities prospered as the leading centres of modernization and international contact for their respective regions. Foreign influence was more direct in Saigon. While Guangzhou established municipal government and services under administrators trained in the West and Japan, Saigon did this under colonial civil servants. The Chinese diaspora played important but very different roles in each city. For Guangzhou and for China as a whole, remittances from overseas Chinese helped balance the purchase of imports. In Vietnam, the ethnic Chinese were concentrated in Cholon next to Saigon (and now part of Ho Chi Minh City) and became the second most important foreign economic presence after the French and later after the Americans.

Guangzhou experienced the vagaries of revolution and war long before the founding of the People's Republic. Its foreign trade rose rapidly until the strikes and boycott of 1925, and afterwards never completely regained its pre-boycott level. Guangzhou's external relationships and privileged position came to an end with the arrival of the People's Liberation Army in October 1949, but the city was not central to the final struggle between the Communists and the Guomindang. By contrast, Saigon became the capital of southern Vietnam for twenty-one years, and its economy was transformed by war and by the American presence.

The PLA entered Guangzhou peacefully, and the initial political leadership of both city and province was a combination of northern cadres, rural southern guerillas, members of the urban underground, and retained Guomindang officials. General Ye Jianying, one of the Communists' pre-eminent military leaders, who was raised in northern Guangdong, was the first regional leader, combining the offices of Head of the Military Affairs Control Commission, first secretary of the Party's South China Sub-Bureau, governor of Guangdong, first secretary of the Guangzhou municipal Party committee, and mayor of Guangzhou. When the local leadership conducted a land reform campaign that the centre considered too moderate, Ye and his subordinates were removed and a new team of leaders headed by Tao Zhu, with Zhao Ziyang as his assistant, arrived in early 1952. The new emissaries from the centre launched a vigorous campaign of thought reform at the universities and a rectification campaign that criticized and removed local cadres from office.

In Vietnam, surrender spared Saigon from direct assault, and the initial leadership constituted a grouping similar to that of Guangzhou. All of the top leaders had served in the Central Committee's Central Office for South Vietnam during the war. Indeed, Nguyen Van Linh had served three separate stints as the Saigon/Gia Dinh Party committee secretary since 1945. After 1975, Linh served a year as chair of the municipal Party committee and was then elected to the Political Bureau in December 1976. Vo Van Kiet moved up from deputy head of the Saigon-Gia Dinh Military Management Committee to replace Linh as the Party committee chair.

The pressure on Ho Chi Minh City to transform its economy in a socialist direction increased after a conference on national reunification in November 1975 decided that the south should "transform" and "reconstruct" simultaneously. Campaigns against "traffickers and speculators" and comprador (mainly ethnic Chinese) bourgeoisie broadened into a comprehensive attempt to bring private enterprise, transportation, construction and retail trade under state control. But progress was slow and uneven.[3] Until spring 1978 about two-thirds of the retail market remained outside state

---

3   Nigel Thrift and Dean Forbes, *The Price of War: Urbanization in Vietnam 1954-85* (London: Allen and Unwin, 1986), pp.104-17, provides an excellent summary of the extensive secondary literature on the socialization effort.

control and the number of small private traders actually increased.[4] Many private businesspeople maintained direct links to Mekong delta peasants and struck deals with Party cadres that left them effectively in control of their enterprises even after ostensible conversion to joint state-private or outright state ownership. Kiet's municipal government set up joint state-private import-export companies that employed Chinese merchants with overseas networks.[5] Agricultural collectivization also stalled in the Mekong delta. As in China, the central government demanded sterner measures, and Linh, who objected, had to cede his chair of the Committee for the Transformation of Private Industry and Trade in the south to Do Muoi, a northerner without previous experience or political base in the south,[6] in February 1978.[7] A severe crackdown followed, ending the incorporation phase.

Both cities' contacts with the outside world declined as trade shifted from private to state companies. In 1950, private companies still carried out 32 per cent of China's foreign trade. By 1954 the private share had fallen to 1.7 per cent.[8] Meanwhile, the direction of China's trade shifted toward the socialist world, which Guangzhou was ill-positioned to service, and Hong Kong gradually assumed Guangzhou's gateway functions between China, Asia, and the West. In Vietnam, the state nationalized the south's export industries and foreign trade in 1976. The virtual termination of aid from the West and Japan sharply reduced the city's capacity to import, and cut it off from traditional export markets, although it managed to continue some trade with Hong Kong, Singapore and Japan.[9] Embargo and socialism, however, obliged it to accept a partial redirection toward the Soviet-bloc nations.

The incorporation phase was more gentle than some urban residents had feared. The regimes in both countries were in firm control nationally and felt no need to demonstrate their power. They recognized the value of the

---

4   The "unorganized market" share of the city's retail trade fell from 78 per cent in 1976 to 62.7 per cent in 1978. *Nien Giam Thong Ke Thanh Po Ho Chi Minh 1976-81*, p.335.

5   Gareth Porter, "The Politics of 'Renovation' in Vietnam", *Problems of Communism*, May-June 1990, p.76.

6   As chair of the Haiphong People's Military and Administrative Committee in 1955-56 and Vice-Minister of Commerce and later Minister of Home Trade in the late 1950s, Muoi had overseen the transformation of the north's private industry and trade after the war with France.

7   See Lewis M. Stern, "The Missing Linh: The Meaning of His Leadership", *Vietnam Commentary*, no.2, May-June 1988, p.5; and Melanie Beresford, *Vietnam: Politics, Economics and Society* (London: Pinter Publishers, 1988), p.222. Vietnamese officials interviewed in November 1995 confirmed that Linh's opposition to accelerated socialization was the reason for his "sacking", as Beresford puts it.

8   *Dangdai Zhongguo duiwai maoyi* [Contemporary China: foreign trade], (Beijing: Dangdai Zhongguo Chubanshe, 1992), vol.1, p.11.

9   From 1978 until the end of 1981, the city reported about half of its trade in Hong Kong dollars. *Nien Giam Thong Ke Thanh Po Ho Chi Minh 1976-81*, p.373.

metropolitan areas under their control, and the establishment of the Party's authority took precedence over the transformation of economic and social structures. The tendency was toward mild policies under cadres with longstanding and high-level connections to the centre who were also locally-rooted. Neither Ye in China nor Linh and Kiet in Vietnam would have got their jobs without central credentials; however, they did not wish to lose standing in the localities now under their control by espousing the increasingly transformative policies of a distant centre. Incorporation was successful in its objectives, but the accommodation to local realities became unacceptable at the level of national leadership when priority shifted to nationally uniform development. The modern resources of cities like Guangzhou and Ho Chi Minh City had to be redeployed for national aims even if the redeployment was unpopular, inappropriate or wasteful at the local level. The end of the incorporation phase was ultimately sealed by the central government's growing frustration with regionally specific and gradualist policies.

2.   Consolidation and Conformity to the National Pattern

The drive to consolidate the state-controlled economy, that intensified in 1952 in China and 1977-78 in Vietnam, attempted to homogenize institutions and policies nationwide, ending the cities' special status. China's "Southern Gate" closed, and an economy that had been built on a privileged commercial role with the outside world became a regional industrial centre on China's periphery. Ho Chi Minh City's external links withered, and the plan directed it to emphasize light industrial manufacturing, leaving heavy industry to the north. A large portion of the city's mainly ethnic Chinese commercial class fled abroad, causing a sharp drop in domestic trade. This phase lasted longer in China than in Vietnam, where institutional weakness and economic crisis forced a grant of exceptions after about one year. In contrast, Guangzhou and Guangdong remained tightly integrated into this national pattern until 1979.

Tao Zhu, Ye Jianying's replacement in Guangzhou in the 1950s, was a successful enforcer of central consolidation policies. He removed well-known local leaders and disciplined lower-level cadres. He transformed Guangzhou's economy into a regional administrative centre and emphasized the development of heavy industry. By the time of the Cultural Revolution in 1966, however, Tao's strong position in Guangdong had become an object of envy to Beijing radicals, and he was criticized and removed for building his own "kingdom".[10] Zhao Ziyang, removed from power along with Tao during the Cultural Revolution, returned to the provincial leadership in 1972-75 but was in no position to make major changes. He was replaced by General Wei Guoqing, a close colleague of Deng Xiaoping.

---

10   See Ezra Vogel's classic study of Guangzhou and Guangdong, *Canton under Communism: Programs and Politics in a Provincial Capital, 1949-1968* (New York: Harper and Row, 1971).

In Ho Chi Minh City, restructuring began under a long-entrenched local leadership. Although Nguyen Van Linh lost his post in the south and membership of the Political Bureau and Central Committee secretariat for opposing rigorous socialization,[11] his associate Vo Van Kiet remained secretary of the city's Party committee. Do Muoi served briefly as the centre's "enforcer" but learned that the policies he was sent to enforce were exacerbating the economic crisis and social turmoil. While the leadership in Guangdong had been an instrument of the centre, dependent on it for authority both to enforce consolidation and to terminate it, the leaders of Ho Chi Minh City had a local power base, representation at the centre, and sympathy from individuals such as Do Muoi, who were discovering the limits of central planning — all of which gave them leverage that their Guangdong counterparts lacked. In both cases, however, the power of regional leaders as well as the regions' developmental capacities assured them leading roles in modernization and openness when the consolidation phase ended.

Given the twenty-five years of consolidation in Guangdong compared with just a year or two in Vietnam's south, it is not surprising that the transformation of economic structures affected Guangzhou more profoundly than Ho Chi Minh City. Table 4 shows that a major restructuring of Guangzhou's economy took place in the 1950s, and the trend continued in later years at a slower pace. The emphasis of the First Five-Year Plan on industrial development, followed by the cooperatization of the service economy in the late 1950s, changed Guangzhou from an economy dominated by service industry to one dominated by manufacturing, and this pattern lasted through the 1970s. But the growth of manufacturing was relatively slow by national standards, and Guangzhou (as well as Guangdong) fell behind national growth rates. Comparable data on this phase in Ho Chi Minh City are unavailable,[12] but the shift was inevitably away from the extreme service-industry bias of the wartime economy. For not only did demand for services wither at war's end, but the first post-war Five-Year Plan emphasized industrial development and neglected the service trades.

Industrial output in Ho Chi Minh City, however, failed to keep up with the national average and began to decline in 1978, subverting the state's attempt to command the heights of the south's economy. The reasons included mismanagement and the inaccessibility of spare parts and supplies in the West and Japan, which mainly affected large state-owned enterprises (SOEs).[13] The

---

11   "Opposition" was the word used by Vietnamese interviewed in both Hanoi and Ho Chi Minh City during November 1995. Also see Stern, "The Missing Linh", p.5.

12   Only very sketchy retrospective System of National Accounts data are available for Ho Chi Minh City; the available Material Product System data count industrial output differently and exclude most services.

13   Tran Du Lich, "Dac Diem Kinh Te Hang Hoa va Quan He Thi Truong O Mien Nam Viet Nam" [Characteristics of commodity economy and market relations in southern Vietnam], in Vien Khoa Hoc Xa Hoi Tai Thanh Pho Ho Chi Minh [Institue for Social

Table 4:   Guangzhou and Ho Chi Minh City GDP by Sectors, 1952-96 (current prices)

Year	100 million yuan Total GDP	Guangzhou Sector Shares (per cent)			billion dong Total GDP	Ho Chi Minh City Sector Shares (per cent)		
		Agriculture	Manufacturing	Service		Agriculture	Manufacturing	Service
1952	0.54	20.01	31.42	48.57				
1957	1.12	13.37	45.74	40.89				
1962	1.24	16.36	49.30	34.34				
1965	1.80	13.88	56.25	29.87				
1970	2.67	11.72	64.09	24.19				
1975	3.66	12.10	62.06	25.84				
1978	4.31	11.67	58.59	29.74				
1980	5.75	10.85	54.52	34.63				
1985	12.44	9.69	52.92	37.39				
1990	31.96	8.05	42.65	49.30				
1991	38.67	7.29	46.53	46.18				
1992	51.07	6.98	47.25	45.77	18,587	3.34	31.83	64.83
1993	74.08	6.42	47.48	46.10	23,722	2.78	34.00	63.22
1994	97.62	6.21	46.79	47.00	28,271	3.80	37.76	58.44
1995	124.31	5.91	46.67	47.42	38,810	3.03	41.23	55.74
1996	144.49	5.62	46.74	47.64	55,068	2.51	42.06	55.44

Sources: *Guangzhou tongji nianjian 1997; Nien Giam Thong Ke Thanh Po Ho Chi Minh 1994, 1997.*

Sciences in Ho Chi Minh City] (ed.), *Mot So Dac Diem Kinh Te cua Mien Nam Viet Nam* [Some characteristics of the economy of southern Vietnam] (Ho Chi Minh City: Social Sciences Publishing House, 1991), p.62.

Table 5: Sector Shares in Industrial Output, 1949-96

Year	Guangdong				Ho Chi Minh City				Vietnam
	State	Collective	Cooperative	Other	State	Collective	Cooperative	Other	State
1949	59.6	0	40.4	0					
1952	68.4	0.9	30.6	0					
1957	69.0	20.1	10.9	0					
1962	71.9	22.8	5.4	0					
1965	76.8	18.3	5.0	0					
1970	75.9	20.7	3.4	0					
1975	71.9	25.0	3.2	0					
1976					77.6	0.2	22.2	0	62.7
1977					76.0	0.2	23.8	0	68.0
1978	67.8	26.1	6.1	0	71.9	6.4	21.7	0	66.0
1979					59.0	7.4	33.6	0	61.8
1980	63.1	27.7	7.3	1.9	67.4	32.6	Non-state	0	57.6
1981	68.2	31.8							55.0
1982	68.2	31.8							
1983	68.2	31.9							
1984	66.2	33.8							
1985	52.5	30.6	12.4	4.6	67.7	32.3		0	
1986	57.5	35.3		7.3					
1987	58.0	32.7		9.4					
1989	43.4	36.9		15.3					
1990	35.0	26.6		2.2	68.0	32.0			66.4
1991	36.8	23.0		24.6	69.2	30.8			67.6
1992	32.5	22.4		27.7	65.0	26.7		8.3	68.5
1993	24.2	20.5		34.9	64.1	27.8		8.1	70.5
1994	17.6	18.8		37.5	63.3	25.1		11.6	71.7
1995	14.3	16.3		44.3	60.0	23.8		16.2	72.4
1996	12.3	15.8		45.0	57.3	23.3		19.4	71.8

Notes: The "non-state" category for Vietnam after 1980 combines data on collective, cooperative, household, and individually-owned enterprise — categories that Vietnamese sources have reported inconsistently and sporadically since that time. Due to differences in method of data collection between the two countries and across time in Vietnam, the figures in this table should be considered as indicative only. Data are unavailable where cells are blank.

Sources: Guangdong tongji nianjian 1985, 1987, 1994, 1997; Guangzhou tongji nianjian 1983, 1988, 1990; Nien Giam Thong Ke Thanh Po Ho Chi Minh 1976-1981; Nien Giam Thong Ke 1981, 1994, 1996.

decline of output by industrial SOEs was absolute in 1978-80 — calamitously so among SOEs managed by the central government[14] and only partly offset by rising output in the collective, cooperative, private and household economies. Relative to other sectors, as Table 5 shows, the state sector's share of industrial output shrank steadily throughout the consolidation phase and more than for the nation as a whole.[15]

The figures for Guangdong (data on Guangzhou were unavailable) by contrast show a much more extensive and durable attempt by the state to dominate industry. Private ownership and output practically did not exist by the 1960s. The traditional socialist model with its emphasis on industry dominated by SOEs thus enjoyed a long run in Guangdong and, by extension, Guangzhou; while in Ho Chi Minh City it began to fail almost from the start, with a partial revival in the early 1980s followed by relative stability.

The shift in emphasis away from foreign trade and commerce and toward industry undercut both cities' economic pre-eminence. Guangzhou's rate of growth was stifled until the effects of foreign trade, investment and the unleashing of the service sector were felt in the 1980s. In Vietnam, the national emphasis combined with a foreign embargo delayed Ho Chi Minh City's recovery until a relaxation of controls touched off a growth spurt in 1981. Retail trade suffered in both cities as well. The number of retail and service units in Guangzhou bottomed out at thirteen per 10,000 persons in 1978 before this sector became re-established during the boom of the 1980s. In Ho Chi Minh City, the ratio held steady at around sixteen per 10,000 residents, but the number of outlets selling food, general goods, pharmaceuticals and books declined during 1977-80.[16]

With the peace that accompanied Communist victory and a rise in social welfare services, life expectancy at birth in Guangzhou's urban districts climbed from sixty-seven years in 1953, to sixty-nine in 1964, to seventy-three in 1982, although this was not a great increase in comparison with rural China or even with other large cities. By comparison, after reunification in 1975 life

---

14 Output by central government SOEs in Ho Chi Minh City declined 40.7 per cent from 1978 to 1980; the share of this sector in the city's total industrial output fell from 70.4 per cent in 1976 to 30.1 per cent in 1981. Ban Phan Vung Kinh Te T. P. Ho Chi Minh [Ho Chi Minh City Regional Economic Committee], *Vai Net Co Ban ve Cong Nghiep Tieu Thu Cong Nghiep Thanh Pho Ho Chi Minh* [Some basic features of industry and handicrafts in Ho Chi Minh City] (Ho Chi Minh City: Ho Chi Minh City People's Committee, 1981), p.49.

15 The industrial output share of state industry in Hanoi, by contrast, slipped less than a percentage point annually in this period, from 79.3 per cent in 1976 to 76.6 per cent in 1980. *So lieu thong ke Ha-Noi* [Statistical summary of Hanoi] *1976-1980* (Hanoi: Hanoi Statistical Directorate, 1980), p.32. Hanoi's large enterprises did not face such severe supply cut-offs as the embargo imposed on those in Ho Chi Minh City.

16 *Nien Giam Thong Ke Thanh Po Ho Chi Minh 1976-81*, p.358.

grew more difficult in Ho Chi Minh City, which experienced economic restructuring in the midst of a national economic crisis.[17] The consolidation phase thus had important similarities and differences in the two cities. The criterion of policy effectiveness for both cities was the execution of uniform national policies. For Guangzhou, this meant transformation from a leading centre of commerce, trade and services to an orientation toward industry, but one in which Guangzhou could not match Shanghai. Consolidation was far less successful in Ho Chi Minh City, as industry faltered under the combined effects of mismanagement and foreign embargo, and like Guangzhou it experienced constrictions of commerce, trade and the service industries. In both cities, it eventually became clear that the natural advantages of each were being sacrificed to national uniformity and domestically oriented trade. In Ho Chi Minh City, local leaders could not spur growth or even govern effectively while remaining faithful to national policy. Non-compliance with central *diktat* was more in congruence with local conditions and could not be prevented, so local leaders ultimately had to choose between failure or disobedience.

3.   Policy Exceptionalism and Experimentation

It might appear from the statistics that while Ho Chi Minh City faltered under national consolidation Guangdong made progress, but in fact the cost of consolidation must be measured by the lost opportunities for more rapid growth under more appropriate policies. By 1979 the leaderships of both countries permitted a tentative readjustment.

This transitional phase lasted in Guangzhou and Guangdong from the central government's declaration of new policies in 1979 to the popularization of experimental policies for coastal areas in 1985. In Vietnam, policy also became more flexible in 1979, initially as a response to crisis that tolerated local experimentalism, until overtaken by national reform in 1985. However, this stage differed considerably in the two places, as Guangzhou had been fully absorbed into the national economy and in any case had less weight in a national context than Ho Chi Minh City. Exceptionalism could only occur in China as the result of a change of policy at the national level; in Vietnam it occurred as the result of Ho Chi Minh City's unresponsiveness to national consolidation followed by recovery under emergency policies that did not officially or explicitly privilege it.

Exceptionalism was premeditated in China, adventitious in Vietnam. Guangdong province occupied a key position in Deng Xiaoping's project to

---

17   Vietnam improved access to social services for the urban poor during this period but could not overcome the immediate effects of embargo, crop failure and war in 1978-79. The caloric intake of state sector workers and their families in Ho Chi Minh City fell almost 12 per cent in 1979. *Nien Giam Thong Ke Thanh Po Ho Chi Minh 1976-81*, p.475.

reorient the Chinese economy. Its foreign trade and capital would greatly facilitate rapid development; overseas Chinese offered easy access to unthreatening foreign economic involvement; and the opening of Guangdong would ease Hong Kong's reintegration into China. While the years of socialist construction had disadvantaged the province compared to many others, its earlier prosperity made it likely that more permissive policies would yield rapid results. As the provincial Party secretary, Xi Zhongxun, said at the time, Guangdong would have developed much faster if it had been an independent country.[18] Reflection on thirty years' experience under the socialist model lay behind the Central Work Conference of April 1979, which led to a series of directives that permitted Guangdong to redevelop its external ties and service economy.

In Vietnam a similar appreciation of Ho Chi Minh City's unique requirements and potential had barely begun to develop.[19] The paramount concern in 1979 was the socialist model's failure amidst economic crisis. The disastrous effects of the crackdown on private trade and a backlash against agricultural cooperativization galvanized the south, while falling output in the state sector, the termination of Chinese and Western aid, and the conflicts with Cambodia and China affected the entire nation. The international situation ruled out a Deng-like opening to the outside world, so economic policy had to stress domestic solutions, which meant legitimizing any practices and productive forces that could immediately boost output. The city Party committee in August 1979 seized this opportunity to propose a number of policies that the Central Committee incorporated in a resolution,[20] the key one from the city's perspective being permission for the private sector to produce goods in which it had a comparative advantage over state enterprises. A subsequent decree permitted enterprises to obtain supplies and sell output in the free market, sanctioning practices that were beginning to spread in the north but had never completely disappeared in the south. Other changes that enterprises in Ho Chi Minh City were quick to exploit were permission to

---

[18]   As quoted in Peter T. Y. Cheung, "Relations between the Central Government and Guangdong", in Yeung and Chu (eds), *Guangdong*, p.25.

[19]   Vietnamese attention in the immediate post-war period focused on the difference in "material results" between north and south despite the earlier heavy dependence of both regions on external support. This difference led some leaders to doubt the wisdom of advancing class struggle over "objective economic laws" and to favour priority for growth over equality. Interview with Tran Bach Dang, former Saigon Party secretary, 13 November 1995.

[20]   Hoang Ngoc Nguyen, "Economic Renovation in Southern Vietnam: Challenges — Responses — Prospects", in Dean K. Forbes et al. (eds), *Doi Moi: Vietnam's Renovation Policy and Performance* (Canberra: Australian National University, Department of Political and Social Change Monograph No.14, 1991), p.35.

introduce piece-rate wages, profit-and-loss accounting, and supply priority for export industries. The plan for the city to concentrate on light industry quietly died.

In Guangzhou, the new flexibility allowed retail trade and services to pick up, and these activities assumed major importance alongside industry (see Table 4). In Ho Chi Minh City, the service sector experienced an even greater renaissance. Political flexibility *vis-à-vis* both cities also allowed accelerated growth of industrial production in non-state sectors, so much so that the SOE share of industrial output in Guangdong went into a steady decline, as it did in Ho Chi Minh City (see Table 5). Growth spurts revealed the potential of both Guangdong and Ho Chi Minh City to advance much more rapidly under looser policies. Guangdong's share in national industrial output rose from 4.3 per cent to 5 per cent, while Ho Chi Minh City's rose from 32 per cent to nearly 37 per cent in just the one year from 1980 to 1981.[21]

But the changes that produced these results in each country were different in three important respects. First, a five-year fiscal contract that allowed Guangdong to retain revenues over an annual quota of RMB 1.2 billion, and other concessions, granted a degree of autonomy to the province that Ho Chi Minh City did not enjoy.[22] Second, Vietnam's policies remained uniform in principle if not in effect, whereas some of China's policies explicitly discriminated between regions. Under the slogan, "special policies, flexible measures", Guangdong received a broad range of privileges and was exempted (or exempted itself) from various national restrictions. And third, Vietnam's policy shift began with a domestic focus, whereas China's was outward-oriented from the start. China in 1979 authorized three Special Export Zones (later renamed Special Economic Zones) for Guangdong and another in Fujian province. These were by no means simply factory sites with special attractions for foreign investment and export production. The largest SEZ, Shenzhen, located across from Hong Kong, had an area of 327 square kilometres, 23 per cent the size of Guangzhou's urban area and more than twice the urban area of Ho Chi Minh City.[23] Massive investments, the wage differential between Hong Kong and China, and cross-border family and ethnic ties supported a dizzy expansion of the SEZs. They quickly became Guangdong's Guangdong, a super-prosperous, externally oriented periphery unlike anything Vietnam could then contemplate. In fact, the SEZs soon surpassed Guangzhou city in per capita income and replaced the provincial capital as the leading edge of provincial economic development.

---

21   *Nien Giam Thong Ke Thanh Po Ho Chi Minh 1976-81*, p.77; and *Nien Giam Thong Ke 1981*, p.18.

22   Peter T. Y. Cheung argues that this was the most important of the centre's concessions to Guangdong during this period, in "Relations between the Central Government and Guangdong", in Yeung and Chu, *Guangdong*, pp.26, 42.

23   Ezra Vogel, *One Step Ahead in China: Guangdong Under Reform* (Cambridge: Harvard University Press, 1989), p.127.

The greater explicitness and depth of policy exceptionalism in China than in Vietnam was partly an effect of differences in leadership. Deng Xiaoping needed to consolidate his power by cultivating regional support and encouraging regions to demonstrate the efficacy of reform. Leaders sent to Guangdong in the Deng era — Xi Zhongxun and Yang Shangkun in 1978, Ren Zhongyi and Liang Lingguang in 1981, and Lin Ruo and Ye Xuanping (son of Ye Jianying) in 1985 — were expected to accelerate Guangdong's economic growth even at the cost of central revenue and national policy uniformity. The right of SEZs to retain their foreign exchange earnings and the right to import, for example, gave the province an enormous advantage in the race to modernize over regions that needed central government approval. Deng could afford to grant such privileges because Guangdong was not a central part of the national economy, and the quick growth of the SEZs and of foreign investment in Guangdong provided proof of the wisdom of his policies. Of course, exceptionalist policies for Guangdong excited the envy of provinces that were not favoured, but the main political effect was to induce other provinces to ask for similar policies.

No equivalent grant of autonomy and privilege for Ho Chi Minh City was conceivable. The centre was still consolidating national unity, there was an atmosphere of national economic crisis, and Ho Chi Minh City was simply too important to the national economy to be bracketed off from general economic management. Formal recognition of Ho Chi Minh City's special character came with the rise of the city's own leaders to national power. This occurred after a conservative retrenchment in the early 1980s provoked southern leaders to develop a comprehensive program whose basic elements foreshadowed *Doi moi*.[24] To promote this, they joined forces with reform-minded leaders at the centre headed by a former Party general secretary and elder statesman, Truong Chinh. Reinstated to the Political Bureau in 1985, Nguyen Van Linh openly criticized past failures to exploit the city's "designed industrial capacity" and advocated making it the "industrial and service centre for the south *and the country as a whole*".[25]

The success of local experiments provided ammunition for reformists to defend reform policies that had been politically vulnerable. In Vietnam, echoing Linh's advocacy of a leading role for the city, Vo Van Kiet, a member of the Political Bureau, deputy premier, and chair of the State Planning Commission since 1982, in 1985 held up the city's Food Trading Corporation as a model worthy of emulation.[26] In China, Deng and Zhao Ziyang made trips

---

[24]   Beresford, "The Impact of Economic Reforms...", p.128.

[25]   Nguyen Van Linh article in *Nhan dan* [The people], 23-24 April 1985, in US Foreign Broadcast Information Service, *Daily Report: Asia & Pacific* (hereafter FBIS-APA), 1 May 1985. Emphasis added.

[26]   Vo Van Kiet, "Transformation of Private Industry and Trade in South Vietnam — Some Practical Problems", *Viet Nam Social Sciences*, no.2, 1985, pp.55-6, referring to an experiment that "replaced" private traders by hiring them and organizing small

to the south to promote coastal development as a central government policy. Reformists in both countries could cite increased flows of revenue. But the only sure way to stabilize and deepen the experiments was to widen them into national policies, and, with that widening, experimentation ceased to be exceptional. Nonetheless, the transition differed between the two cases. In Guangdong, exceptionalist activities made the local leadership a natural ally of the national reform leadership but also a target of more conservative national leaders, while in Ho Chi Minh City local leaders rose to national prominence because of their opposition to discredited conservative policies.

4.   Reform Vanguardism

The best defence for the reform trend was further success, plus constant pressure for deeper and broader reforms. Guangzhou, Guangdong and Ho Chi Minh City developed especially strong stakes in this reform project because their advanced economies generated interests that pressed for further reform. They pushed for reforms that would further open and diversify the economy, though not so far as would weaken the national framework that was essential to their success. The point is not that the two cities pushed for similar policies but that they pushed for a generalization of policies that favoured their own growth, with success in this effort riding on politics in the national capital.

The effectiveness of local assertiveness in such politics continued to depend on connections to, and the balance between, factions at the centre. For Guangdong, the patronage of central leaders was crucial. Zhao Ziyang's new policy of enhancing coastal development by extending Guangdong's privileges to other areas led the province to propose a reformulation of its special status that would have increased its autonomy. It was the leading province making such demands, and its requests were not granted. The combination of Zhao's national leadership and Ye Xuanping as provincial governor led to new attempts in 1987-89 to confirm greater provincial autonomy, and Guangdong received designation as a "comprehensive reform area", but Ye's proposals were never implemented due to the change in central leadership.

Ho Chi Minh City by contrast took liberties with existing policy (specifically by loosening some controls on retail trade and price-setting),[27] and then saw this boldness validated in December 1986 by the inauguration of *Doi Moi* and the appointment of Nguyen Van Linh to the post of Party general secretary. The removal of restrictions on the private sector's involvement in trade and transport, a new foreign investment law, the reduction of rationing, and devaluation of the *dong* during 1987 were highly consistent with the city's

---

merchants to sell rice at market prices. In 1995 the Food Trading Corporation was bankrupt, leaving US$10 million in debts, with no apparent consequences for Kiet or other reformists.

27   Hanoi radio, 13 May 1986, in FBIS-APA, 16 May 1986.

interest in the market economy and openness to foreign trade. Reforms a year later that formally recognized the private economy, unified the official and open-market exchange rates, and separated commercial and state banking functions had strong support from, and at times followed proposals made by, the Ho Chi Minh City government.[28] Price reform, fiscal reforms, the removal of import duties on industrial inputs, the termination of export subsidies and legalization of private production of export commodities and trade with foreign partners in 1989 were all favourable to the opening and expansion of the city's economy.

The city's collusion with reformist leaders in the central government, however, was by no means solely responsible for pushing *Doi Moi* forward. Further reform was the only way Vietnam could cope with challenges China did not have to face. These challenges included a low state capacity to offer alternatives to local initiatives, severe inflation, the demonstration effect of reform elsewhere, and impending termination of economic cooperation agreements with the USSR and Eastern European countries. International events in 1989 intensified Vietnam's need to redirect its foreign economic relations. There was a sudden need to capitalize on Ho Chi Minh City's assets, particularly the access of its ethnic Chinese minority to regional markets and sources of capital.[29] External shocks helped the reformists get a single exchange rate, *dong* convertibility, liberalization of foreign trade and permission for private sector participation, and a more general opening of the economy to foreign competition and investment.

Events abroad had less effect on China in 1989 than its own tragedy in Tiananmen Square. This was traumatic for external relations and especially so for Guangdong. Besides the abrupt change in the international political climate, the province also lost some of its reformist friends at the centre and had to cope with attempts by Li Peng to reassert central control and to acquire a greater share of national revenue. Ye Xuanping opposed these efforts with a fair amount of success. Although he and Lin Ruo retired in early 1991, their replacements, Xie Fei and Zhu Senlin, were natives of Guangdong (Zhu had been mayor of Guangzhou) and well-known reformers.

---

[28] The clearest case of acceptance by the centre of a city proposal was the one on the separation of state and commercial banking, presented by the city in spring 1987. Hanoi radio, 4 May 1987, in FBIS, *Daily Report: East Asia* (hereafter FBIS-EAS), 8 May 1987. The city also led in obtaining approval of measures, *inter alia*, that released municipal SOEs from plan controls, liberalized foreign trade and encouraged the formation of joint state-private enterprises. Interview with Ton Si Kinh, 10 November 1995.

[29] By December 1992 two-thirds of all foreign capital invested in Vietnam was estimated to have come from overseas Chinese sources. Voice of Vietnam, 10 December 1992, in FBIS-EAS, 11 December 1992. And while the rest of the nation conducted 29.6 per cent of its trade with Taiwan, Hong Kong and Singapore, the city conducted 47.6 per cent of its trade with these partners. *Nien Giam Thong Ke 1993*, pp.238-9; *Nien Giam Thong Ke Thanh Po Ho Chi Minh 1994*, pp.190-2.

In early 1992 Deng Xiaoping made a well-publicized southern tour in which he encouraged Guangdong and Shenzhen to catch up with Hong Kong, Taiwan, South Korea and Singapore in twenty years. This trip became a decisive watershed for central government support of reform policies. As a result, some of Guangdong's wishes finally became national policy. Even the Pudong project in Shanghai was a consolidation of Guangdong's achievements, in part a response to Shanghai's lagging behind the growth rate of Guangdong.

Ho Chi Minh City by contrast never enjoyed privileges like those of Guangdong. The one concession that might be styled a privilege was the permission given in 1991 to establish export processing zones at sites near the city, but permission was soon granted to Haiphong, Danang and Can Tho as well.[30] Guangdong-style privileges would have clashed with the goals of reducing north-south differences and spreading the wealth outward from Ho Chi Minh City.[31] Preferential treatment was not essential to the city's success anyway. All it needed were national policies that permitted it to exploit its advantages. In return, it acquiesced to pressure for a redistribution of state outlays, mainly toward central and northern provinces, for capital construction and for the siting of foreign investments.[32] In Vietnam's case, preoccupation with repairing the effects of war, and in China's case a desire to stabilize and popularize the reforms, compelled the reform leaders in both countries to frame their demands as national policies.

Generalization of policy, however, did not completely eliminate frictions over the reforms' pace and direction, and in some ways exacerbated them. In the summer of 1995 China adopted its Ninth Five-Year Plan, which laid a basis for the eventual cancellation of the remaining preferential policies for coastal areas and a shift of investments toward inland areas. Arguments were made, infuriating Guangdong leaders, that with the opening of the reform policies to the entire nation the Shenzhen SEZ was no longer needed. Ho Chi Minh City for its part chafed under the central government's tight credit

---

[30]   In late 1995, only Tan Thuan, a joint venture of the Ho Chi Minh City people's committee and two Taiwanese firms, was deemed to be "nearing success", and the government decided to convert unsuccessful EPZs to industrial zones in which domestic firms would be allowed to invest and sell on the local market. *Business Vietnam*, vol.7, no.10 (October-November 1995), pp. 28, 34.

[31]   In 1993 Ho Chi Minh City accounted for 43 per cent, in 1995 about 38 per cent, of total foreign capital invested in the country. *Economy and Finance of Vietnam 1986-1992* (Hanoi: Statistics Publishing House, 1994), p.51; *Vietnam Economic Times*, no.15, July 1995, p.10.

[32]   The unsuccessful attempt in 1995 to have the French oil firm Total participate in a refinery project at Dung Quat, far from Ho Chi Minh City or the industry's service centre in Vung Tau, was only the most publicized of several such incidents.

policies and a highly-centralized revenue system, inaugurated in 1991, that allocated the city substantially less than it collected.[33]

The disproportionate prosperity of Ho Chi Minh City makes it a target of various national attempts to equalize opportunities among regions and to improve regulatory and fiscal control. But even though tensions between national and regional interests have re-emerged, the basic policy direction is no longer called into question. National commitments have made the reforms secure.

But reform is not static. In both countries, the current stage in economic and political transformation began with a dominant focus on the relaxation of central controls and then matured as localities became more concerned with the state's promotion and regulation of the national economy. Both Guangdong and Ho Chi Minh City appealed in the 1980s to the central government to reduce competition among exporters, and in the 1990s they were driven by the increasing complexity of the economy to support demands by central government leaders for administrative reorganization and professionalization at all levels. The agendas of the two countries' regional reformers thus evolve dialectically, in a direction that tends to strengthen integration rather than nourish latent separatism, despite the frictions this may sometimes produce.

Significant Differences

The stages of national-local relations discussed above demonstrate that there is much in common between Guangzhou and Ho Chi Minh City. Indeed, in this respect these two cities have more in common with each other than Guangzhou has with the Chinese city of Xi'an or Ho Chi Minh City has with Hanoi. Nevertheless, our brief discussion of these stages reveals that the experience of each city has also been different. The main factors accounting for this difference involve the relative mass of each, the state's capacity, the timing and duration of stages, the historical antecedents of war in Vietnam versus leftism in China, and the recent international situation.

The magnitude of the difference in relative mass of Guangzhou and Ho Chi Minh City has already been discussed in the first section of the chapter, so the remaining task is to highlight how this has affected political and economic development. Both cities were significant enough to merit careful treatment in the initial stage of incorporation, but relative mass became important at the stage of consolidation. Guangzhou was not so big as to prove indigestible to national policy. It was reshaped into a regional centre of administration and state industry, and only a change in national priorities among the post-Mao

---

[33]   Every Ho Chi Minh City economist, businessperson and official interviewed in November 1995 cited the centre's obsession with macroeconomic stability as an unreasonable restraint on the city's growth, and the revenue system as involving a perhaps more justifiable city "contribution" to inter-regional equality.

leaders caused a reconsideration of this policy. The exceptionalist policies applied in Guangdong became a matter of localized experimentation, but the discretion enjoyed by its innovative leadership was granted by the centre. It could be said, however, that the disproportionate success of Guangdong has increased its relative mass within China, and that it is now less tractable and more directly influential in the national political economy than it was in the early 1980s. Nevertheless, its success has also undermined the rationale for the privileged treatment of Guangdong and Guangzhou, and it does not have the clout by itself to resist redistributive tendencies originating in inland provinces.

By contrast, Ho Chi Minh City was too big to be digested. It did not confront the central government and oppose national consolidation, but the consolidation policy produced policy failure rather than transformation. Because its resources were so important to the central government, the failure of policy forced a national leadership that still preferred socialist consolidation to permit local leaders to act more pragmatically. But Ho Chi Minh City was also too big to be a haven for special policies. The contrast of its pragmatic success with dogmatic failure put a direct pressure on national policy and leadership. Having played a key role in turning the national leadership toward reform, the city's leaders earned national prestige. In an era that glorifies economic achievement, the very size and prospects of Ho Chi Minh City's economy guarantee it a major role in the shaping of national policy.

The second factor, differences in state capacity, is related to relative mass but not identical to it. Clearly, if the Vietnamese leadership had had the resources available to it that the Chinese leadership did, then the stage of consolidation in Ho Chi Minh City might have been more successful. Concessions to Ho Chi Minh City were only part of a pattern of emergency policies adopted in the 1980s to cope with dire shortages of goods, a stagnant economy, galloping inflation and international isolation. The subsequent successful policies of marketization and decontrol have had other serious consequences in undermining state services and creating economic polarization. In China, the reform policies, including Guangdong's experiments, were adopted in order to accelerate growth in an economy that was beginning to lose steam rather than to avert looming disaster, and the national and local governments were better able to sustain their respective infrastructures. China has a more powerful and effective governmental engine, and so its "takeoff" has been smoother and steeper.

The third factor is the temporal pattern of stages. The two cities have each experienced four stages, but Guangzhou has spent forty-six years in the process while Ho Chi Minh City has been at it for only twenty. There are two major effects of this difference in temporal patterns. First, Guangzhou had experienced an entire generation of socialism. By contrast, the two years of unsuccessful consolidation in Ho Chi Minh City were not enough either to succeed or to establish a new identity. Also, China has been the leader in policy innovation in the reform period, and even though Vietnam is loath to copy the Chinese experience publicly, clearly it has been an important referent for Vietnamese policy-making. While the most recent phase of reform in both countries began in 1985, it should be remembered that Deng Xiaoping initiated the general reorientation of China in 1979, and the experimentalist policies in Guangdong were part of an extraordinarily bold and successful set of reforms already five years old by 1985.[34]

The fourth and fifth factors are deeper contextual differences between China and Vietnam rather than factors specific to Guangzhou and Ho Chi Minh City. The fourth factor concerns the domestic context, in which the most prominent difference is that Vietnam was at war from 1941 to 1975 and then in hostile isolation from 1979 to 1995, while China was able to accumulate resources and to build on the successes and failures of its own domestic politics. To be sure, Chinese politics was quite tumultuous from 1957 to 1976, and its leftism led to serious economic chaos in the Great Leap Forward and political chaos in the Cultural Revolution. But the country was not, like Vietnam, plunged into war or destroyed by competing armies. Any negative judgement of the performance of the Vietnamese leadership should be tempered by the acknowledgement that the war and continuing hostilities put it in a situation of chronic emergency and privation continuing into the present day. According to a World Bank study, fifty-one per cent of Vietnam's population remained in poverty in the early 1990s, compared to twenty-one per cent in the Philippines, sixteen per cent in Thailand, fifteen per cent in Indonesia, and nine per cent in China.[35] Clearly war, rather than socialism, is the cause of Vietnam's poverty. If Vietnam had enjoyed forty-one years of peaceful, unified development after the Geneva Accords it might well have fared somewhat better than China, since it would not have suffered the idiosyncrasies of Mao Zedong's leftism.

Another important effect of war was to create vastly different experiences in north and south Vietnam. This difference was not effectively erased by the subsequent political domination of the north after victory and the imposition of policies aimed at forcing the south to catch up with the socialist north. By contrast, the extremes of leftism in China were a national rather than a regional experience. Within that context, Guangdong had, if anything, rather mild experiences during the Great Leap Forward and Cultural Revolution, while neighbouring Guangxi province suffered terribly from violence during the Cultural Revolution. Localism is a powerful tendency in Chinese politics, but if the Guomindang had managed to hold on to southern China until 1975, regionalism would be a more critical issue than it is today.

The last factor is that of differences in international context. These differences are clearly reflected in the two countries' most international cities.

---

[34] Notice that the stages we have identified are somewhat different from those that Adam Fforde finds for China and Vietnam in his chapter.

[35] World Bank, *Viet Nam Poverty Assessment and Strategy*, Report No.13332-VN, East Asia and Pacific Region (Washington, DC: World Bank, 23 January 1995), p.121.

Here again, relative weight is significant. China's population is twenty-one per cent of the world's total; Vietnam's is just sixteen per cent of Southeast Asia's total. To put it metaphorically, China opened its door and expected the world to walk in, which it has. Vietnam opened its door and expected to go out and find the world, adjusting to global tastes. Guangdong is not simply a province with ambitions of participating in the world market; it is a vestibule to the potentially massive China market. The Vietnamese domestic market is not insignificant in its potential, but it is in no way comparable. Vietnam's economic path is more immediately dependent on regional and global markets, and the country has been more agile and cosmopolitan than China in pursuing opportunities. It is not an accidental linguistic difference that China insists on things "... with Chinese characteristics", while Vietnam only requires that things be "... appropriate to Vietnamese conditions".

Moreover, China — and especially Guangzhou and Guangdong — is benefitting from a special relationship with Hong Kong. To some extent, Hong Kong deprives Guangzhou of a leadership role. A glance at the current economy of Guangdong shows that prosperity radiates from Hong Kong rather than from Guangzhou, and in the 1980s Guangzhou had a reputation of being rather stodgy compared to the new frontier towns of the Pearl River Delta, which took their lead from the opportunities presented by Hong Kong. Hong Kong has been and continues to be an invaluable asset to China, not only in terms of its own considerable investment activity, but even more so as a world-savvy mediator of regional and international interests. To a great extent, China — and especially Guangdong — deals with the world through Hong Kong, not Guangzhou.

Vietnam and Ho Chi Minh City do not have a buffer between themselves and the regional and world economies. Although Hong Kong and Taiwan are also top investors in Vietnam, they do so as part of the regional economy, which is largely dominated by overseas Chinese, rather than as fellow ethnics and intermediaries with the outside world. Ho Chi Minh City faces the world economy more directly than does Guangzhou. Its industries and markets are less protected, and its investment climate is also more predictable and transparent to outsiders. In general, Vietnam's hope and expectation is to become another small dragon within the region, while China remains a singularly large dragon, with no external role model.

Conclusion

Two basic dimensions of disparity emerge from this comparison of Guangzhou and Ho Chi Minh City. Guangzhou is at once larger, more prosperous and more economically developed, and was all of these things from the beginning of China's reform period. But it is Ho Chi Minh City that has had the greater economic role and significance in its respective national setting. Ho Chi Minh City also has the political clout of a major province, whereas Guangzhou is only one among many large cities in China and must approach the centre through the intervening layer of Guangdong province. Our comparison reveals that leaders in both cities entertained visions of reform-led growth in their localities but interacted differently with their respective national governments to fulfil them. In both cases, however, the centre-region dynamic contributed significantly to driving reform forward to the point where it became irreversible. That has not only restored the two cities to their status as centres of commercial modernization within their respective countries, it has also positioned them to remain in the forefront of reform, riding the crest of the internationalization and commercialization sweeping East and Southeast Asia.

FIVE

Agrarian Transformations in China and Vietnam

Benedict J. Tria Kerkvliet
and
Mark Selden*

In the half century since 1945, China and Vietnam have each completed two far-reaching agrarian transformations whose broad parameters exhibit striking institutional and temporal similarities. The first transformation, from 1945 through to the end of the 1970s, began with redistributive land reforms and continued with collectivization. Land reform eliminated tenancy and hired labour, equalized land ownership within villages, broke the power of the dominant landed classes, and consolidated the position of the Communist Party at the village level. Collectivization transferred authority over land and labour from rural households to local authorities, increased the scale of cultivation, and sharply restricted but never eliminated household production and markets. The collectives in both nations reduced labour mobility and increased the ability of the state to control consumption, to extract resources at fixed state prices, and to regulate most aspects of rural life.

In the second transformation, beginning in the late 1970s, households in both countries received contractual rights to cultivate small plots of land, and most of the other collective property was distributed, leased or sold. Households re-emerged as independent producers, as the state and collective relaxed controls over agricultural production, prices, labour and accumulation. Markets revived, with diverse forms of private and mixed ownership enterprises. Legacies from the first period, however, continue to influence rural society in both countries in the second period.

*   We thank Paul Bowles, Anita Chan, Adam Fforde, Edward Friedman, Carl Riskin and Jon Unger for comments, criticisms and suggestions on an earlier draft. Ben Kerkvliet would like to thank Pham Thu Thuy for assisting with research on Vietnam.

This Chapter explores the forces that propelled these transformations and the changing institutional landscapes and economic outcomes that they have produced. Two themes run through both periods. One is the tension between the central state and local authorities, and between cadres and households with respect to ownership, production and control over land and labour. The second is the consistently stronger role of the Chinese state and collectives in controlling land, labour and markets during both periods, with important developmental and social outcomes.

The First Agrarian Transformation

Land Reform

The late 1940s and early 1950s comprised an era of land reform throughout the grand arc that includes Japan, Korea, China, Taiwan, the Philippines, Vietnam and India.[1] Across the region, post-colonial outcomes were contested across multiple axes: between forces associated with nationalism and colonialism, between core and peripheral nations, between socialism and capitalism, and among social classes. On the eve of their land reforms, China and Vietnam were densely populated agrarian nations whose rural structures were deeply etched by inequalities of landed wealth and power. In China, the 10 per cent that were landlord and rich peasant households owned 56 per cent of the land while, at the other pole, 68 per cent of rural smallholders, tenants and hired labourers owned just 14 per cent.[2] Land ownership was most heavily concentrated and tenancy rates the highest in the central and southern rice-growing areas. In north Vietnam on the eve of land redistribution, about five per cent of the rural households plus the Catholic Church and French citizens owned one-third of the agricultural land. Poor peasants and labourers, comprising 62 per cent of the rural population, owned just 13 per cent.[3] In Cochinchina, in southern Vietnam, concentration was even more pronounced: less than three per cent of the landowners owned 45 per cent of the cultivated

1   Hung-chao Tai, *Land Reform and Politics: A Comparative Analysis* (Berkeley: University of California Press, 1974).

2   Joseph Esherick, "Number Games: A Note on Land Distribution in Revolutionary China", *Modern China*, vol.7, no.4 (October 1981), Table, p.405. Cf. Carl Riskin, *China's Political Economy: The Quest for Development Since 1949* (New York: Oxford University Press, 1987), p.26; Victor Lippit, *Land Reform and Economic Development in China* (White Plains: M. E. Sharpe, 1974); Carl Riskin, "Surplus and Stagnation in Modern China", in Dwight Perkins (ed.), *China's Modern Economy in Historical Perspective* (Stanford: Stanford University Press, 1975); Linda Arrigo, "The Economics of Inequality in an Agrarian Society: Land Ownership, Land Tenure, Population Processes and the Rate of Rent in 1930s China", PhD dissertation, State University of New York, Binghamton, 1996.

3   Edwin Moise, *Land Reform in China and North Vietnam* (Chapel Hill: University of North Carolina Press, 1983), p.164.

area while 72 per cent of the owners possessed just 12 per cent. Nearly three-quarters of the rural households in Cochinchina owned no land and worked mainly as tenants and labourers for middle-sized and large landowners.[4]

In both China and Vietnam, land reform coincided with civil and international conflict. The reforms began with programs to reduce rent and interest rates consistent with "united front" efforts directed against the Japanese and French forces in China and Vietnam respectively. In subsequent phases of land reform, Vietnamese and Chinese village activists pressed ahead with land seizures and redistribution, often in advance of Party directives. In parts of northern and central Vietnam, land reform also meant the restoration of communal land that had been privatized during French colonial rule. In both China and Vietnam, land redistribution and the destruction of the property and power bases of the landlords gave rise to a rural population comprised of roughly equal owner-cultivators.

In south Vietnam, land redistribution was bitterly contested in the context of the war and took much longer than in the north. In Viet Minh and National Liberation Front strongholds, rent reduction and land redistribution campaigns spanned the wars against the French and the Americans. The US-supported Saigon government also implemented a "land to the tiller" program in parts of the region after 1968. By 1975, the combined effect of the guerrillas' and the Saigon government's land reforms saw a significant reduction both in large landholdings and landless families. After reunification in 1975-76, the Communist government accelerated the drive to create a countryside of small landholders.[5]

Land reform in both countries strengthened the forces fighting against foreign armies and the revolutions' domestic foes. In both countries, too, land reform improved the position of small owner-cultivator agriculture as well as contributing to the power and penetration of the state at the village level.[6]

---

4   Quang Truong, *Agricultural Collectivization and Rural Development in Vietnam: A North/South Study, 1955-1985* (Amsterdam: Academisch Proefschrift, 1987), pp.136-7.

5   Nguyen Thu Sa, "Van de Ruong Dat o Dong Bang Song Cuu Long" [The land problem in the Mekong delta], in *Mien Nam trong Su Nghiep Doi Moi cua Ca Nuoc* [The south in the renovation of the country]   (TP Ho Chi Minh: NXB Khoa Hoc Xa Hoi, 1990), pp.144, 147-8; Robert Sansom, *The Economics of Insurgency in the Mekong Delta of Vietnam* (Cambridge, Mass: MIT Press, 1970); Charles Stuart Callison, *Land-to-the-Tiller in the Mekong Delta* (Lanham: University Press of America, 1983).

6   Christine Pelzer White, "Agrarian Reform and National Liberation in the Vietnamese Revolution: 1920-1957", PhD dissertation, Cornell University, 1981; Moise, *Land Reform*; Callison, *Land-to-the-Tiller in the Mekong Delta*; and Robert Sansom, *The Economics of Insurgency*; Mark Selden, *China in Revolution: The Yenan Way Revisited* (Armonk: M. E. Sharpe, 1995); Edward Friedman, Paul Pickowicz and Mark Selden, *Chinese Village, Socialist State* (New Haven: Yale University Press, 1991); Victor Lippit, *Land Reform and Economic Development in China* (White Plains: M. E. Sharpe, 1974); John Wong, *Land Reform in the People's Republic of China: Institutional Transformation in Asia* (New York: Praeger, 1973).

Politically, power in the villages of both countries shifted from landlords and rich peasants — who were stripped of property, humiliated, and sometimes imprisoned and killed — to land reform activists and demobilized soldiers, many of them from the ranks of the poor.[7] While violence and vengeance in applying class categories appear to have been greater in China, a powerful backlash against land reform rocked the Vietnamese Party and society. In the face of petitions and protests — some in front of the Communist Party's Central Committee headquarters in Hanoi — the leadership acknowledged serious mistakes, and in 1957 and 1958 a movement throughout north Vietnam rectified many of the excesses that had been associated with land reform.[8]

Collectivization

While the land reforms in China and Vietnam embodied both bottom-up and top-down processes, collectivization was an initiative pressed from above by Party leaders, not something that villagers clamoured for. Party leaders in both countries viewed collectives as the keystone of the socialist transition in the rural areas, even as they sought to avoid the disasters associated with the Soviet Union's forced collectivization.[9]

While heading in broadly similar collectivist directions, however, their paths diverged. Following several years of experimentation with small mutual-aid teams and low-level cooperatives, China's leaders collectivized the entire

---

[7]   For graphic documentation on the treatment of landlords, see Liu Shaoqi, "Report to the CC Concerning Each Locality's Report to the Land Conference and Suggestions for the Future", Central Party Archives, in Tony Saich, *The Rise to Power of the Chinese Communist Party* (Armonk: M. E. Sharpe, 1996), pp.1287-95. Estimates of killings in China's land reforms spanning the years 1947-53 and coinciding with a bitter civil war range from the hundreds of thousands to the tens of millions. While abundant evidence of violence exists, in the absence of release of archival materials, calculations are at best crude estimates. The best estimates suggest killings that were the direct product of land revolution may have been in the range of several hundred thousand to more than one million. Stephen Shalom's *Deaths in China Due to Communism: Propaganda Versus Reality* (Tempe: Center for Asian Studies, Arizona University, 1984) provides a critical look at the estimates. Estimates of killings during Vietnam's land reform in the north are also wide-ranging — from very few to half a million. The most credible figures are between 3,000 and 15,000. Moise, *Land Reform*, pp.216-22.

[8]   Bui Tin, *Following Ho Chi Minh* (London: Hurst, 1995), p.31. Also see Moise, *Land Reform*, ch.12.

[9]   We use the term "collective" for what both Vietnam and China call a high-level cooperative (*hop tac xa bac cao* in Vietnamese; *gaoji hezuoshe* in Chinese) in which land and other means of production have collective ownership and local cadres organize and allocate labour. The term refers to "high-level" comprehensive cooperatives similar to the kolkhoz type in contrast to "low-level" cooperatives which, typically, were smaller, involved less comprehensive organization, and paid dividends on investment of land and other means of production as well as labour.

countryside within one year in 1955-56.[10] China's collectivization drive reduced villagers' autonomy and their control over land, which passed without compensation to the collectives and tightened the state's control over the rural surplus. Basic decisions about the allocation of labour and resources passed from households and the market to cadres and the state. In 1954-56, the Chinese state virtually eliminated the market for grain, cotton and vegetable oil and initiated a system of compulsory crop sales to the state at low fixed prices.

Vietnam's Communist leaders, who simultaneously fought against the United States and the Saigon government, proceeded more cautiously. Collectivization, which began in 1955-57, stretched over many years and was never thoroughly implemented, not even in the northern half of the country. In 1960, official statistics record that 86 per cent of north Vietnam's rural households were members of cooperatives, most of a "low-level" type in which members retained rights to their land. Not until 1969 did the Party claim that 92 per cent of rural households in the north were in collectives.[11] In the south, no attempt was made to form even low-level cooperatives prior to the US military defeat.

Collectivization coincided with increased state control over markets, in that the Vietnam government required collectives to buy inputs and consumer goods from the state and to sell crops at official prices. But it did not eliminate free markets for numerous items, nor could it eliminate the black market in goods that could not be legally traded. In contrast to China, the Vietnamese state did not ban the selling of staples in the open market until 1974.[12] Even then, in order to procure rice and other key commodities from the countryside, state agencies in the mid and late 1970s moved away from fixed quotas and prices to higher negotiated prices paid to the collective producers.[13]

China's Great Leap Forward of 1958-60 carried collectivism to extremes in an effort to fully tap popular energies. By expanding each collective to a scale of up to one hundred villages and mobilizing untapped labour (particularly female labour), the Leap was supposed to usher in an era of universal prosperity. Soon, however, the bubble burst and China hurtled into a famine that exacted a toll of 15 to 30 million lives.[14]

---

[10]   Mark Selden, *The Political Economy of Chinese Development* (Armonk: M. E. Sharpe, 1993), pp.62-108; *The People's Republic of China: A Documentary History of Revolutionary Change* (New York: Monthly Review Press, 1978).

[11]   Quang Truong, *Agricultural Collectivization*, pp.58-9.

[12]   Adam Fforde, *The Agrarian Question in North Vietnam, 1974-1979: A Study of Cooperator Resistance to State Policy* (Armonk: M. E. Sharpe, 1989), p.82.

[13]   Christine Pelzer White, "Agricultural Planning, Pricing Policy and Cooperatives in Vietnam", *World Development*, vol.13, no.1 (January 1985), pp.101, 105, 111.

[14]   Friedman, Pickowicz and Selden, *Chinese Village, Socialist State*, ch.9; Penny Kane, *Famine in China, 1959-61: Demographic and Social Implications* (New York: St. Martin's, 1988).

Great Leap Forward fundamentalism broke the links between productive labour and remuneration (public dining halls for a brief time provided free food for all and household plots of land were abolished) and between collective institutions and communities (tens of millions of villagers were sent to work on projects far from home). Radical decentralization left the central government unable to plan and the localities frequently without resources to produce. The pressures to claim ever greater leaps in production also destroyed the statistical bases for planning. A flood of villagers into the cities seeking industrial jobs at the height of the Leap, followed by three years of famine, prompted the state in 1960 to impose far-reaching controls over population movement (the *hukou* household registration system), dividing city from countryside and binding rural people to their villages in subsequent decades.

Vietnamese policy similarly restricted population movements by requiring all citizens to have residency papers in order to find housing, obtain ration coupons, purchase food in state stores, and secure other goods and services such as education and health care. But Vietnam had no equivalent to China's Great Leap Forward. Vietnam's state initiated a series of campaigns to expand collectivization in the north and, briefly after 1975, in the south. Successful collectives were held up as models for all others to emulate. Mobilization efforts, however, were less intense than in China, downplaying class struggle and leaving more space for the household economy. The national need to mobilize resources for the war and to recover from the damage inflicted by the American bombing raids of 1965-68 and 1971-72 placed a premium on maintaining popular unity.

An ongoing struggle in the collective experiences of China and Vietnam concerned the locus of authority and power over labour, land, and the distribution of produce. The state and its local representatives, the Party and collective officials, tried to maximize control of all three spheres. Pulling in the opposite direction, in an attempt to retain as much control as possible, were village lineages, households and individuals. In both countries, for instance, the Communist Party repeatedly tried to enlarge the accounting unit of collectives beyond previous groupings among villagers. Rural people, however, tried to keep as much control as possible over the fields and harvests in which they were directly involved.[15] Overall, the Chinese state was more successful in such contests than its Vietnamese counterpart.

In the early 1960s, following the failure of the Leap, a three-level system of commune, brigade and team was established as the basis for China's rural collectives for the next two decades. Communes were reduced in size to approximately 3,000-3,500 households. As of the mid-1970s, each production brigade — a village or cluster of hamlets — averaged 200-250 households,

---

15   Fforde, *Agrarian Question*, pp.80-1; Francois Houtart and Genevieve Lemercinier, *Hai Van: Life in a Vietnamese Commune* (London: Zed Books, 1984), pp.31-2; Selden, *Political Economy of Chinese Development*, chs. 2 and 3.

and each team contained some 30-40 households.[16] This three-level collective structure coincided with the resurgence of a limited household economy restricted to private plots and a small window of opportunity in local free markets, as well as the development of rural sidelines and industry.

Collectives in north Vietnam by the early 1960s averaged 60 to 85 households, somewhat larger than a Chinese team but a fraction the size of a Chinese brigade. By 1970 the average collective was 150 households; and in 1980, 370 households.[17] This was somewhat larger than a Chinese brigade in the mid-1970s but a small fraction of the size of a Chinese commune.

Agricultural collectives in Vietnam were supposed to be the size of the state's lowest administrative unit (*xa*). They were also supposed to have production groups (*doi san xuat*) that specialized in particular phases of farming and that raised livestock (especially pigs) collectively. By the mid-1970s, however, most collectives were smaller than a *xa*. As many as 70 per cent had no specialist production groups, and had little or no collectivized pig-raising. At the same time, the non-specialist production groups often exercised more control than the collective's managers over farming, labour, draft animals and land.[18] In these weak collectives, more so than the minority that met the state's standards, members could withhold produce from the collective's managers and, hence, the state. That, in turn, meant villagers kept for themselves more of the harvest than they were supposed to and production group leaders might personally profit at the expense of other producers.

The household in both nations remained significant in villagers' lives, not merely as a unit of consumption and socialization but also in private production. Although substantial control over resources, accumulation and labour power passed to the collective, the household economy survived in part because villagers insisted, and because officials realized, that it filled productive roles that collective labour could not. As in the Soviet Union, the stability, indeed survival, of the collective system hinged on allowing both household production and a free market, even as national leaders often labelled these as capitalistic activities that should eventually be eliminated.[19]

The space officially allowed the household economy was larger in Vietnam than in China, and Vietnamese villagers were often more successful

---

16   Jean Oi, *State and Peasant in Contemporary China* (Berkeley: University of California Press, 1989), p.5; Frederick Crook, "The Commune System in the People's Republic of China, 1963-1974", in Joint Economic Committee, US Congress, *China: A Reassessment of the Economy* (Washington, DC: US Government Printing Office, 1975), pp.374-5.

17   *So Lieu Thong Ke Nong Nghiep 35 Nam* [35 years of agricultural statistics] (Hanoi: NXB Thong Ke, 1991), Tables 7, 10, 15, 16, 17.

18   Fforde, *Agrarian Question*, esp. pp.50-5, 80-3.

19   Mark Selden, "Post-Collective Agrarian Alternatives in Russia and China", in Barrett McCormick and Jonathan Unger (eds), *China After Socialism: In the Footsteps of Eastern Europe or East Asia?* (Armonk: M. E. Sharpe, 1995), pp.7-28.

than Chinese villagers in widening its scope beyond what was authorized. Collectives in both countries distributed five-per-cent of their land to individual households to use (*ziliudi* or self-retained land in Chinese; *dat nam phan tram* or five-per-cent land in Vietnamese). In Vietnam, however, informal arrangements within the brigades combined with villagers' surreptitiously taking over fields for themselves resulted in 7 to 20 per cent of many collectives' lands being farmed by individual households.[20]

Over the decades, household production that included private plots, animal husbandry, orchards and crafts provided critical supplies of food and cash to the collectivized households in both nations. The household sector was, however, substantially more important for the Vietnamese throughout the entire collective era. In China, collectivized production quickly became the primary source of subsistence and income for most rural households, and this pattern was sustained and intensified in the course of two decades of collective agriculture. In north Vietnam, the proportion of household income derived from private plots, petty trading, pig and chicken raising, and other household activities was some 50 per cent in 1961 and 54 per cent in 1967.[21] By the mid and late 1970s, with the national economy in decline, it rose to more than 60 per cent.[22] Comparable figures for China are elusive. But throughout the years 1956-78 the state launched repeated campaigns to control and restrict private plots and the household economy. For example, in much of north China in the 1970s, private plots were reduced in size and collectively cultivated; private marketing was also tightly restricted. National sample surveys suggest that the household sector amounted for 27 per cent of net rural household income in 1978 at a time when the state had begun to encourage the development of this sector. Data on a number of villages suggest that the household sector rarely accounted for much more than one-fourth of household income throughout the collective era, and frequently the figure would have been less than ten per cent.[23]

---

[20]   Quang Truong, *Agricultural Collectivization*, p.91; and "Hoi Quan He Giua Kinh Te Tap The va Kinh Te Phu Gia Dinh, Doi Song Xa Vien" [The relationship between collective economy and subsidiary family economy and the lives of cooperative members], p.E-3, and Table 3 "Ruong Dat Do Cac Ho Xa Vien va Ca The Su Dung" [Land used by cooperative and non-cooperative households], both apparently prepared by the Tong Cuc Thong Ke [National Statistics Office, Hanoi] undated, circa 1971 (phong Tong Cuc Thong Ke, ho so 993, vinh vien, National Archives Number 3, Hanoi).

[21]   Tong Cuc Thong Ke, "Nhung Chi Tieu Chu Yeu ve Tinh Hinh Phat Trien Nong Nghiep cua Nuoc Viet Nam Dan Chu Cong Hoa Tu Nam 1955-1967" [Principal targets in agricultural development in the Democratic Republic of Vietnam, 1955-1967], Table 287, 1968 (phong Tong Cuc Thong Ke, vinh vien, ho so 670, National Archives Number 3, Hanoi).

[22]   Fforde, *Agrarian Question*, p.218.

[23]   Terry Sicular, "Agricultural Planning and Pricing in the Post-Mao Period", *The China Quarterly*, no.116 (December 1988), pp.636-7; David Zweig, "Restricting Private Plots", *Agrarian Radicalism in China, 1968-1981* (Cambridge, Mass: Harvard University Press,

Dynamics of Change

With the crucial exception of the Great Leap famine years, the Chinese state assured subsistence for its growing rural population and invested the revenues that it extracted from the countryside. By mobilizing large numbers of labourers to develop the rural infrastructure, particularly irrigation and soil improvement, and by launching a green revolution based on a combination of high-yielding seeds, irrigation and chemical fertilizers, China increased per capita grain output from 306 kilograms in 1957 to 319 in 1978. The other side of the coin, leading to mounting rural discontent, was the state's program of low consumption and high extraction of agricultural surpluses that resulted in stagnation in rural income throughout the two decades of the collective era.[24]

Collectivization nevertheless provided a foundation for China's industrialization by assuring high rates of accumulation (averaging nearly 30 per cent for the years 1957-80) and by enabling the state to transfer much of this rural surplus to urban industry and urban consumption as well as to foster rural industrialization. Between 1949 and 1978, industry's share of national income expanded from 13 to 49 per cent while agriculture's share dropped to 33 per cent. The combination of assured subsistence diets and the provision of basic health care enabled China to raise life expectancy to nearly 70 years by the end of the collective era.[25] But these achievements could not ameliorate rural discontent with the high exactions and stagnating incomes.

In north Vietnam, industrial output grew by 15 per cent and the output of capital goods increased by nearly 20 per cent per year in the early 1960s before US bombing campaigns caused heavy damage.[26] Economic conditions for most rural people in north Vietnam had also improved by the late 1950s and early 1960s.[27] The production of staple foods (*luong thuc*) per capita,

---

24   Mark Selden, "Rethinking China's Socialist Economic Development", *Political Economy of Chinese Development*, p.30.

25   Nakagane Katsuji, *Chugoku keizairon: Noko kankei no seiji keizaigaku* [On the Chinese economy: studies in the political economy of agricultural-industrial relations] (Tokyo: Tokyo University Press, 1992), p.27; Arthur Ashbrook, "China: Economic Modernization and Long-term Performance", in Joint Economic Committee, US Congress, *China Under the Four Modernizations* (Washington, DC: US Government Printing Office, 1982), p.104; *Zhongguo tongji nianjian 1994* [Statistical yearbook of China 1994] (Beijing: China Statistical Publishing House, 1994), p.33.

26   Melanie Beresford, *Vietnam: Politics, Economics and Society* (London: Pinter, 1988), p.132.

27   Besides the information that follows, this statement is based on 1993 and 1996 interviews by Kerkvliet with farming families in villages of Da Ton (rural Hanoi) and Nghiem Xuyen (Ha Tay province), and on assorted Vietnamese sources, including Nguyen Huy, "35 Nam Thuc Hien Duong Loi Phat Trien Nong Nghiep cua Dang" [35 years of implementing the Party's line for rural development], in Dao Van Tap and Chu

converted into an equivalent measure of rice, rose from 223 kilograms in 1939 to 318 in 1961, almost precisely the per capita production reached in China. Yields in the north continued to improve until the end of the war, from 1.7 metric tons per hectare in 1955 to 2.4 tons in 1974, a rise of some 41 per cent, due to more double and triple cropping, new rice varieties, more fertilizer, and expanded irrigation networks constructed by thousands of work teams under the Communist Party's direction.[28]

Despite Vietnamese achievements in the teeth of US bombing and mobilization for war, discontent with the collectives was rife.[29] Many villagers blamed the collective system, more than anything else including the war, for the fact that life remained arduous. They could see that standards of living had peaked in the early 1960s, at the beginning of collectivization, and then declined.[30] Rice production per capita barely managed ultimately to keep abreast of population growth. It had been increasing in the early 1960s, but fell to 242 kilograms by 1974, a kilogram less than in 1955. And actual food consumption per capita dropped significantly between 1965 and the late 1970s. Only during the 1980s, as decollectivization gathered momentum, did per capita staple-food consumption begin to increase again.[31] With economic deterioration in the 1970s, ever more people looked to the household economy and the market to improve their livelihood. Higher yields on household plots reinforced the view that collectivized production was floundering. Unlike China, where collectivization provided the framework both for channelling the

---

Bien, *35 Nam Kinh Te Viet Nam, 1945-1980* [35 years in the Vietnamese economy, 1945-1980] (Hanoi: NXB Khoa Hoc Xa Hoi, 1980), pp.115-17, 121-2, 154-8.

[28]   The figures in this paragraph on rice and other food production come from or are calculated from statistics in Tong Cuc Thong Ke va Bo Nong Nghiep & CNTP [National Statistics Office and Ministry of Agriculture], *So Lieu Nong Nghiep Nam, 1956-1990* [Agricultural statistics 1956-1990], (Hanoi: National Statistics Office and Ministry of Finance, 1991), pp.87, 89; and "Sau 30 Nam Hop Tac Hoa Nong Nghiep" [30 years of agricultural cooperativization", in Nguyen Luc (ed.), *Thuc Trang Kinh Te Xa Hoi Viet Nam Giai Doan 1986-1990* [Social-economic situation in Vietnam in the 1986-1990 period], (Hanoi: Tap Chi Tong Ke, 1990), pp.28, 47. "Staple food" (*luong thuc*) is primarily rice plus potatoes, casava, corn, and some vegetables.

[29]   For elaboration, see Benedict J. Tria Kerkvliet, "Village-State Relations in Vietnam: The Effect of Everyday Politics on Decollectivization", *Journal of Asian Studies*, vol.54, no.2 (May 1995), pp.402-7.

[30]   Interviews with villagers in Da Ton villagers (rural Hanoi) and Nghiem Xuyen (Ha Tay province), 1993 and 1996.

[31]   Tong Cuc Thong Ke, *Bao Cao Phan Tich Thong Ke: 30 Nam Hop Tac Hoa Nong Nghiep, 1958-1988* [Statistical analysis: 30 years of agricultural cooperativization, 1958-1988], (Hanoi: Tong Cuc Thong Ke, July 1989), pp.138, 143. Also see references in footnote 28. One factor contributing to the continued decline in food availability in the second half of the 1970s is that food assistance from allied countries, which had been critical to the ability of the state to make up for domestic production shortfalls, sharply decreased after the war ended in 1975.

rural surplus toward industrialization and diversifying the rural economy, Vietnam's industrialization stalled and rural collectives remained largely restricted to agricultural production.

The war against the United States profoundly affected the course and outcomes of collectivization in north Vietnam. The state needed villagers to fight. Whether village resistance to the collectives was stronger or their bargaining power greater than that of Chinese villagers given the wartime situation, north Vietnamese villagers enjoyed substantially greater latitude for household activities within the collective framework. Vietnamese leaders in the end chose not to risk alienating villagers and upsetting what progress had been made in mobilizing food, troops, money and local militia by pressing collective demands to the extreme. Villagers who went to the war-front took some comfort in knowing that back home even weak collectives provided their families with some food, medical and educational needs and physical security. And the wounded and lame upon returning home were given a share of the collective's production, even if they could not work, as well as receiving state stipends that were funnelled through the collective. Moreover, because the mobilizations for collectivization and for the war were often interwoven, villagers realized that outright opposition to collective farming could be interpreted as unpatriotic.

For many Vietnamese, the end of the war ended a major justification for collectivization. Yet precisely at this juncture the Party accelerated efforts to make all collectives conform to the model ones, to increase their size in the north, and to extend collectivization to the south. National leaders and many rural people were on a collision course whose gravity intensified with the decline in agricultural production after 1975 despite the return home of demobilized troops.

In north Vietnam both during and after the war, direct confrontation was rare and resistance often took the form of discreetly ignoring or evading collective regulations. But occasionally, villagers did refuse to work, petitioned against enlarged units, and asked to farm their own land — actions that their counterparts in China, whose resistance was far less direct, dared not take.[32] By the mid to late 1960s and during the 1970s, villagers in many of Vietnam's northern provinces quietly shifted more collective production back to households. This expansion of household production often had the tacit consent of local officials eager to raise output and meet quotas as well as to improve the livelihood of fellow villagers.

---

[32]   "Tong Thuat, Phan Tich He Thong, Quan Diem cua Dang trong Cac Van Kien Ve Nong Nghiep va Phat Trien Nong Thon" [Analysis and Party views in official documents regarding agriculture and rural development], report prepared by members of the Central Agricultural Committee, Communist Party (November 1992), p.23; Tran Duc, *Hop Tac Trong Nong Thon Xua va Nay* [Cooperation in the countryside: past and present], (Hanoi: NXB Hong Nghiep, 1994), pp.80-2; Hy Van Luong, *Revolution in the Village: Tradition and Transformation in North Vietnam, 1925-1988* (Honolulu: University of Hawaii Press, 1992), p.197.

After re-unification in 1975-76, southern villagers, especially in the Mekong delta, spurned and fled the small agricultural production cooperatives that local officials had established as a prelude to collectivization. Of the more than 13,000 that had been formed in the Mekong delta, only 3,700 remained by 1980. A few collectives were established, but most of these functioned poorly.[33] In some parts of the central coast and highlands in southern Vietnam, villagers were receptive to cooperatives and collectives, but often these were places with low population densities that had suffered massive destruction from the war. Such conditions made the pooling of resources sensible in a concerted effort to recover use of the land.[34]

By the late 1970s, defiance of collectivization in the south, mounting discontent among villagers in the north, pervasive household production, and an economy in crisis forced Vietnam's leaders to re-think the viability of collectivization.[35] They concluded that an improvement in agricultural performance would require embracing household-based production.[36]

In China's countryside, pressure against collectivization, which existed throughout the collective era, came to a head following the death of Mao in 1976. China's collective system guaranteed villagers employment and subsistence, yet it also sustained vast rural under-employment (perhaps 150 to 300 million people), left 120 million villagers in chronic poverty, and yielded few income gains. Without fanfare, villagers in the late 1970s, sometimes supported by local and regional officials, pressed to expand the scope of the household and market. Bound to land they did not own and could not leave, villagers were locked into a system that denied them control over their labour power and the surpluses they produced, prevented them from selling or buying much in the shrivelled markets, and limited them to incomes in kind pegged at low subsistence levels. When a significant group among China's leaders, following the rise of Deng Xiaoping, also concluded that the collective was an economically and politically costly anachronism, pressures from above and from below combined to open the way to a second transformation.[37]

---

33   Lam Quang Huyen, *Cach Mang Ruong Dat o Mien Nam Viet Nam* [Land revolution in southern Vietnam] (Hanoi: NXB Khoa Hoc Xa Hoi, 1985), pp.191-2. Also see Vo Tong Xuan, convenor, *Phat Trien Tong Hop King Te Xa Hoi Nong Thon qua 7 Nam Xay Dung va Phat Trien Tinh An Giang* [Seven years of rural socio-economic development in An Giang Province] (An Giang: Chuong Trinh Phat Trien Nong Thon An Giang, 1994), pp.31-4.

34   Quang Truong, *Agricultural Collectivization*, pp.207-10, 222, 261, 270-1.

35   The importance of bottom-up pressures for policy changes is the theme in Kerkvliet, "Village-State Relations in Vietnam". Also see, inter alia, Fforde, *Agrarian Question*; and Quang Truong, *Agricultural Collectivization*.

36   Chu Van Lam et al., *Hop Tac Hoa Nong Nghiep Viet Nam: Lich su, Van De, Trien Vong* [Agricultural cooperativization in Vietnam: History, problems, and prospects] (Hanoi: NXB Su That, 1992), pp.78-9.

37   Kate Zhou, *How the Farmers Changed China: Power of the People* (Boulder: Westview

There are two notable differences between the two countries' transitions from collectivized to household farming. One is timing. The household contract system in China, which returned land cultivation rights to households, was virtually completed within four years between 1978 and 1982. The transition took much longer in Vietnam. Officially sanctioned experiments there, allowing households to do a few farming tasks on their own (*khoan san pham*), commenced in the late 1970s and were extended to the entire country in 1981. But not until 1988 did the state authorize local officials to redistribute land to households and permit them to farm the land as their own (*khoan ho*).

The second difference relates to the circumstances facing the rural economies of both countries at the time of decollectivization. Vietnam's began in the late 1970s in a climate of economic crisis. The initial steps, together with other slight shifts away from a command economy, contributed to some economic improvement, but not until land redistribution in the late 1980s did the Vietnamese rural economy make a strong recovery. Decollectivization was not the only factor but it contributed significantly to accelerated growth in the rural economy and much improved living conditions for most Vietnamese villagers.[38]

In China, however, redistribution of collective land in the form of household contracts coincided with a period of dynamic gains in the rural economy that peaked in the years 1978-84. The gains may be traced back a decade to the 1970 North China Agricultural Conference, which initiated a process of "conservative modernization" associated with Zhou Enlai. This led to accelerated rural industrialization and state investment in irrigation, and a comprehensive green revolution package that was implemented under collective auspices. Starting in the late 1970s, the state encouraged agricultural diversification (ending "grain first" practices) and provided an immense boost for rural producers in the form of increased agricultural purchasing prices. These measures stimulated agricultural production and increased rural incomes during 1978-84, when agriculture achieved very impressive gains. Yet in most areas, decollectivization and a return to family farming were not widely implemented until 1982-83, suggesting that the major gains in

---

Press, 1996) makes a compelling case for change from below; also see Daniel Kelliher, *Peasant Power in China: The Era of Rural Reform 1979-1989* (New Haven: Yale University Press, 1992). Jonathan Unger has argued the case for initiation and direction of the reforms by the highest levels of Party leadership in "The Decollectivization of the Chinese Countryside: A Survey of Twenty-Eight Villages", *Pacific Affairs*, vol.58, no.4 (Winter 1986), pp.585-600. David Zweig explores the relationship between impulses from below and from above in *Freeing China's Farmers: Rural Restructuring in the Reform Era* (Armonk: M. E. Sharpe, 1997).

[38]   Adam Fforde and Stefan de Vylder, *From Plan to Market: The Economic Transition in Vietnam* (Boulder: Westview Press, 1996), pp.88-9, 156-7, 179-91, 304-77 inter alia; and World Bank, Country Operations Division, *Vietnam: Poverty Assessment and Strategy* (January 1995), p.9.

agricultural productivity and rural incomes were the product of a complex package of which household farming was only one component.

The Second Agrarian Transformation, 1970s to the Present

In both China and Vietnam, three key institutions of the first period of transformation changed significantly in the second: land use, labour allocation and markets. From the early 1980s, villagers in both nations regained considerable control over land and labour and the authority to consume, sell or invest a larger share of their own product and income. National leaders now made improved living conditions through the market economy the principal yardstick for success and the key to building popular confidence in their regimes.[39]

Neither Vietnam nor China, however, made a wholesale shift from collective to private ownership. As the following discussion will show, the legacy of China's stronger collective system would continue to be felt in the form of deeper collective and state involvement in China's rural economy.

Land and Property Rights

In both Vietnam and China, land was allocated to villagers rather equitably, reminiscent of the land reform of the 1940s and 1950s.[40] One difference, though, is that in the 1950s households owned the land, including the rights to sell it.[41] In recent years, however, Vietnamese and Chinese households have held long-term use rights to the fields they farm with periodic adjustments of land to account for changes in household size. Land in Vietnam, formally speaking, belongs to "the entire people" with the state responsible for managing it.[42] Authority over agricultural land and forests in Vietnam resides with rural districts, towns and provincial cities, but in practice the village officials normally distribute and manage the land.[43] In China, land ownership

---

39   In Vietnam, Party Secretary General Do Muoi made this connection clear in a speech to Party cadres. "Bai Noi cua Dong Chi Tong Bi Thu Do Muoi tai Hoi Nghi Can Bo do Ban Bi Thu Trieu Tap tai Ha Hoi, ngay 3-3-1994" [Speech of Secretary General Do Muoi to the Secretariat's Conference, Hanoi, 3 March 1994], in Ban Tuyen Giao, Thanh Uy Ha Noi, "Tai Lieu Pho Bien den Dang Vien va Can Bo cac Doan The" [Materials for Party members and association cadre], 4 April 1994, p.4.

40   Indeed, Chinese and northern Vietnamese villagers were apt to refer to the redistribution of previously collectivized land as the "second land reform" (For Vietnam see *Nhan Dan* [The people], 16 April 1993, p.1).

41   In China, as land reform gave way to the mutual aid and cooperative movements in the early 1950s, the right to buy and sell land became nominal. In north China, in the early 1950s, farmers were pressured not to buy or sell land. See Friedman, Pickowicz and Selden, *Chinese Village, Socialist State*, ch.5.

42   *Luat Dat Dai 1993* [1993 Land Law] (Hanoi: NXB Chinh Tri Quoc Gia, 1993), article 1.

43   Ibid, article 24.2.

is vested in villages whose officials assign rights to households for extended periods.

In Vietnam, and to a lesser extent in China, conflicts erupted during the distribution of collectivized land to households.[44] One example of this, common in upland areas of Vietnam, involved minority groups seeking to reclaim lands they believed the government and lowlander immigrants had wrongly taken from them during previous decades. In some parts of northern Vietnam and China where land redistribution between villages had occurred decades earlier, the villages struggled to re-establish old boundaries and claims to fields that collectivization had erased. In areas of south Vietnam where collectivization had been minimal, former landlords often tried, sometimes successfully, to take back land that local authorities had turned over to tenants in the mid-1970s.[45] Former landlords in China and north Vietnam, to the best of our knowledge, invoked no such claims.

In Vietnam, the rights and obligations of rural landholders were spelled out in a 1993 land law passed by the National Assembly following extensive public debate.[46] Significantly, not only Party officials but many villagers opposed privatization of land ownership rights. While favouring the long-term distribution of use rights to the fields, many preferred periodic redistribution in order to maintain equity, a pattern with roots in pre-revolution village praxis. Land use conditions are similar in China.

Villagers may not own land; they may only hold "use rights" to it — twenty years for annually cropped land and fifty years for perennially cropped land in Vietnam and, since 1992, thirty years or more in China depending on the type of land. During the period of tenure, however, households may cultivate the land or they may transfer, lend, or rent it out, and can transfer the use rights to heirs.[47] In return, Chinese and Vietnamese landholders pay taxes

---

44   See Benedict J. Tria Kerkvliet, "Rural Society and State Relations", in Kerkvliet and Doug J. Porter (eds), *Vietnam's Rural Transformation* (Boulder and Singapore: Westview Press and the Institute of Southeast Asian Studies, 1995), pp.74-6; Elizabeth Perry, "Rural Violence in Socialist China", *The China Quarterly*, no.103 (1985), pp.414-40; David Zweig, "Struggles over Land in China: Peasant Resistance After Collectivization, 1966-1986", in Forrest Colburn (ed.), *Everyday Forms of Peasant Resistance* (Armonk: M. E. Sharpe, 1989), pp.151-74; personal communication, Kate Xiao Zhou, 1996.

45   Lam Quang Huyen, "Mot So Van De Ruong Dat o cac Tinh Phia Nam" [Land problems in southern provinces]; and Nguyen Phuong Vy, "Ket Qua Dieu Tra Ruong Dat o cac Tinh Phia Nam" [Survey results regarding land in southern provinces]. Both are papers in the "Chinh Sach Ruong Dat o Nong Thon" [Land policy in the countryside] series of the National Research Program on Rural Development, KX08, December 1993, Hanoi.

46   Kerkvliet, "Rural Society and State Relations".

47   *Luat Dat Dai 1993*, article 3, paragraph 2. Mark Selden and Aiguo Lu, "The Reform of Land Ownership and the Political Economy of Contemporary China", in Selden, *The Political Economy of Chinese Development*; Jiang Bing, "The Emergence of a Land Market in China: Issues in the Reform of the Planned Land Management System and the

to the state and are also often liable for other charges such as irrigation fees and payments to village funds, and for such service obligations as road and irrigation repairs and other corvee labour.

An enduring legacy of the 1950s land reform in China and Vietnam is that land distribution since decollectivization has been remarkably equal. This provides a safety net and limits the growth of large inequalities in wealth and power based on land concentrations such as those found in India, the Philippines and Brazil.[48] Vietnamese law allows up to three hectares of annually cropped land per household; local authorities have the option of reducing that size. China has imposed no limits on the size of leased holdings.

In both Vietnam and China during the 1990s, villagers with other sources of income often sublet their land or hire labourers to do some or all of the farming. This has occurred on a large scale in China's coastal and suburban areas where resident villagers can secure lucrative industrial jobs. In some areas, a few households have cultivated (often using hired migrant labour) most or all of the land in an entire village while other villagers specialize in non-agricultural work. For example, in Changshu City, Jiangsu, 1,230 farm households have signed contracts to cultivate 6,887 hectares, an average of 5.6 hectares per household. Wuxi County has established 761 village-run farms in which small numbers of villagers cultivate all the village lands on behalf of the community, freeing others for different jobs.[49] These are areas where collective traditions have remained strong in both farming and rural industries. In many parts of Guangdong's booming Pearl River delta, however, much of the land is being privately tilled for households by hired migrant workers, mainly from Hunan and Hubei.[50]

With the exception of the small number of large farms, subsistence conditions prevail for most Vietnamese and Chinese farm households that lack off-farm incomes. A 1989 Chinese sample survey found that the average household contracted 9.7 plots of land totalling 0.62 hectares.[51] In the lowlands of northern and central Vietnam, households commonly have five or more small fields that add up to less than a third of a hectare. In the less densely populated south, including the Mekong delta, those with two or three

Development of a Land Market with Chinese Characteristics", PhD dissertation, University of Adelaide, 1994.

48   Jim Matson and Mark Selden, "Poverty and Inequality in China and India", *Economic and Political Weekly*, 4 April 1992, pp.701-15; Amartya Sen, "How is China Doing?", *New York Review of Books*, vol.29, no.20 (16 December 1982), pp.41-45. This is no assurance that other forms of inequality will not arise. Indeed, income inequality has risen significantly in rural China in the 1990s. Personal communication with Carl Riskin, November 1997.

49   Li Ning, "Rural Southern Jiangsu Pursues Modernization", *Beijing Review*, vol.38, no.41 (9-15 October 1995), pp.8-9.

50   Mark Selden, personal observation, June 1997.

51   Vaclav Smil, *China's Environmental Crisis. An Inquiry into the Limits of National Development* (Armonk: M. E. Sharpe, 1993), p.148.

times as much land are still extremely poor.[52] In short, in both China and Vietnam, equal land distribution has assured subsistence but not a higher standard of living.[53]

Organization of Labour and Production

Following the redistribution of land to families, local authorities in most of China and Vietnam also sold, gave away or contracted to households the farm machinery, draft animals, sideline enterprises and other means of production that the collectives had previously monopolized. Consequently, rural households emerged as the primary locus of agricultural production and many other economic activities. Later, other households, individually or at times jointly, started their own industrial, service and commercial establishments. These are far more numerous, prosperous, and export-oriented in coastal China than in the country's inland areas, or in any part of Vietnam.

Only between 10 and 20 per cent of the collectives in Vietnam at the beginning of the second transformation made the transition to a new type of cooperative providing marketing assistance, irrigation, loans and other services to their members.[54] The rest have either completely disappeared or retain a few features such as an irrigation system that villagers continue to operate collectively.

Meanwhile, villagers in many parts of Vietnam have formed their own small-scale "cooperatives" involving varying degrees of organization. Many households exchange labour during ploughing, planting and harvesting seasons, arrangements that require minimal organization.[55] Somewhat more complicated have been collaborations among village households to secure

---

[52]   According to survey data, the average agricultural and forest land per household in the Red River delta is 0.28 hectares and in the north central region the figure is 0.40 hectares. In the Mekong delta, the average land area per household is 1.1 hectares. For the nation, the average area per household is 0.64 hectares. Vietnam, State Planning Committee and General Statistics Office, *Khao Sat Muc Song Dan Cu Viet Nam/Vietnam Living Standards Survey 1992-1993* (Hanoi: State Planning Committee and General Statistics Office, 1994), p.151.

[53]   For elaboration on land distribution, rural poverty and socio-economic inequality, see the following Chapter by Hy Van Luong and Jonathan Unger.

[54]   The lower percentage is from a survey, apparently done in 1994, reported in the government study "Tom Tat Bao Cao Ket Qua Dieu Tra Hop Tax Xa Nong Nghiep o Viet Nam" [Summary of survey results regarding agricultural cooperatives in Vietnam], (Hanoi: TCP/VIE/4452A, undated, circa 1997). The higher percentage comes from Dao The Tuan, coordinator, "Kinh Te Ho Gia Dinh va cac To Chuc Hop Tac Co So" [The family economy and cooperative organizations], paper of the National Research Program on Rural Development, KX08, undated, circa 1994, Hanoi, pp.20-1.

[55]   Drawn from Tran Duc, *Hop Tac*, pp.141-4, and newspaper articles on the countryside in the *Nhan Dan* and *Nong Thon Ngay Nay* [The countryside today] (previously named *Nong Dan Viet Nam*), 1993-1996.

credit from lending agencies or to pool and lend funds to each other. There are also reports of fellow villagers cooperating in longer-term economic and welfare activities. Families in a village in Ha Tay province, for instance, created their own pension program. Each season members deposit specified amounts of rice in a fund from which they will receive an annual rice allocation after they reach retirement age.[56] Other examples of cooperation include clusters of households in Nghe An and Ha Tinh provinces that have pooled savings to buy and raise deer and then share the profits.[57] People living in different villages have also cooperated in order to market their goods and secure other mutual advantages. Examples from the south include an association of lemon growers in Ben Tre province and an association of cashew nut producers in Song Be province; in the north there is a handicraft association in Hai Hung province.[58]

These and many other cooperative and collective forms can be found in far greater numbers in rural China.[59] A 1991 Ministry of Agriculture report noted that since the early 1980s, over two million village and sub-village groups — some 26 per cent of former production teams — have retained or re-instituted collective farming activities. Their machines plow more than 35 per cent of all the farmland and water 70 per cent of irrigated acreage.[60]

In contrast to China, few Vietnamese rural cooperatives are industrial producers for urban markets or for export, and few have attracted foreign investment. One successful example is a silkworm and weaving cooperative in Duy Xuyen district, Quang Nam-Da Nang province, that has become a factory with 3.5 billion *dong* ($350,000) capital investment and 570 workers.[61] Thus far, this is exceptional. A 1992 survey indicates that less than one per cent of all rural enterprises are cooperatively owned and an even smaller percentage are state owned.[62]

---

56   *Nhan Dan*, 24 January 1994, p.2.

57   Tran Duc, *Hop Tac*, pp.184-90.

58   "May Van De ve Thiet Che Chinh Tri Xa Hoi Nong Thon Hien Nay" [Matters concerning political institutions in rural society at present], paper in the National Research Program on Rural Development] (KX08, topic 09), circa 1994, p.8; *Nhan Dan*, 16 May 1994, p.3.

59   Mark Selden, "Household, Cooperative and State in the Remaking of China's Countryside", in Edward Vermeer, Frank Pieke and Woei Lien Chong (eds), *Cooperative and Collective in China's Rural Development—Between State and Private Interests* (Armonk: M. E. Sharpe, 1998).

60   Bowles and Dong, "Current Successes and Future Challenges". These figures probably exaggerate the extent of village-organized agricultural production. Yet numerous examples attest to the resurgence of various forms of group farming at the village or sub-village level.

61   *Nhan Dan*, 22 March 1994, p.1ff.

62   Nguyen Duc Minh and Bui Bich Hoa, "Rural Industries in Vietnam", paper for a conference on "Rural Development: An Exchange of Chinese and Vietnamese

Vietnam's countryside has had a flurry of small-scale private activity since the mid-1980s. Leading the way are family enterprises, some in the north tracing their beginnings to illegal operations in the 1960s.[63] In the south, a sizeable minority date from the 1970s and some prior to re-unification.[64] Virtually all rural enterprises are run by households (with most of the work done by family members) and most employ fewer than ten workers.[65] As of 1994, nearly 80 per cent of Vietnam's rural households were farming, but even though this was still very large, it represents a six per cent drop from 1989. Survey data for 1992-93 showed that two-thirds of the farming households had other sources of income; only 30 per cent were purely agricultural.[66]

Rural China's economy, already far more diversified than Vietnam's prior to the reform era, expanded and industrialized more rapidly in the 1980s. The walls between urban and rural, between industry and agriculture, and between collective and private have been breached (although hardly eliminated) as a result of twenty years of explosive growth of rural industry and trade, and of migration to towns and cities to work. In coastal and suburban regions, only a minority of households now depend predominantly on agricultural incomes, and these are generally the poorest.[67]

Since the late 1970s, China's rural township and village enterprises (TVEs) have been the most dynamic sector of the economy, a magnet for

---

Experiences", Hanoi, 28 February to 2 March 1995, p.8. A 1991 survey in selected provinces of northern and southern Vietnam shows about the same results: slightly more than one per cent of rural enterprises were cooperatively owned. In analysing that data, Per Ronnas notes that the distinction between private and cooperative businesses is "somewhat ambiguous" because "... many cooperative enterprises have been de facto privatized following economic difficulties, but retain their official status as cooperatives". Per Ronnas, *Employment Generation through Private Entrepreneurship in Vietnam* (Geneva: International Labor Organization, 1992), p.12.

[63]   Hy Van Luong, "The Political Economy of Vietnamese Reforms: A Microscopic Perspective from Two Ceramic Manufacturing Centers", in Turley and Selden (eds), *Reinventing Vietnamese Socialism*, p.124.

[64]   Ronnas, *Employment Generation*, p.62.

[65]   Nguyen Duc Minh and Bui Bich Hoa, "Rural Industries in Vietnam", pp.7-8; Ronnas, *Employment Generation*, pp.128-9.

[66]   Luu Bich Ho and Khuat Quang Huy, "Main Issues, Trends and Problems in Rural Development and in the Diversification of the Rural Economic Base in Vietnam", paper for conference on "Rural Development: An Exchange of Chinese and Vietnamese Experiences", pp.7, 13-14. Also see Li Ta Na, *Peasants on the Move: A Study on Rural-to-Urban Migration in the Hanoi Region* (Singapore: Institute of Southeast Asian Studies, 1995).

[67]   Jeffrey Taylor, "Rural Employment Trends and the Legacy of Surplus Labour, 1978-1989", in Y. Y. Kueh and Robert Ash (eds), *Economic Trends in Chinese Agriculture: The Impact of Post-Mao Reforms* (New York: Oxford University Press, 1993), pp.273-310.

foreign investment, the largest source of new employment and income generation, and the cutting edge of China's rapidly growing exports and trade surpluses.[68] TVE ownership is multi-layered, involving not only township and village but at times also the county and higher levels of the state, sometimes entwined with private and even foreign capital. This mixture of local government and private capital, blurring the boundaries between state, private and collective, does not readily lend itself to decisive labelling as "socialist' or "capitalist", as "statist" or "private".

Why have TVEs developed in China but not in Vietnam and why has rural industrialization advanced much farther and faster in China during the reform era? Part of the answer may be understood from the trends already evident in the collective era. Agricultural collectives — the forebears of TVEs and pioneers in rural industrialization — were more widely developed in China than in Vietnam. The southern half of Vietnam had few collectives, and most of those evaporated soon after the state stopped pressing for them. In the north, household production continued to be as important to most villagers as their earnings from collectivized production. Most important, northern collectives concentrated overwhelmingly on agricultural products. Another factor was China's emphasis on self-reliance in the late 1950s and 1960s, which led to an emphasis on decentralized industry, including rural industry, and to the beginnings of the emergence of the cadre-entrepreneur.[69] Nothing comparable occurred in Vietnam.

Another contributing factor may have been the different timing and manner in which China's economy opened up through deepening involvement in international trade and investment compared to Vietnam.[70] Although decollectivization of agriculture began in Vietnam in the late 1970s, and then gathered momentum in the early 1980s, the opening of Vietnam's economy to domestic and international market forces did not begin in earnest until the second half of the 1980s. The state almost simultaneously removed price controls, allowed private investment, and opened the door to the free marketing of goods and services. China, by contrast, continued to protect state enterprises even as its TVE and private sector expanded and foreign investors stimulated the formation of new export-oriented enterprises. In this

---

[68]   Yan Shanping, "Export-oriented Rural Enterprises", *China Newsletter*, no.118, September to October 1995, pp.8-16, 22; "Situation in China's Economic Reform for 1995: Zhu Rongji's Closed-Door Speech at End of December 1994", *Kaifang* [Open Magazine], February 1995.

[69]   Carl Riskin, "China's Rural Industry: Self-reliant Systems or Independent Kingdoms?", *The China Quarterly*, no.73 (March 1978), pp.77-98; Christine Wong, "Rural Industrialization in the People's Republic of China: Lessons from the Cultural Revolution Decade", Joint Economic Committee, US Congress, *China Under the Four Modernizations*, pp.394-418; Samuel Ho, *Rural China in Transition: Non-Agricultural Development in Rural Jiangsu, 1978-1990* (Oxford: Clarendon Press, 1994), pp.103-5.

[70]   On this, see Adam Fforde, "From Plan to Market: The Economic Transition in Vietnam and China Compared", unpublished paper, January 1998.

environment, China's TVEs were able to take advantage of the emerging opportunities, competing effectively and at times cooperating with both state enterprises and private capital.

International conditions reinforced these differences. Substantial foreign capital flowed into China through Hong Kong, notably from Chinese in Asia, Europe and North America. These investments spurred export-oriented manufactures by TVEs in the coastal areas. While Vietnam faced an international trade embargo imposed by the United States until 1994, China's second transformation took place in the context of the US-China opening and benefitted from access to American and other global markets.

Markets

A third major change since the 1980s involves markets and services. Chinese and Vietnamese rural households gained control over the land they worked, became more mobile, and could freely buy and sell both their labour and commodities. The state also substantially reduced its presence in the market, particularly in Vietnam. The Vietnamese government ceased to control the domestic marketing of rice and other crops, no longer intervenes in the sale of fertilizer or machinery to rural households, and no longer limits the amount of rice or other goods households may buy. Coupons and rationing vanished in the late 1980s. The role of the Vietnamese state in rural markets is now comparable to Indonesia, Malaysia and many other Asian countries. It influences market prices through its purchasing power and fiscal policies, but does not set prices, even for rice and other basic commodities. The state agricultural bank, once the primary source of rural credit, provided by the mid-1990s less than 25 per cent of farm households' borrowings.[71]

From the late 1970s, the Chinese state reduced its monopoly position in markets in general and rural purchasing and supply markets in particular. The state has continued, however, to impose compulsory sales quotas for grain, cotton and other crops at lower-than-market prices while permitting the markets to function only in a supplementary capacity for these commodities. Although Chinese procurement quotas were reduced in the 1990s, in contrast to Vietnam they are far from having been eliminated. The Chinese state also continues to control the supply and price of critical agricultural and industrial inputs such as fertilizers and pesticides, in the context of a mixed system in which private markets provide these to households at premium prices. In sum, the presence of the state in many aspects of the rural economy — from TVEs to crop purchasing quotas, to rationing — remains greater in China than in Vietnam, as it was throughout the collective era.

---

[71]   *Khao Sat Muc Song Dan Cu Viet Nam*, p.22. This source, among others, reports that most rural credit comes through informal arrangements among individuals and families.

Conclusion

Twice within the last fifty years, China and Vietnam have radically reorganized the structure of farming and the rural economy and society. In the first transformation, the state dramatically expanded its reach in an attempt to control production and markets. It was an effort to transform the character of rural society, initially through a land reform that broke the power of landed elites and then through collectives and sharp restrictions on household enterprises and markets. In the second transformation, direct state and collective involvement in all of these realms was reduced and altered but not eliminated, while the scope of households and markets expanded. In both countries, powerful pressures to transform key features of the agrarian arrangements emerged "from below" — from villagers discontented with the collective regime, its associated institutions, and with long-term income stagnation. And in both countries the new order came to fruition when authorities from the national to the local levels endorsed and provided direction for reform agendas.

While noting striking institutional similarities, we have highlighted important differences in the outcomes. While the consequences of land reform were very much alike, the subsequent collectivization in China appears to have penetrated far more deeply and to have had more profound economic and social consequences than in Vietnam. Little of southern Vietnam was collectivized, and even in the north, where collectives were established, the household economy survived on a scale far beyond that in China. An important reason for the differences is that Vietnam was a divided country preoccupied with fighting a major war at the very time that the Communist Party-led state was trying to implement land reform and establish rural collectives. China's land reform also coincided with civil war, but collectivization took place only after the power of the People's Republic had been consolidated.

In part because collectivization was more pervasive in China, its legacy has been greater in the second transformation. China's TVEs, which have proven central to recent rural industrialization, have their roots in the industrialization of rural collectives in the Cultural Revolution decade. The Chinese state has also continued, well into the second transformation, to have a much more direct hand in pricing and distributing rural produce. In sum, the intertwined legacies of deeper collective penetration and rural industrialization characteristic of China's collective era leave their stamp on the mixed economy of the present period. With the resurgence of the household economy in Vietnam, the traces of the collective era leave far less of an imprint.

SIX

Wealth, Power, and Poverty in the Transition to Market Economies: The Process of Socio-economic Differentiation in Rural China and Northern Vietnam

Hy Van Luong and Jonathan Unger

Both Vietnam and China have experienced rural economic reforms that in many respects are parallel; but the socio-economic consequences have been noticeably different. This chapter seeks to show how differences between China and Vietnam in the interplay of rural industrialization, government policies and community processes have led to greater inter- and intra-community differentiation in China and the faster emergence there of a composite moneyed rural elite of officials and entrepreneurs.

In making such a comparison, a distinction regarding Vietnam needs to be noted between the northern and southern halves of the country.[1] In the south, the process of agricultural collectivization was never completed:[2] by 1985, the

---

[1]   For statistical purposes, Vietnam is usually divided into seven socio-economic regions. The north is divided into the Red River delta and "the rest" (the uplands); the centre into the central highlands, the south-central coast, and the northern panhandle (which was a part of North Vietnam until 1976); and the south into the Mekong delta and the southeast (including Ho Chi Minh City). In this chapter we are focusing on the northern half that includes the Red River delta, the northern highlands, and the northern panhandle of central Vietnam — the regions that comprised the Democratic Republic of Vietnam, or North Vietnam, from 1954 to 1976.

[2]   See Hy Van Luong, "The Marxist State and the Dialogic Re-Structuration of Culture in Rural Vietnam", in D. Elliott, H. V. Luong, B. Kiernan and T. Mahoney, *Indochina: Social and Cultural Change* (Keck Center for International and Strategic Studies, Monograph No.7) (Claremont: Claremont McKenna College, 1994), pp.90-1; Chu Van Lam et al., *Hop Tac Hoa Nong Nghiep Viet Nam: Lich Su Van De Trien Vong* [Agricultural cooperativization in Vietnam: History, problems, and prospects] (Hanoi: NXB Su that, 1992), pp.47-8; Le Minh Ngoc, "Thu Nhin Lai Qua Trinh Hop Tac Hoa

percentage of rural households joining agricultural cooperatives, often merely nominal, had reached only 3.7 per cent in the Mekong delta, 15 per cent in the southeast (the provinces around Ho Chi Minh City), and 42 per cent in the central highlands.[3] And even in those southern communities which collectivized, villagers could still retain private ownership of other means of agricultural production, such as water pumps and small tractors, and they provided services on a contract basis to the agricultural cooperatives. In all these respects, the situation differed considerably from the north, and it is not surprising that before Vietnam officially introduced a return to family farming, rural socio-economic differentiation was considerably greater in the south.

And so it remained. By the late 1980s, even in those southern delta communities that had carried out a socialist land reform in the late 1970s as a way-station on the road to collectivization, much of the agricultural land had been returned to the pre-collectivization owners, and many of the farmers who received shares of land after 1975 had in turn been dispossessed.[4] A class of rural landless has re-emerged there, and the main basis for socio-economic differentiation today lies in the initial property owned by each family, in

---

Nong Nghiep o Nam Bo" [A retrospective view on the process of agricultural cooperativization in South Vietnam], in Nguyen Quang Vinh et al. (eds), *Nhung Van De Xa Hoi Hoc o Mien Nam* [Sociological issues in the south] (Hanoi: NXB Khoa Hoc Xa Hoi, 1992), p.31. Also see the preceding chapter by Kerkvliet and Selden.

[3]   Vietnam General Office of Statistics and Ministry of Agriculture Institute of Planning, *So Lieu Nong Nghiep Viet Nam 35 Nam (1956-1990)* [Agricultural data for 35 years (1956-1990)] (Hanoi: NXB Thong Ke, 1991), p.39. Cf. Ngo Vinh Long, "Reform and Rural Development: Impact on Class, Sectoral, and Regional Inequalities", in William Turley and Mark Selden (eds), *Reinventing Vietnamese Socialism: Doi Moi in Comparative Perspective* (Boulder: Westview, 1993), p.184.

[4]   For the village of Khanh Hau in the Mekong delta, where one of the co-authors, Hy Van Luong, conducted field research in 1992, the percentage of landless households stood at about 9.8 per cent. This figure was below the 15.8 per cent of landless recorded in Long Hoa hamlet of Thoi Long village (Hau Giang province), but above the 4.2 per cent rate of landless households in Long Hoa village in the municipality of Can Tho in the same province. See Nguyen Thu Sa, "Suy Nghi Tu Nhung Khao Sat Moi ve Van De Ruong Dat o Dong Bang Song Cuu Long" [Ideas from new studies on the land problem in the Mekong delta], in Nguyen Quang Vinh et al. (eds), *Nhung Van De Xa Hoi Hoc o Mien Nam*, p.45. According to the Vietnamese Ministry of Agriculture and Rural Development, almost 5 per cent of peasant households in the southern third of Vietnam were landless in the mid-1990s. See Gi An, "Khong Co Dat Cam Lua" [No land to grow paddies], *Thoi Bao Kinh Te Viet Nam* [Vietnam economic times], no.79 (332), 1 October 1997, p.14. According to official reports, 30 per cent of those cases involved dispossession in order to return the land to those who owned it prior to collectivization (ibid.). Because the issues of landlessness and land dispossession are of great political sensitivity to policy-makers in Hanoi, those official figures for the southern third of Vietnam might not represent the real magnitude of the problem in the mid-1990s.

particular the amount and quality of farm acreage.[5] In the central highlands of Vietnam, to the extent that collectivization had been carried out after 1975, its effects became increasingly nominal, as numerous households established private plantations to cultivate cash crops for export (most notably coffee).

Only the northern portion of rural Vietnam encounters circumstances fundamentally similar to rural China. Both there and in China, farmers experienced several decades of collectivization and, after subsequent decollectivization, were provided with an essentially equal per capita share of crop-land. In order to focus on the similarities and dissimilarities in the effects of decollectivization, our comparison will therefore centre entirely on income differentials and class formation in rural China and *northern* Vietnam.

We will rely partly on our own field research. Our analysis of rural northern Vietnam is based in large part on Hy Van Luong's in-depth anthropological fieldwork from 1987 to 1994 in four villages (two primarily agricultural, one industrialized, and one with a mixed economic base), and our analysis of China largely derives from Jonathan Unger's interviews with Chinese farmers and local officials during a number of research projects between the mid-1970s and 1997.[6] The aggregate socio-economic data that has become available on rural China and Vietnam will be used to complement our fieldwork information.

Socio-economic Differentiation in the Collective Period

In both China and northern Vietnam under the collectives, income differences within the same village were relatively small. In both countries, farmers accumulated labour points for performing specific tasks assigned to them, and the value of each point increased when the collective unit achieved higher crop yields. Since the labour points accumulated by a person did not significantly differ from those of their workmates of similar age and gender, the main source of differentiation in living standards between neighbouring

---

5   A World Bank-sponsored study in 1992-93 has also concluded on the basis of large-scale survey data that "in the south, the poorest households rely more on off-farm income sources, whereas the wealthiest households are mostly concentrated on the farm". World Bank, *Vietnam: Poverty Assessment and Strategy* (Washington, D.C.: World Bank, 1995), p.66. The situation in northern Vietnam, as in China, is the reverse.

6   This research in China included an extended trip to Yunnan province in 1988, during which interviewing was conducted in 13 poor and middle-income villages. A second research trip in 1991 allowed Unger to conduct interviews in 19 hill-country villages in the three south-eastern provinces of Guangxi, Guizhou and Yunnan. A third trip in late 1993 took Unger into a similar number of villages, both prosperous and poor, on Hainan Island, China's southernmost province. They complement Unger's interviews, in collaboration with Anita Chan, about what has become one of the richest parts of China, Guangdong province. These covered half a dozen villages in the 1970s, two more in the mid-1980s, seven villages in 1989, and an extremely wealthy rural district in the Pearl River delta in 1997.

households depended upon the differing numbers of labouring hands in each family and the numbers of its dependents, which altered cyclically as children grew up and the elderly passed away. Income differences between neighbours also resulted from the differing yields from household garden plots (amounting to about 5 per cent of the total cultivated land in both countries) and the relatively meagre incomes earned by craft specialists and traders in the informal economy. Local cadres gained some slight economic advantages for themselves and, on the other side of the fence, the former rich peasants and landlords and their descendants faced discrimination. However, political power and class background were not as important in rural Vietnam as in China in creating a basis for socio-economic differentiation, due to the wartime conditions in northern Vietnam (the war with the US, the Sino-Vietnamese conflict and the Cambodian war) and the north Vietnamese state's consequent emphasis on domestic political unity during this period.

Although essentially egalitarian standards of living prevailed within each village, the bulk of the villages were quite impoverished in both countries, though even more so in Vietnam than China. At the same time, in Mao's China more than in Vietnam, village life was riven by tensions and repression, with recurrent government-sponsored political campaigns that obliged farmers to single out neighbours for attack.[7] In this respect, Chinese villages were far from being closely-knit "moral communities", and many farmers were glad in the 1980s to be released from the Maoist campaigns and the tight rein of the collectives. In Vietnam, the long period of war from 1960 onwards again had the effect of softening divisions within villages.

The level of income inequality between village neighbours appears to have been roughly equivalent for both countries. If the official statistical data on socio-economic differentiation are reliable, which they very well may not be, towards the end of the collective era the Gini co-efficient [which measures inequality of incomes] for the Vietnamese Red River delta stood at .25, compared to .21 in rural China.[8] Thus, if anything, the income differentials may possibly have been somewhat greater within Vietnamese villages. If so, this would reflect, among other factors, the greater importance of the household and informal economy in rural Vietnam, where household incomes were more differentiated than the incomes from the official collective economy. Vietnamese official statistics suggest that the percentage of peasant

---

7   On these frightening campaigns, see Anita Chan, Richard Madsen and Jonathan Unger, *Chen Village Under Mao and Deng* (Berkeley: University of California Press, 1992), Chapters 1-9.

8   For Vietnam, see Dao The Tuan, "Kinh Te Ho Gia Dinh cua Nong Dan va Su Thay Doi Xa Hoi o Viet Nam" [The peasant household economy and social change in Vietnam], *Xa Hoi Hoc* [Sociology], no.44, 1993, p.16; for China, see Tang Ping, "Wo guo nongcun jumin shouru shuiping ji chayi yanjiu" [Research into the levels and disparities in income among China's village residents], *Jingji yanjiu cankao* [Economic research reference materials], no.158 (14 October 1994), p.27.

incomes derived from the household and informal economy increased from 42 per cent in 1959 to 54 per cent in the 1966-75 period, and to 61 per cent in 1976-80.[9] These percentages in northern Vietnam were considerably higher than the estimated figures of 10-25 per cent for the 1960s and 1970s in rural China.[10]

The Initial Effects of Decollectivizing Agriculture

During the 1980s, the distribution of farm fields to families on a long-term basis in both Vietnam and China (discussed in the preceding chapter by Kerkvliet and Selden) was carried out in a relatively egalitarian fashion. In China, land was of such key importance to the farmers that any favouritism or corruption in the distribution of fields would have discredited the new system of landholding, with bitter recriminations and political repercussions for decades to come. In most villages, land was divided among the households on the basis of an equal share for every member of the production team, children included, and farm tools and draught animals were distributed free of charge among the families. Interviews with farmers from a number of Chinese villages reveal that these land and asset distributions were supervised by county officials, who saw to it that the distribution proceeded with a minimum of corruption.[11] Hillside orchards and fishponds were leased out to private households, and it was here — not in the distribution of farm fields — that village officials sometimes took undue advantage of their position to obtain lucrative leases for themselves or relatives.

In northern Vietnam, an ideology of equality has similarly strongly shaped the distribution of farm fields in most rural communities, although this ideology operates largely within the village and in turn has exerted pressure on national policy. Unlike in China, Vietnam's land redistribution guidelines in 1988 initially proposed that in order to increase agricultural efficiency, the better cultivators should be given the opportunity to make bids to contract the more fertile agricultural land with higher production quotas. However, many of the villagers reportedly complained about the auction of village land to the highest bidders and about its supposed effects in enriching those who were

---

9   Nguyen Sinh Cuc, "Sau 30 Nam Hop Tac Hoa Nong Nghiep: Doi Song Nong Dan va Van De Quan Ly San Xuat Nong Nghiep Hien Nay" [After thirty years of agricultural cooperatization: Peasant life and the problem of agricultural production management at present], in Nguyen Luc (ed.), *Thuc Trang Kinh Te — Xa Hoi Viet Nam Giai Doan 1986-1990* [The reality of Vietnamese economy and society in the 1986-1990 period] (Hanoi: NXB Thong Ke, 1990), p.48. See also Dao The Tuan, "Kinh Te Ho ...", p.10.

10   William Parish and Martin K. Whyte, *Village and Family in Contemporary China* (Chicago: University of Chicago Press, 1978), p.119.

11   Jonathan Unger, "The Decollectivization of the Chinese Countryside: A Survey of Twenty-eight Villages", *Pacific Affairs*, vol.58, no.4 (Winter 1985-86), p.594.

better off.[12] In many communities, these complaints hindered the implementation of the 1988 policy. As a result of the national leadership's desire to maintain socio-political stability, by 1994 the majority of the communities in northern Vietnam had switched to a more egalitarian system. They retained few fertile farm fields for annual bidding and had divided most of the fields among the villagers on a strictly egalitarian long-term basis[13] (although the state, in the name of agricultural efficiency, allowed the subsequent sale by families of their rights to fields). As in China, in the northern Vietnamese villages where Hy Van Luong has conducted field research there were no informal complaints by villagers about the village leadership's favouritism in land allocation.

In both China and northern Vietnam, in light of the varying quality of village fields, to ensure equity a household usually received its land in 3-12 small pieces in different locations. Each family's share of fields became inheritable, and in that sense today resembles private property. But particularly in China, to ensure continued egalitarian distribution, villages have been prone to redistribute marginal bits of land periodically as families grow or shrink over time. Surveys of Chinese farmers' attitudes in the mid-1990s showed that this system of periodic marginal redistributions of farm land as family sizes change is favoured by most villagers, rather than *de jure* permanent private land ownership.[14]

---

[12]   Dang Canh Khanh, "Ve Su Phan Tang Xa Hoi o Nong Thon Hien Nay" [On social stratification in the countryside at present], in Ban Nong Nghiep Trung Nong (ed.), *Kinh Te — Xa Hoi Nong Thon Viet Nam Ngay Nay* [Vietnamese rural economy and society at present], vol.2. (Hanoi: NXB Tu Tuong Van Hoa, 1991), p.348. Ben Kerkvliet (personal communication) has suggested that this bidding system was not necessarily regressive because its proceeds could be used to support collective programs (pre-schools, social welfare). It should be added, however, that in communities where not much land was available for bidding, these programs were still supported, primarily through the imposition of additional "local taxes" on land. While in the former system the funds to support those programs are collected from the supposedly efficient producers who have privileged access to some of the most fertile fields, in the latter system funds are collected from all the producers, who have equal access to these fields. In our opinion, the latter is a more egalitarian system.

[13]   On the basis of provincial guidelines, the village of Trung Trac, Hai Hung province, where Hy Van Luong has made field visits, adopted this policy in 1994. Even in a commercialized village in Ha Bac province that increasingly engaged in retail trade in Hanoi, the percentage of village reserve land had been reduced from 20 per cent in 1990 to 13 per cent in 1994, and the rest was allocated on a long-term and egalitarian basis to all villagers, regardless of age and gender. At this point systematic data is not available on land distribution for all of northern Vietnam, but it appears to have moved in the direction of greater equality since 1988.

[14]   James Kai-sing Kung and Shouying Liu, "Farmers' Preferences Regarding Ownership and Land Tenure in Post-Mao China: Unexpected Evidence from Eight Counties", *The China Journal*, no.38 (July 1997), pp.33-63.

There were, however, also a number of strings entirely unwanted by farmers that were attached to the distribution of fields throughout most of the 1980s. In both China and northern Vietnam, households could only retain the surplus above a production quota, usually in grain, that was attached to each piece of land and that had to be sold to the state at a low state-fixed price. The state also still monopolized the supply of many of the inputs into agriculture. In Vietnam, these restraints gradually eased up and by 1989 had mostly evaporated. China, however, still retained most of these restrictions and, as will be observed, this has affected socio-economic differentiation.

Overall, in both countries the distribution of land among the farming households was equivalent to an egalitarian land reform, leaving in its wake communities of small independent farmers. Given this initial base, even today there exists a lower degree of economic differentiation among households within the same village than is found throughout most of the developing world. Yet it will also be observed that even though this remains true for both countries as of the late 1990s, in China rural socio-economic differentiation has progressed at a much more rapid pace than in Vietnam. One important reason was that rural China stood poised for a boom in the early 1980s, unlike northern Vietnam. But it will also be seen that particularly in China, rural economic development has varied greatly by region, with important effects. The disparities in different regions in the opportunities to generate income will be briefly surveyed first for China and then, in comparison, for Vietnam.

Regional Differentiation

China

From the start, the great majority of farmers in China benefitted noticeably from the return to family farming. A major reason was that in the early 1980s the government also allowed them to diversify their crops rather than just plant grain. At the same time, the Chinese government began providing better farm-gate prices for most of the produce, and farmers thereby doubly benefitted from their increases in productivity.

Perhaps of greatest importance, though, was that villagers were now allowed to seek ways to earn money beyond their crops. Especially in villages within striking distance of cities, families with know-how and surplus labour began raising large numbers of hogs and poultry, or rented village ponds and raised fish for urban consumption. Other families became heavily involved in cottage industry, even during the growing seasons, or sent a daughter to work in the new factories that were sprouting in the rural market towns that lay within reach of a city. Some men, even from families short of labour, left their village during the agricultural off-season to work at urban construction sites, where wages were relatively good by Chinese standards, leaving the winter agricultural chores in the hands of wives and children.[15] Through these diverse means, enterprising families greatly expanded their incomes. They have been building larger homes and buying colour TVs, VCRs, washing machines and refrigerators.

For those families in China who remained largely in agriculture, however, the terms of trade for their produce began to turn less favourable after 1984 as government policy changed and the quota price for agricultural goods was pressed downward in real terms. Farmers' living standards began to stagnate and in a great many cases declined. Taking all rural household income into account, real income had risen dramatically by some 10 per cent annually in rural China between 1978 and 1984, but during the next four years increased at a slow annual rate of only 2 per cent. It dropped precipitously in 1989 and stagnated in 1990, providing the same real per capita rural income in 1990 (¥338) as in 1984-5 (¥336).[16] Throughout the 1980s, off-farm income in the more commercialized parts of the Chinese countryside had continued to rise, but this had been offset by a marked decline in real *agricultural* income during the last half of the decade. Those families who were stuck entirely in farming were very noticeably hurt.

With opportunities outside agriculture varying dramatically across different regions, inter-regional income differentials have widened considerably and the richer parts of China have drawn ever further away from the poorer parts. Rates of poverty remain substantial in China's interior, but are far lower in the coastal provinces, where off-farm opportunities are far greater, especially in rural industry. Whereas industry had accounted for only a quarter of the rural Chinese economy in 1983, a decade later it accounted for close to half. And this rapid industrialization was disproportionately located in the booming eastern region of China, where it accounted for more than 60 per cent of the rural economy by 1992, compared to 30 per cent in central China and under 20 per cent in western China's laggard economy.[17] Parallel to this,

---

15   Extensive fieldwork in a well-off village in Sichuan province by a group of Danish scholars in 1987 has illustrated clearly the importance of such off-the-farm income. See Peter Fenger, Steen Folke, Allan Jorgensen, Peter Milthers and Ole Odgaard, "Occupational Patterns and Income Inequality in a Sichuan Village", *Copenhagen Papers in East and South-east Asian Studies*, no.5, 1990, p.78; for a rural site near Nanjing, see Flemming Christiansen, *The De-rustication of the Chinese Peasant? Peasant Household Reactions to the Rural Reforms in China since 1978*, PhD dissertation (University of Leiden, 1990), p.121; for sites in Henan province, see Zhu Ling, *Rural Reform and Peasant Income in China* (London: Macmillan, 1991), pp.78, 80. Also see Carl Riskin, "Income Distribution and Poverty in Rural China", in Keith Griffin and Zhao Renwei (eds), *The Distribution of Income in China* (New York: St. Martin's Press, 1993); and Azizur Khan et al., "Household Income and Its Distribution in China", *The China Quarterly*, no.132 (December 1992), pp.1029-61.

16   On these trends see Scott Rozelle, "Stagnation Without Equity: Patterns of Growth and Inequality in China's Rural Economy", *The China Journal*, no.35 (January 1996).

17   ibid.

while the incidence of severe rural poverty had slumped, by World Bank estimates, to under 1 per cent in the south coastal province of Guangdong by 1989, 34 per cent of households in the western province of Gansu remained below that poverty line.[18] More recently, as labour and land costs continue to rise on China's east coast, industry has begun to move inland, perhaps presaging a diminution of the long-term widening of income disparities between the coast and the interior. But the interior starts from a low base, and in absolute terms the gap between the coast and the interior continues to widen.

The overall net effect, as some families increasingly prosper off the farm, and as the coastal regions and the more fertile districts take advantage of the reforms, is that the Gini coefficient of rural income inequality has progressively widened since the reform period commenced in 1979, as can be seen in Table 1.

Table 1: **The Gini Coefficient for Chinese Villagers' Incomes and the Differentiation between the Richest and Poorest 20 per cent of the Rural Population**

	Gini Coefficient	Highest:Lowest 20% of Incomes
1978	.2124	2.88 fold
1980	.2366	3.16
1985	.2635	3.65
1987	.2916	4.16
1988	.3014	4.68
1990	.3099	4.50
1991	.3072	5.00
1992	.3135	5.06
1993	.3300	5.54

Source: Tang Ping, "Wo guo nongcun jumin ...", p.27. A second Chinese source calculates the Gini coefficient as being even wider — standing at .34 in 1988 and reaching .43 by 1994. See *Xinhua wenzhai* [New China digest], no.2, 1996, pp.16-19.

---

18   World Bank, *China: Strategies of Reducing Poverty in the 1990s* (Washington, D.C.: World Bank, 1992), p.37.

Vietnam

While socio-economic differentiation has increased markedly in rural China, it has not done so in rural north Vietnam. The official statistics show that in the Red River delta it had increased only marginally from .25 in 1978 to .26 in 1993, and in 1993 was even lower in the northern highlands at .245 and the north central panhandle at .25.[19] A main reason, as will be seen, is the comparative dearth of rural industrialization in Vietnam.

However, to the limited extent that differentiation between poor and prosperous households exists today in northern Vietnam it has centred, as in China, on off-farm income. Vietnam's government surveys show that since the onset of economic reforms, households with non-agricultural incomes have fared considerably better than strictly agricultural households. As a World Bank report has noted, citing 1992-93 data, "In the three regions of the North, the poorest households work only on the farm, while the wealthiest households have mostly off-farm income".[20]

Again similar to China, this can be seen in terms of inter-regional differentiation. Vietnamese surveys in 1989 and 1990 found that despite the relative equality in average land holdings, rural households in the Red River delta enjoyed a higher average income than in the north central panhandle and the northern highlands: principally because the Red River delta has had a more developed handicraft and trading system. For the same reason, the Red River delta had almost the same level of average income as the central coast despite the lower average land holdings (3,231 square metres vs. 5,468 square metres). The availability of off-farm wage employment, according to a 1995 World Bank report,[21] is lowest in the regions with the most widespread poverty, the north central and northern highland regions; and seen from the opposite side of the socio-economic spectrum, the regions now with substantial numbers of prosperous rural households are those with off-farm opportunities.

---

[19]   World Bank, *Vietnam: Poverty Assessment and Strategy*, p.27 (cf. Nguyen van Thieu, "Su Phan Tang Xa Hoi o Nong Thon Viet Nam" [Social differentiation in rural Vietnam], *Nghien Cuu Kinh Te* [Economic studies], no.204 (April 1995), p.25); and Dao The Tuan, "Kinh te ho ...", p.16. It should be added, however, that the Gini coefficients within various northern communities are considerably lower: they range from .11 to .15 in selected communities with different degrees of market orientation (Dao The Tuan, op. cit., p.13). The Gini coefficients of .24-.26 for northern Vietnam in 1993 were lower than the figures of .29, .37 and .30 for the rural central highlands, the southeast (around Ho Chi Minh city), and the Mekong delta (World Bank, op. cit., p.27). A Vietnamese study provides higher figures of .39, .42 and .43 respectively for these three latter areas. See Nguyen van Thieu, op. cit., p.25).

[20]   World Bank, *Vietnam: Poverty Assessment and Strategy*, p.66.

[21]   ibid., p.67.

Table 2: Main Income Sources and Poverty Rates in Rural Northern Vietnam, 1992-93, by Region

Income Sources	Northern Highlands	Red River Delta	North Central Panhandle
Agriculture/ forestry	63.1%	39.9%	47.0%
Non-farm self-employment	19.8%	36.5%	34.1%
Salaries/wages	11.1%	16.6%	12.2%
Other	6.1%	7.0%	7.7%
Household-reported per capita income (US$)	$73	$100	$69
Poverty rate	63%	55%	74%[22]

Sources: Vietnam State Planning Commission and General Statistical Office, *Khao Sat Muc Song Dan Cu Viet Nam* [Vietnamese survey of living standards, 1992-93] (Hanoi: State Planning Commission, 1994), pp.217, 219; World Bank, *Vietnam: Poverty Assessment and Strategy* (1995), pp.10-11, 65.

In sum, in both China and northern Vietnam, some villages and districts have developed relatively high levels of off-farm income, with commensurate income gains for local residents. Meanwhile, the more remote villages remain largely reliant on subsistence agriculture. In terms of socio-economic

[22] In Vietnam, the World Bank has defined the poverty line in terms of the price of a 2,100 kcal/day food basket, plus the average costs of non-food commodities and services typically consumed by the poor (World Bank, *Vietnam: Poverty Assessment and Strategy*, pp.5-8). The Vietnamese rural poverty line in 1995 was accordingly set at 1,040,000 *dong* per person per year (ibid., p.141). The Vietnamese government calculated a poverty rate of only a bit over 30 per cent of the rural populace because it considered food intake of 1,500 kcal a day sufficient (see the official 30 per cent+ statistic in *Vietnam Investment Review*, 4-10 April 1994). See also Pham Do Nhat Tan, "Ngheo Doi, Nhan Dien, Nguyen Nhan va Giai Phap" [Poverty: Diagnosis, causes and solutions], in Do Nguyen Phuong (ed.), *Ve Su Phan Tang Xa Hoi o Nuoc Ta Trong Giai Doan Hien Nay* [On social differentiation in our country in the present period] (Hanoi: Chuong Trinh Khoa Hoc Cap Nha Nuoc Kx 07, 1994), pp.74-8). Elsewhere in Vietnam the rural poverty rate, using the World Bank's criteria, was lowest in the southeast (in provinces around Ho Chi Minh City, at 45.2 per cent), and slightly exceeded 50 per cent for the remaining three regions (Mekong delta, central highlands, and south central coast). World Bank, *Vietnam: Poverty Assessment and Strategy*, p.65.

differentiation *within* villages, as will be seen, these two types of communities — subsistence-oriented and market-oriented villages — occupy quite different worlds. In light of the major differences in the causes of socio-economic differentiation in the two types of villages, we shall discuss them separately.

Differentiation Inside Subsistence-oriented Communities

China

With greater levels of commercialization in Chinese agriculture, a smaller proportion of the farming population than in Vietnam appears still to live in subsistence-oriented communities. These are overwhelmingly located in the Chinese interior, in agriculturally marginal districts where only relatively small surpluses can be wrested from the soil and in areas, too, where transport linkages with urban centres are inadequate.

In such villages, government policies over the past decade and a half have exacerbated rather than reduced socio-economic differentiation. In particular, in three dozen remote subsistence-oriented communities in southwest China where Jonathan Unger conducted household interviews during 1988 and 1991, a sinking under-class of totally immiserated families has emerged that has been hurt by the Chinese government program of cheap grain requisitions. At the time of decollectivization and the division of fields among households, these grain quotas were apportioned among the families along with the fields and became the families' personal responsibility, much like a fixed tax in kind. Households that subsequently became more prosperous are not obliged to provide any more low-priced grain to the state than the most impoverished families of their village.[23] In most villages, if a household cannot raise enough grain to feed itself after its sales of requisitioned grain to the state, the family simply goes hungry.[24]

Simultaneously, local taxes in the impoverished regions discriminate against the poorest households. A survey based on 500 rural households, selected randomly from poor regions spread across China, concluded that "the taxes appear to be highly regressive, with households in the lowest quintile

---

[23] Though the government announced in 1985 that this grain-quota system would be abolished and replaced with a system of contracts between the farmer and state, in most of the villages visited in China the policy change has been in name only. The shift to so-called "contracts" seems to have been aimed at regions where grain production was rising rapidly and where the state wanted to free itself from an obligation to buy more grain than it needed. In the regions which did not see such sharp rises in grain production, the state has chosen to continue to extract grain from the villages on the same terms as previously.

[24] Some villages that are desperately poor are excused from their grain sales to the state, but this relief usually applies only to whole villages, not to individual families. Thus, a family that is financially at its wits' end in a village that does not qualify for this concessionary arrangement still has to hand over its grain levy *in toto* to the state.

paying a higher *absolute* amount than those in the top quintile" of the surveyed households from these poor regions.[25]

The poor farmers' chances of producing enough grain to feed themselves are damaged by a third government practice — they are denied access to chemical fertilizers. Such fertilizers are particularly needed given the very infertile soils of the inland hill country. Household interviewing by Unger in the impoverished hill country of China's southwest revealed close to a doubling in grain output by families that could afford sufficient fertilizers, improved seeds and insecticides compared with those who could not afford any. To buy this fertilizer and other inputs, many of the farm families in this region seek short-term credit from the local government credit association at the beginning of the growing season. The credit associations' personnel, however, have come under strong pressure from the state to be business-like in their operations. They therefore normally reject the poorest households' requests for loans on the grounds that such households cannot guarantee repayment, as they do not possess collateral in the form of draught animals or pigs or other movable assets. These families do not have the wherewithal to raise such animals because, without fertilizers, they cannot grow enough to feed themselves, let alone livestock. Overall, in the three dozen impoverished villages that Unger visited in China's Yunnan, Guangxi and Guizhou provinces, somewhere between 5 and 15 per cent of the households had fallen into this trap, unable to afford any chemical fertilizers whatsoever. Harnessed to requisitioned grain "contracts" that they had difficulty fulfilling, a few of the families visited could not even afford to buy matches or salt.

But these families occupy only a comparatively small marginalized minority, out of sight in China's more remote districts, and comprising a relatively small minority even there. They are all but ignored by a government whose sights are set on the nation's richer districts and on the rapid development occurring there.

Vietnam

In contrast to China, the majority of northern Vietnamese villages have not been able to expand economically beyond their agricultural bases. One Vietnamese researcher estimates that in these communities, the percentage of strictly agricultural households varies between 75 per cent and 95 per cent; and the proportion of non-agricultural households is negligible. Most of the farming households produce crops not for the market but for their own consumption. Ninety per cent of the respondents in one village replied that they would store any surplus grain for future use instead of selling it. Even in a village close to a prosperous district market, only 7.5 per cent of the

---

25   Wu Guobao, Sue Richardson and Peter Travers, "Rural Poverty and its Causes in China", *Working Papers of the Chinese Economy Research Unit*, no.96/2 (University of Adelaide, 1996), p.12. Word italicized in the original.

respondents sold their surpluses, and almost three-quarters of this small minority did so in the village market.[26] Similarly, in a 1992 study the majority of the households in 13 out of 16 northern and central Vietnamese communities still produced for their own use; and even in the remaining three more-commercialized villages, households produced more for their own consumption than for the market.[27]

Not only does a higher percentage of the rural population remain subsistence-oriented in Vietnam than in China. A higher percentage of the population is also trapped in dire poverty. According to one estimate, 5-10 per cent of the total rural population in Vietnam remains desperately poor,[28] whereas we have noted that the truly desperately poor in China are confined largely to the most agriculturally marginal inland regions. Far larger numbers in both countries fall below the poverty line. If we use the common standards of poverty for both China and Vietnam adopted by the World Bank in 1992, 11.5 per cent of the Chinese rural population (98 million people) lived in poverty in 1990, down from 33 per cent in 1978,[29] while 57 per cent of rural Vietnamese remained below the poverty line in 1992-93.[30]

---

[26] Dang Canh Khanh, "Ve Su Phan Tang ...", pp.345, 350, 355.

[27] Dao The Tuan, "Kinh Te Ho ...", pp.9, 14.

[28] Hoang Viet, "Orientation and Major Solutions for Developing the Household Economy in the Vietnam Countryside", paper presented at the conference on "Rural Development: An Exchange of Chinese and Vietnamese Experiences", held in Hanoi, February-March 1995.

[29] The World Bank study in China defined the poverty line on the basis of the cost of a 2,160 kcal/day food basket, plus the costs of a modest level of non-food goods and services. World Bank, *China: Strategies for Reducing Poverty*, p.21. The Chinese rural poverty line was set at ¥275 per year, and the rural poverty rate was judged to be 11.5 per cent in 1990 (ibid., p.23). In a personal communication to us, Carl Riskin, who has conducted detailed analyses of rural Chinese poverty rates, estimates that the figures should be higher, at 120 million people, which by our estimates would amount to close to a 14 per cent rate of poverty. Given the stagnation in agricultural income in more recent years, we can estimate that an equivalent percentage of the rural Chinese populace remains below the poverty line today. A Chinese study separately shows the poverty-stricken populace to have comprised 9.7 per cent of the population in 1990, but observes that some of the provincial figures on which its tables are based relate only to extreme poverty. See Liu Nanchang, "Wo guo nongcun pinkun wenti yanjiu he fazhan qushi yuce" [Research into the issue of China's rural poverty and prediction of development trends], *Jingji gongzuozhe xuexi ziliao* [Study materials for economic workers], no.35 (1994), esp. pp.35-7.

[30] In Vietnam, the rural poverty rate of 57 per cent for the entire country was considerably higher than the urban one of 26 per cent. (See footnote 22 above for World Bank criteria of poverty for Vietnam.) There are no reliable data in Vietnam on whether the percentage of the rural population living below the World-Bank-defined poverty line has declined in the past decade and a half in northern Vietnam. In 95 per cent of the 120 surveyed communities, respondents indicated that the quality of life had improved in the

More recently, in 1996, the World Bank recalculated its estimates for China based on "the international standard of poverty [which] is substantially above [China's] norms of minimum welfare", and on this basis the World Bank now defines the poverty threshold in China as equivalent to US$1 per person per day, not its previous standard of roughly 60c per day.[31] By this new calculation, some 350 million Chinese lived below the poverty line as of 1993. The vast majority of these were rural, and by our own rough calculation they comprised close to 40 per cent of China's rural population. If the incidence of rural poverty in Vietnam is to be recalculated upward using the same criterion, the percentage in Vietnam who fall below the poverty line is, by this international standard, exceptionally high, encompassing the overwhelming majority of the rural population.

Nevertheless, even in some of the subsistence-oriented villages, a small number of Vietnamese villagers are in a position to bid for additional village fields when these are made available and to acquire such household commodities as electronic equipment and motorcycles. Dang Canh Khanh reports that in the largely subsistence-oriented village of Dong Duong, more than 20 per cent of the households had hired labour for ploughing, insecticide spraying and harvesting. At the other end of the spectrum, in this village some 10-20 per cent of the strictly agricultural households cannot even pay off their taxes to village governments.[32]

Even though socio-economic differentiation in these villages has been growing, the elimination of the Vietnamese state's mandatory grain procurements and of a two-tiered grain price system have helped to raise the standard of living in subsistence-oriented and market-oriented communities alike. Moreover, these twin reforms appear also to have slowed the widening of the gap between rich and poor within each village. Prices in rural Vietnam are now mostly in accord with market principles; and importantly, the state's procurement price for rice rose from 12 per cent of the market price in 1978 to 100 per cent in 1988[33] when agricultural land was divided on a long-term basis

---

last five years (World Bank, *Vietnam: Poverty Assessment and Strategy*, p.9). Vietnamese sources have reported that for the country as a whole, the percentage of the rural population with a monthly per capita income of less than 20 kilograms of rice declined from 32.9 per cent in 1976-80 to 9.4 per cent in 1989. In the same period, the percentage of rich households, earning more than 60 kilograms of rice per person a month, increased from 12.5 per cent to 18.4 per cent. See Vietnam, Communist Party [Agriculture Commission], "Danh Gia Thuc Trang Kinh Te Xa Hoi Nong Thon" [An evaluation of rural socio-economic realities], in *Kinh Te Xa Hoi Nong Thon Viet Nam Ngay Nay*, vol.1, pp.45-56).

[31] World Bank, "Poverty in China: What do the Numbers Say?", *Background Note: The World Bank* (1996), 6 pp.

[32] Dang Canh Khanh, "Ve Su Phan Tang ...", pp.351-2.

[33] Ngo Vinh Long, "Some Aspects of Cooperativization in the Mekong Delta", in David Marr and Christine White (eds), *Postwar Vietnam: Dilemmas in Socialist Development* (Ithaca: Cornell University South-east Asia Program, 1988), p.170.

to households. In fact, in the northern villages that Hy Van Luong has visited, by 1990 local Vietnamese authorities preferred not to collect agricultural taxes in kind in order to avoid the delivery of poor quality grain. Instead, they used the local market prices to convert grain taxes into a cash amount to be collected from households.[34] The prices of agricultural inputs, including chemical fertilizers, have also been set by market supply and demand since then. In all these respects, China's reforms lagged behind. (In one and only one regard, this has been beneficial to China's peasantry: a portion of the fertilizer sales continued to be subsidized.)

Rural credit in Vietnam is now also largely determined by market forces. In 1992, when the annual inflation rate stood at 17.5 per cent, the monthly interest rates on agricultural credit from formal institutions averaged 3.5 per cent, amounting to a very high annual interest rate of 42 per cent.[35] Notwithstanding this, a large number of farmers took out small loans. A 1992-93 World Bank survey of 120 rural Vietnamese communities reports that among the poorest 13 per cent of the rural population, formal credit from the cooperatives and from banks (carrying lower interest rates) amounted to 17.5 per cent of their total credit. This compared to an average of 26 per cent among the rest of the farming population, with no significant variations among this less impoverished 87 per cent of the rural populace.[36] In China, by comparison, the poorer sectors of the community do not normally have any access to such loans. Yet this distinction is not necessarily to the advantage of Vietnam's poor. The loan requirements in Vietnamese villages stipulate land

---

[34] In 1989, the Vietnamese government divided agricultural land into 7 categories on the basis of yield. Agricultural taxes depended on field classification and region. Land yielding more than 5 tons of paddy a year was classified into category 1. Annual taxes for this category amounted to 700 kilograms in the lowlands, 650 kilograms in the midlands and 580 in the highlands. In the bottom category was land yielding less than 1.5 tons of paddy a year. Annual taxes for this category were set at 100 kilograms in the lowlands, 80 kilograms in the midlands and 60 kilograms in the highlands. See Vietnam, *Cac Van Ban Phap Luat ve Thue Nong Nghiep* [Legal documents on agricultural taxes], (Hanoi: NXB Phap Ly, 1992), p.6. In 1993, there remained only 6 categories of land, and land taxes no longer varied with region. Taxes were reduced to 550 kilograms for category-1 land, and to 50 kilograms for category-6 land. See "Luat Thue Su Dung Dat Nong Nghiep (10-7-1993)" [Tax law on the use of agricultural land (10 July 1993)], in *Cac Van Ban Phap Luat Ve Dat Dai, Nha O, va Thue Nha Dat* [Legal documents on land, houses, and land and housing taxes] (Hanoi, NXB Chinh Tri Quoc Gia, 1993), p.318.

[35] World Bank, *Vietnam: Poverty Assessment and Strategy*, p.73. In the summer of 1992, in the village of Khanh Hau in Long An province (Mekong delta in south Vietnam) where Hy Van Luong did field research, the actual monthly rate on short-term agricultural credit amounted to 5 per cent. This rate included administrative fees on the loans.

[36] World Bank, *Vietnam: Poverty Assessment and Strategy,* p.74.

as collateral and an absence of overdue taxes.[37] This has presented a problem for the poorest villagers who have not been able to pay their taxes. Even more important, because the state has allowed the transfer of usufruct rights since 1993, the poorest households now risk losing their land, either by defaulting on loans or by voluntarily selling their right to land in order to meet the expenses of life crises. While a landless peasantry has not yet clearly emerged in northern Vietnam, due to the short period of time since the authorization of usufruct land sales and due also to the extensive networks of reciprocal assistance in the villages, the emergence of a landless class is probably only a matter of time.

In sharp contrast, in China the poor cannot legally be alienated from their rights to village land. But, as earlier observed, this advantage comes at a price. Unable to use their rights to land as collateral, China's rural poor in the subsistence-oriented villages in China's interior do not possess sufficient property to secure loans to buy the fertilizer and other inputs that they so desperately need.

Differentiation Inside Market-oriented Communities

Our research suggests that in both Vietnam and China, three factors underlie the degree of a village's market orientation. These are: i) proximity to markets; ii) traditions of craft and trade specialization; and iii) access to non-agricultural wage employment. This can be observed most readily through examples drawn from our field research.

(i)   Proximity to Markets

The impact of proximity to urban centres or regional marketing nodes is exemplified in Vietnam by the village of Hoai Thi, where Hy Van Luong has conducted fieldwork. Numerous villagers there have been employed since 1987 in Hanoi's construction industry and have also taken to peddling goods in the city, in particular hogs, tea and a famous rice alcohol from a nearby village. In 1990, the average income from retailing and construction work among a sample of 24 households in Hoai Thi was more than twice what they gained from agriculture,[38] and the average real per capita income in the village

---

[37]   Banks can seize collateral (usufruct rights on agricultural fields) in the case of a loan default. However, this does not seem to occur frequently because agricultural credit is usually small and short-term (no more than six months). Peasants rarely have trouble repaying the loans at the time of harvest.

[38]   For this sample, off-farm earnings were equivalent to 620 kilograms of paddy per household member, in comparison to their average net income of 275 kilograms from agriculture. See Hy Van Luong, "Economic Reform and the Intensification of Rituals in Two North Vietnamese Villages, 1980-1990", in Borje Ljunggren (ed.), *The Challenge of Reform in Indochina* (Cambridge, Mass.: Harvard Institute for International Development/Harvard University Press, 1993), pp.265-8. A village leader estimated in

in 1989 had more than tripled since 1980.[39] The degree of socio-economic differentiation in communities such as Hoai Thi, however, remained limited because in both the construction industry and retail trade, capital investments were considerably less important than a trader's physical strength; after all, the only equipment required for transporting goods to nearby Hanoi was a bicycle. In general, households with members in their twenties and thirties and older members available to take care of young children earned more from retail trade and the construction boom than others. One important basis for socio-economic differentiation in Hoai Thi was therefore the demography of household memberships. Households were more differentiated than in subsistence-oriented communities, but the degree of differentiation was probably less than in other villages with a longer tradition of market orientation.

Parallel to Hoai Thi village, in China the community of Chen Village, within range of both the Hong Kong and Canton markets, was able to take advantage of its location during the first half of the 1980s, before the district became inundated with foreign-owned factories. Immediately after decollectivization, the Chen farmers switched to producing vegetables for the nearby urban markets, and some households, even more profitably, converted low-lying rice paddies into commercial fish ponds to provide fresh carp for Hong Kong's tables. A number of other villagers stopped working in the fields altogether, and brought in field labour from poor inland counties to work their land as share-croppers. Some of them, particularly women, went to work instead in factories in the rapidly industrializing county capital, which had begun recruiting workers from within the county at urban wage scales. Through a combination of specialized market-oriented agriculture and urban work, by 1983-84 the average villager was earning many times more than had been possible in 1980.

Within a few more years, socio-economic differentiation was widening very noticeably in Chen Village as a small minority of the households, having accumulated capital through their endeavours or from relatives in Hong Kong, began carving out increasingly capital-intensive ventures. One household first rented a fish pond, then parlayed the proceeds into leases on groves of lychees, which it exported to Hong Kong, then hired labour to plant a 20-acre hillside orange orchard, and finally pioneered a large commercial chicken operation, with an annual output of some 40,000 chickens. Another villager made money through trade, used it to establish a sizeable modern hog-raising operation, sold it for a good profit, and invested the proceeds in a large new brickworks

---

1991 that of the 162 village households, some 30 were engaged in the hog trade, 50 in alcohol delivery, 20 in retailing other items, and 60 in the construction industry.

39   Hy Van Luong, "Local Community and Economic Reform: A Microscopic Perspective from Two Northern Villages", in T. Rambo, N. M. Hung and N. Jamieson (eds), *The Reconstruction of Vietnam: Challenges and Issues* (Fairfax and Honolulu: George Mason University Indochina Institute and East-West Center, 1992), pp.26-39.

to supply the nearby urban markets. Such households were soon many times richer than their neighbours.[40]

(ii)   Traditions of Craft and Trade Specialization

This is the second major factor underlying market orientation and socio-economic differentiation in many Chinese and Vietnamese villages. Hy Van Luong's fieldwork has revealed that with the reduction in the Vietnamese government's role in the trading system and with the re-emergence of private firms, a number of traditional handicraft villages (such as the conical hat centre in the village of Chuong in Thanh Oai district, the silk manufacturing centre of Van Phuc in Ha Dong, and the ceramics centre of Bat Trang) were quickly able to take advantage of market opportunities. So has Ninh Hiep village in Ha Bac province, which has a strong tradition of long-distance trade that has seen its residents actively engaged over the past few years in buying and transporting goods from the Sino-Vietnamese border to the rest of northern Vietnam.

In China, similarly, local craft and trade specializations were rapidly revived after the rural reforms were introduced. Memories of such skills had survived the quarter-century collectivist period during which government policy had all but decimated these local specializations. Villages near Beijing which before the revolution had produced special foods such as noodles for urban sale or had been known for quilts or tin-smithing quickly went back to those trades.[41] One example suffices to show how successfully some of these Chinese rural districts and villages could rejuvenate money-making skills that had not been practised for many decades. Unger spent two weeks in 1997 in Xiqiao, a rural township in Guangdong province, which until the 1930s economic depression had been a major rural centre of silk-textile production. Starting in the mid-1980s peasant entrepreneurs revived the local textile industry almost from scratch. This former commune now contains 1,600 textile factories, all of them privately owned by local residents. In the space of little more than a decade this small rural district has emerged as one of the major profitable textile-manufacturing areas in China.

(iii)   Access to Non-agricultural Wage Employment

Access to off-farm wage employment is, as earlier noted, very unequally distributed across regions and, within each locality, unequally distributed among households. This has been true for both China and northern Vietnam. But in light of the far greater commercialization and industrialization of the

---

[40]   On this, see Chan, Madsen and Unger, *Chen Village Under Mao and Deng*, esp. Chapters 8 and 10.

[41]   This information was gathered by Jonathan Unger in Beijing in 1993.

Chinese countryside, the impact of wage employment has been felt there far more than in northern Vietnam.

In northern Vietnam, a full macroscopic view of rural industrialization is yet to emerge because Vietnamese industrial data are broken down primarily by forms of ownership (state, cooperative, private, household), and only to some extent by any rural/urban distinction. According to the 1989 population census, 1.6 million workers (6.7 per cent of the active rural workforce of 23.8 million) worked in rural industries (including the construction field).[42] In the years since, rural industrial employment has not increased significantly, if at all, because the majority of the handicraft cooperatives that had dotted the rural landscape have collapsed. Many of the provincially-owned and district-owned state enterprises have also been dissolved. The available data for northern Vietnam (both urban and rural) reflect this collapse. It seems to have affected more severely the rural sector with its smaller and less competitive enterprises: the number of state enterprises, which are mostly urban, declined only slightly from 1,469 in 1989 to 1,225 in 1992; whereas the number of industrial and handicraft cooperatives plummeted from 13,261 to 3,761 in the same period. The output of the state industrial sector stagnated at 3,114 billion *dong* in 1989 and 3,133 billion *dong* in 1992, while that of cooperatives dropped by more than half in the same period, from 642 billion *dong* to 246 billion *dong*.[43] The reasons include a drastic reduction in state subsidies, the collapse of the export markets for low-quality handicraft products in the former Soviet Union and Eastern Europe, and competition from smuggled goods from China and Thailand in certain categories, such as textiles and ceramics.

Small private rural enterprises have emerged from the ashes of this structural transformation.[44] Normally employing fewer than 50 workers, they fill small niches in the domestic market. The emergence of these private firms was facilitated by the state's relinquishment of its virtual trading monopolies in industrial raw materials as well as its dominant role in the distribution of agricultural and manufacturing products. A survey of 505 small and medium-size firms in 1991 in three northern and three southern provinces revealed that approximately two-thirds of the firms in the northern sample and half of those

---

42   Vietnam, Central Census Steering Committee, *Ket Qua Dieu Tra Toan Dien* [Complete census results], vol.4 (Hanoi: Central Census Steering Committee, 1994), p.458.

43   The state industrial workforce declined from 511,000 employees in 1989 to 373,977 in 1992, while the cooperative industrial workforce plummeted from 560,000 in 1989 to only 144,000 employees in 1992. Vietnam, General Statistical Office, *So Lieu Cong Nghiep Viet Nam, 1989-1993* [Industrial data on Vietnam, 1989-93] (Hanoi: NXB Thong Ke, 1994), pp.79-80, 92-3, 118-19.

44   The Vietnamese government distinguishes household enterprises from private ones. The former use primarily family labour, while the latter hire mostly labour from outside the family. In reality, the line between these two types of enterprises is not clear-cut, and we refer to the enterprises in both categories as private firms.

in the southern sample had been established since 1988.[45] Most provided goods and services to local communities, and employed workers from within the same village. The only exceptions were private firms in a number of traditional handicraft villages that had quickly taken advantage of market opportunities and employed many people from outside the community.

In Bat Trang, a village with over 4,000 people that has successfully found a market in Asia and Europe for its traditional ceramics, a small household kiln costs US$200-500 to construct, while the larger ones cost approximately US$3,000 each. With over 1,000 household firms, the village regularly hires 1,500-2,000 workers from other communities in order to supplement its workforce. Because they are employed primarily in non-skilled positions during the agricultural slack seasons, these workers tend to receive considerably lower pay than the skilled workers from within the handicraft village. Thus the major differentiation in wealth emerges between the more successful entrepreneurs in specialized villages such as Bat Trang and the hired labourers who come primarily from surrounding communities, be it to work on the remaining agricultural fields, in trade, or in handicraft production. A Vietnamese researcher has estimated that the incomes of successful entrepreneurs exceeded those of such labourers by 200 times in Ninh Hiep and 30-100 times in other handicraft or trading villages.[46]

---

[45]   Vietnam, Ministry of Labour, Institute of Labour and Social Affairs, *Doanh Nghiep Nho o Viet Nam* [Small enterprises in Vietnam], (Hanoi: NXB Khoa Hoc va Ky Thuat, 1993), p.113. According to a 1992 survey of 60,019 rural industrial enterprises, private and household firms comprised 98.95 per cent of all rural industrial units, while cooperative and state firms made up respectively only .88 per cent and .17 per cent. See Chu Huu Quy (ed.), *Phat Trien Toan Dien Kinh Te Xa Hoi Nong Thon Viet Nam* [Towards the holistic socio-economic development of rural Vietnam], (Hanoi: Ministry of Science, Technology and Environment, 1993), p.13. The private firms employed 21 workers on average, including 6 family members, 8 regular non-family employees and 7 seasonal ones. Fifty two per cent of rural firms were in the food-processing industry, 18 per cent in construction materials, 12 per cent repaired and manufactured simple machines, and 10 per cent were in traditional crafts (ibid.). In a survey of rural industrial enterprises in Ha Bac province, a major northern centre of handicrafts and industry, the four main sectors were traditional crafts and arts (29 per cent), machine repairs and manufacturing (24 per cent), wood and paper processing (18 per cent), and construction materials (12 per cent). See Luu Bich Ho and Khuat Quang Huy, "Main Issues, Trends, and Problems in Rural Development and in the Diversification of the Rural Economic Base in Vietnam", paper presented at a conference on *Rural Development: An Exchange of Chinese and Vietnamese Experiences.* held in Hanoi, February-March 1995, p.17. According to the 1989 population census, the rural industries with the largest numbers of workers were textiles, food processing, machinery, garments, and construction materials. See Vietnam Central Census Steering Committee, *Kat Quo Dieu Tua Toan Dien* [Complete census results], vol.5 (Hanoi, 1995), pp.23-4.

[46]   Danh Canh Khanh, "Ve Su Phan Tang ...", p.341. Labourers' wages tend to be extremely low. As the 1995 World Bank report notes, "While there are greater opportunities for non-agricultural wage earning in the densely populated Red River Delta due to its

But villages like Bat Trang and Ninh Hiep are exceptions rather than the rule. Only 6.7 per cent of the Vietnamese rural labour force in 1989 gained a livelihood primarily from industrial employment. Processing industries accounted for only 7.2 per cent of rural GDP in 1990 and 7.5 per cent in 1995.[47] The weakness of rural industry in Vietnam in comparison to China means that it provides employment for a considerably smaller proportion of the rural populace and employs far fewer workers from outside local communities. Consequently, too, rural accumulation of wealth and economic differentiation among households are far more limited in Vietnam than China.

We noted earlier that the greatest single factor accounting for increases in Chinese rural incomes since 1985 has been the surge of rural industrialization, far more than any other type of off-farm employment, and that this industrialization has been concentrated in the richer districts within reach of convenient transport routes and urban areas. By 1993, about 28 per cent of the rural workforce (120 million people) worked full-time or part-time in such rural enterprises.[48]

China's rural factory workers derive from two distinctly different types of backgrounds. Those who are locally recruited generally earn incomes higher than is available locally from farming. There is therefore competition to obtain such jobs, and those recruited tend to come from the better-connected families in the district. Often, their numbers include relatives of village officials and of the factory's own managers. In many rural districts, some of the other workers have bought their way in: their families can only secure a factory job for them by purchasing a fixed number of shares in a company. In short, precisely the families who are already well-connected and/or already more successful in agriculture tend to gain access to the higher earnings in local industry. The disparities in income between families thus further widen.[49]

---

proximity to urban areas, wage incomes are low, particularly for the poor. The low earnings probably result from an over-supply of unskilled labour relative to the employment opportunities". World Bank, *Vietnam: Poverty Assessment and Strategy*, p.67.

[47] Dang Tho Xuong et al., *Nong Nghiep Nong Thon Trong Giai Doan Cong Nghiep Hoa Hien Dai Hoa* [Agriculture and the countryside in the period of industrialization and modernization] (Hanoi: NXB Chinh Tri Quoc Gia, 1997), p.53. According to the same source, in the 1990-94 period, rural industries grew at an annual average rate of 3.7 per cent in the north and 10.1 per cent in the south (p.52). For comparison, construction accounted for 2.6 per cent of rural GDP in the entire country in 1990 and 6.7 per cent in 1995 (ibid.). See also Nguyen Sinh Cuc, *Thuc Trang Nong Nghiep, Nong Thon, va Nong Dan Viet Nam* [The reality of agriculture, the countryside, and the peasantry in Vietnam] (Hanoi: NXB Thong Ke, 1991), p.63.

[48] See *Renmin ribao* [People's daily], 11 May 1995.

[49] For an excellent case study of this, see Minchuan Yang, "Reshaping Peasant Culture and Community: Rural Industrialization in a Chinese Village", *Modern China*, vol.20, no.2 (April 1994), p.159.

Increasingly, though, in order to secure cheaper labour, rural factory workers are being pulled in from afar from China's poorer districts. The status and circumstances of this second type, workers who now number in the millions, are altogether unlike those enjoyed by rural workers of local origin. For instance, in the rural districts of Guangdong province near Shenzhen where Unger has conducted fieldwork, in each of the local factories two discrete labour markets have been created so as to ensure relatively high pay in a fixed number of factory positions for employees from the nearby villages. For performing similar jobs in these same factories, immigrant workers from elsewhere in China earn far less.[50]

These in-migrants greatly outnumber local recruits in the most heavily industrialized parts of rural China such as this Guangdong district. They sometimes work under genuinely awful conditions. But the current situation nonetheless may be preferable to what prevailed during the collective era when, starting with the mid-1950s, labour mobility and such wage labour were all but banned and the peasants from the poorest districts were forced to stay at home and to rely entirely upon the resources of their own villages. This went against their interests, since their villages generally did not possess an adequate climate or soils to develop ample food production. Over the two decades between the mid-1950s and the mid-1970s, therefore, the gap in living standards substantially widened between the better-off and poorer rural districts.[51] Today, the money remitted by the new emigrant workforce to their families at home helps to reduce the plight of those remaining in the poorer districts.

In previous decades, however, with the best-off and worst-off communities isolated from each other, the chasm in incomes between them had few political and social consequences. By the 1990s, in contrast, within the richest communities across China sizeable groups of poor immigrant labourers, hired both in industry and agriculture, were living literally next door to the most fortunate of the rural populace,[52] and this has given rise to growing tensions between the two groups.

---

50   On this see Chan, Madsen and Unger, *Chen Village Under Mao and Deng*, pp.304-7.

51   Nicholas Lardy, *Agriculture in China's Economic Development* (Cambridge: Cambridge University Press, 1984), ch. 4; and Peter Nolan and Gordon White, "The Distributive Implications of China's New Agricultural Policies", in Jack Gray and Gordon White (eds), *China's New Development Strategy* (London and New York: Academic Press, 1982).

52   One example is a rural township of non-Chinese hill peoples in Yunnan province that has become wealthy on the proceeds of village- and township-owned mines. There — and in Chen Village, too — most of the farming and almost all of the heavy labour is done by impoverished immigrants. This wealthy township is discussed in Jonathan Unger and Jean Xiong, "Life in the Chinese Hinterlands under the Rural Economic Reforms", *Bulletin of Concerned Asian Scholars*, vol.22, no.2 (April 1990), esp. pp.11-12.

At the same time, the rapid development of industry in such districts has sometimes enriched only a minority of the *local* population, a fact that overall statistics usually conceal. The Chinese Ministry of Agriculture investigated four rural towns in Jiangsu province that boasted average local incomes of more than ¥2,000 per capita. It was discovered that 32 per cent of the 2,260 local households were engaged in private industry or construction, and these households averaged ¥14,000 per capita. But among the remaining local households, which presumably were still largely farming, incomes averaged only ¥720 per capita, and 26 per cent of the village's households lay below ¥400 per capita, the government's poverty line.[53] A flourishing private industry had generated a widening gulf in local living standards.

The Personal Origins of Entrepreneurship

In both China and northern Vietnam since the return to family farming, the success of some households as opposed to their local neighbours appears to be due to a combination of individual drive, skills and favourable connections with the authorities. An education also seems to prove helpful, as does prior experience as, say, a tractor driver or mechanic under the collectives. But two categories of rural people appear to have had the greatest success since decollectivization — those with experience as cadres and those with family traditions of money-making skills prior to the revolution.

It is not just 'connections' and corrupt practices that have given the former local cadres a head-start over their neighbours. The socialist era provided them, unlike the ordinary farmers, with a good training in business: in handling sizeable sums of money, managing groups of workers, dealing with the officialdom, and taking charge of managerial decisions in a complex agricultural regime. In short, many of the people favoured with leadership positions during the collective era have, for that very reason, benefitted subsequently from the demise of agrarian socialism.

The other salient factor — family history — comes through clearly in a survey showing which families in a middle-income north China village have become well-off and which have not. Forty-one per cent of the families of pre-Liberation middle-peasant stock in this village had become prosperous since decollectivization, compared to less than 10 per cent of the families from pre-Liberation poor peasant origin.[54] One apparent reason for this marked difference in outcomes is that the pre-Liberation middle peasants and their children, unlike the former poor peasants, had had to learn to be particularly conscientious in their work habits under the collectives, lest they be criticized as politically retrograde. But a second and probably more important factor in

---

53   *China Focus*, vol.3, no.2 (1 February 1995), p.4.

54   Yan Yunxiang, "The Impact of Rural Reform on Economic and Social Stratification in a Chinese Village", *The Australian Journal of Chinese Affairs*, no.27 (January 1992), pp.9-10.

the success of these middle-peasant families lies in the traditional knowledge of economically useful techniques and the cultural skills that have been passed down within these families.[55]

Similarly, in the northern Vietnamese village of Hoai Thi where Hy Van Luong has conducted field research, 46 per cent of the sampled households with at least middle-peasant backgrounds produce an agricultural surplus, while only 14 per cent of those with poor-peasant and landless backgrounds fall into this category. Meanwhile, 36 per cent of the households with poor-peasant and landless backgrounds have trouble making ends meet, while none of those with at least middle-peasant backgrounds fall into this category.

However, the skills and the drive to succeed that are passed down within families may not be altogether sufficient in China and northern Vietnam to achieve success. Such endeavours often require the acquiescence and cooperation of local authorities.

In China, this favouritism is officially encouraged by a "wager on the strong" bias in programs. The government provides special financial backing to so-called "specialized households" (*zhuanye hu*) — prosperous peasant families who are chosen to receive favoured access to subsidized inputs *because* they are already generating a higher income than their neighbours.[56] A pertinent example is a hill village that was visited in Yunnan province where, under a provincial government program to sow and fertilize hill pastures, 30 of the wealthiest families, less than 10 per cent of the village's households, had been granted near-permanent leases in 1987 to most of that village's common pasturelands.[57] This "wager on the strong" bias can also be observed clearly in China's Hainan province, where in late 1993 Unger supervised a random survey of 69 farming families in six relatively prosperous rural townships that specialize in growing winter vegetables. Among these 69 families, only nine — 13 per cent — had succeeded in securing loans from the government Agricultural Bank or Credit Association during the previous year. These families' average household income amounted to ¥63,000, and they borrowed, on average, ¥26,000 apiece. This compared to an average household income of only ¥8,500 among the other households. Interviews revealed that the majority of these latter families had also wanted to borrow for investment purposes, but official banking policy favoured loans to those already rich.

In all, Unger's 1993 survey of 214 rural households in this and other parts of Hainan revealed that only 9.8 per cent of the families had received any

---

55   Ivan Szelenyi has discovered through surveys in rural Hungary that successful rural entrepreneurship there also clusters in the households that before the socialist era were middle peasant. Ivan Szelenyi, *Socialist Entrepreneurs: Embourgeoisement in Rural Hungary* (Madison: University of Wisconsin Press, 1988).

56   Jean Oi, "Peasant Households Between Plan and Market", *Modern China*, vol.12, no.2 (1986), pp.240-1.

57   On this particular case, see Unger and Xiong, "Life in the Chinese Hinterlands ...", p.8.

formal loan during the past year. In one district, according to a deputy township head who was interviewed, almost all of the loans went to the relatives of township and village officials and to wealthy households, who reportedly often used the money to rent the land of neighbours who were short of capital. In yet another district, the head of a township confided that much of the credit went to households who had relatives employed at the Agricultural Bank and local credit associations. In Hainan, and throughout rural China, it appears that both the better-connected and the financially better-off households enjoy a distinct edge in getting access to whatever grants or credit become available.

Not only loans but also the Chinese tax system is regressively skewed to the advantage of the rural wealthy. One study has shown that the richest 10 per cent of the rural Chinese population receives 26 per cent of the total rural income but pays only 13 per cent of the taxes[58] — that is, they are taxed at only half the rate paid by the rest of the rural population. (One reason is that taxes are largely on land, which each family in a village, rich or poor, possesses in relatively equal measure, while non-agricultural sources of income are lightly taxed, if at all.) In China today, those who enjoy a head start then get assisted by the government's lending and tax policies and pull yet further ahead of their neighbours.

In Vietnam, the main policy bias in favour of the better-off families lay in the 1988 agricultural reform guidelines, which suggested that in order to increase agricultural efficiency, the better cultivators should be given the opportunity to obtain contracts for the best land. In northern Vietnam, however, this policy encountered resistance at the local level, as earlier noted, and as a result, by 1993 most communities in northern Vietnam had divided almost all of their fields on an egalitarian basis among villagers, regardless of gender and age. In general, the dynamics of government policies and community pressures in northern Vietnam has helped to contain the wealth gap, while in the case of China, the lack of strong community pressures in the face of the government's wager-on-the-strong policies have had regressive effects on income distribution within communities.

The consequence throughout rural China, more so than in Vietnam, is that wealth is becoming increasingly concentrated in the hands of the most prosperous households. As we have seen, this is due partly to the entrepreneurial initiative of a capable minority and partly to government policies that favour the already affluent — but sometimes it is due, too, to "official connections" in the form of nepotism and corruption.

Not surprisingly, Chinese farmers declare themselves to be far less resentful about wealth that has been acquired through what they consider legitimate means — hard work and skill — than wealth acquired through such

---

[58]   Azizur Rahman Khan, Keith Griffin, Carl Riskin and Zhao Renwei, "Sources of Income Inequality in Post-Reform China", *China Economic Review*, vol.4, no.1 (1993), p.24.

official connections.[59] The extent of these latter practices, and their impact on the creation of a new moneyed class, should not be under-estimated, especially in the market-oriented communities.

Self-enrichment among Rural Officials

China

With the return to family farming in China in the early 1980s, the rural officialdom lost control over the daily work of the peasantry, and the cadres' arbitrary power over the peasantry was accordingly weakened. But the state's deliberate pullback from its domination of village life simultaneously weakened the central government's hold over the conduct of rural officials. Increasingly, networks of local officials have taken advantage of this pullback to favour their own private interests and those of their favourites, unimpeded by fears of anti-corruption campaigns or purges. And they are able to do so not only by positively intervening in behalf of their friends and kin but also by using their power directly to secure pay-offs from other families.

Chinese local officials have been able to benefit more than their Vietnamese counterparts. The former retain more leverage over the rural population, who remain dependent upon the goodwill of village and higher-level rural cadres to get access to fertilizers, credit, new housing sites and licences to engage in business. Chinese peasants frequently need to resort to currying these cadres' favour through gifts and shows of deference.

Corruption is most certainly involved here. But to consider it simply as corruption may miss an important ingredient undergirding these transactions — new types of patronage networks are emerging. Even where entrepreneurial families do not already have any special *guanxi* relationships in place, by persistently giving small gifts they can curry the favour of the diverse officials who might be helpful to the operation and expansion of family enterprises. Under the collectives, of course, patron-client relationships between cadres and peasants also existed, but now an already prospering peasant family's wealth provides a distinct advantage in sealing such relationships.

Previously, under the collectives, the range of a family's potential patrons was greatly restricted. Because only a small group of local cadres controlled all of a village's economic and political affairs, all patronage flowed through them. Now a more pluralistic structure of patronage is developing. For different sorts of favours, farmers can go to different patrons. For example, farmers who hope regularly to get preferential access to, say, special fertilizers or insecticides have developed *guanxi* connections with various marketing bureau personnel. Such procurements no longer need be funnelled through a

---

[59]   See, for example, Isabelle Thireau, "From Equality to Equity: An Exploration of Changing Norms of Distribution in Rural China", *China Information*, vol.5, no.4 (1991), p.56.

single set of village cadres. This growth of diffuse patron-client networks provides the peasants with considerably greater freedom to manoeuvre; and their autonomous building of patronage links has further eroded the former rigid structuring of rural power.

The farmers do not appear to resent cadres who, as patrons, accept small gifts and dinners, but they are disturbed when rural officials grab for more than that. Yet the upper levels of the Chinese state permit such corruption in part, it appears, because they see this as necessary if they are to win the local officialdom's acquiescence to the economic reform programs. The cadres are thus being allowed to trade off some of their power for wealth, placing their own families into the new moneyed elite that is emerging.

Throughout the Chinese countryside, even in the poorest districts, such a trend was evident from the very start of decollectivization. Even though the distribution of ordinary agricultural land was egalitarian and relatively free of corruption, the leasing or sale of production-team and village assets other than farm fields — orchards, fishponds, village factories and equipment — all too frequently favoured the families of the Chinese officials involved in their disbursement. Sometimes they improperly sold or very cheaply leased these assets to themselves. Other times, though the bidding processes were technically open and fair, they were the only villagers with sufficient know-how and market connections, and thus the only ones to make a bid.[60]

Whatever the particular mechanisms that were at work, a survey of a north China village discovered that fully 54 per cent of the village's officials who have held positions during or since decollectivization had become wealthy by local standards. This compares with only 16 per cent of the villagers as a whole. Interestingly, too, only 17 per cent of those who had once been village officials but no longer held office at the time of decollectivization have become wealthy since then. Regardless of the skills they had earlier acquired as local cadres, without power over village resources they have done no better economically than the ordinary farmers.[61] Here and elsewhere in rural China, power and influence can be crucially important for attaining wealth.

If this is true of current-day Chinese village officials, their counterparts in the market towns and county capitals hold even greater opportunities to divert money into their own pockets. This is especially true in the rich coastal and suburban districts, where they control an array of collective factories that can be milked, and where local private entrepreneurs are getting into businesses that require licences and frequent interaction with local government offices. The pickings are far more meagre in the hinterlands: not one of the six impoverished counties in the interior of China where Unger conducted

---

[60]   See, for instance, Jonathan Unger, "Decollectivization in a Guangdong Village: An Interview", in John P. Burns and Stanley Rosen (eds), *Policy Conflicts in Post-Mao China: A Documentary Survey, with Analysis* (Armonk: M. E. Sharpe, 1986), p.277.

[61]   Yan Yunxiang, "The Impact of Rural Reform ...", p.10.

research in 1991 contained even a single private factory, and publicly owned factories were few and far between.

The richer areas have not only spawned a vigorous growth of both private and collective industrial and commercial activity. They have also, in tandem, given rise to two types of wealthy elite households: first, some of the cadres and their relatives, who have been converting official positions into sources of revenue; and, second, entrepreneurs who have risen through their own skill and resourcefulness. Before, under the collectives, there was a single hierarchy that was grounded in differential access to power; now there are two. One is still intimately associated with political and administrative power, but with power increasingly perceived as a means to wealth; and the second originates independently in ownership of economic assets, which in turn are used to buy political cooperation and protection. In certain circumstances these two sets — the mandarins and the entrepreneurs — have come into conflict, with the officialdom of some districts fitfully moving to suppress or to ruinously milk the latter. But increasingly the two elites have developed a *modus vivendi* and, indeed, have begun to coalesce.[62] In some cases it is through business partnerships. Even more often, the sons of officials have placed themselves among the entrepreneurs with their parents' strong assistance. In yet other cases, strategic marriages have emerged between the offspring of officials and those of wealthy entrepreneurs, bringing such families directly into the same fold.

The development of this new hybrid class does not bode well for the poorer sectors of the rural populace. As just one example, intervention by local officials sometimes becomes the only available means to ameliorate the harsh Dickensian work regime in some of the private rural factories. But a merging of the local power elite and the new moneyed elite would be likely to spell an end to the willingness of local officials to intervene in defence of workers.

Vietnam

Although a number of rural Vietnamese cadres have taken advantage of their position to enrich themselves and their relatives, the evidence suggests that thus far the problem is less severe than in China. In 1989, 15 per cent of the 40,000 grievances received by peasant associations at various levels had to do with abuses of power by rural cadres, but such charges did not necessarily entail corruption.[63] In the early 1990s, a source within the Vietnamese

---

62   Based on research in Sichuan, Ole Odgaard has separately come to similar conclusions in "Entrepreneurs and Elite Formation in Rural China", *The Australian Journal of Chinese Affairs*, no.28 (July 1992), pp.89-108.

63   Cam Ngoan and Van Cong, "Thuc Trang Dan Chu, Cong Bang Xa Hoi va Thuc Hien Phap Che Xa Hoi Chu Nghia o Nong Thon" [The real conditions regarding democracy, social equity, and the implementation of socialist laws in the countryside], in *Kinh Te —*

Communist Party estimated that only 10 per cent of rural officials were corrupt and oppressive.[64] Similarly, a Vietnamese government survey in 30 villages in 1989 revealed that respondents considered 75 per cent of their three key village leaders (Party secretary, president of the people's committee, and president of the agricultural cooperative) to be of high moral calibre, as well as 70 per cent of the occupants of the ten key village positions (the aforementioned three, plus the heads of the Party organizational committee, village police, village militia, the Fatherland Front, and of the youth, women's, and peasant associations).[65] The rest were considered to have problems ranging from unsatisfactory work-style to corruption. In four villages in the district of Chi Linh in the northern province of Hai Hung, 72 per cent of the respondents considered the occupants of the ten key positions to be people of integrity, and the 2 per cent who mentioned major problems cited only work style.[66]

If the statistical data are reliable, the household incomes of village and cooperative officials, while better than average, were not higher than local teachers, who did not wield any formal power in the local administrative system.[67] In a 1992 survey of well-off households whose annual per capita incomes approached at least 1 million *dong*, the percentage whose pre-1988 backgrounds involved state power and employment was considerably higher in the northern part of the country than in the former South Vietnam (see Table 3). This could, though, simply reflect the fact that a higher percentage of the northern population had directly served in the state apparatus due to the greater role of the state in north Vietnam. It can also be argued that because the state controlled more land and other resources in the north, local cadres there, more than in the south, could exercise favouritism toward their colleagues when allocating resources. In one of the northern communities

---

Xa Hoi Nong Thon Viet Nam Ngay Nay [Vietnamese rural economy and society at present], vol.2 (Hanoi: NXB Tu Tuong Van Hoa, 1991), p.425. In one case in the south, for example, peasants charged that rural cadres were arresting people for complaining about the land issue, which in the southern context had mostly to do with disputes concerning the claim to land by former owners (ibid., p.426).

[64] Ho van Thong, "Tinh Hinh Cac To Chuc Chinh Tri Co So o Nong Thon Nuoc Ta" [The situation of the rural political organisational infrastructure in our country], in *Kinh Te — Xa Hoi Nong Thon Viet Nam Ngay Nay*, vol.2, p.414.

[65] Nguyen Minh Nien, "Ve Doi Ngu Can Bo o Co So Nong Thon Hien Nay" [On the cadre force in rural organisations at present], in *Kinh Te — Xa Hoi Nong Thon Viet Nam Ngay Nay*, vol.2, pp.469-72. The respective percentages ranged from 59 per cent and 53 per cent on the central coast and central highlands to 88 per cent and 76 per cent in northern Vietnam.

[66] ibid., p.472.

[67] Among five Vietnamese provinces studied in 1989, the households of village and cooperative officials earned clearly more than those of local teachers only in the central coastal province of Binh Dinh, and significantly less than the latter in the northern highland province of Hoang Lien Son.

where Hy Van Luong has conducted field research, for instance, two ranking officials obtained construction material provided by foreign aid agencies although they were not strictly qualified to be the recipients. But corruption appears to be more prevalent in urban areas of Vietnam, where contractors, for example, often give kickbacks to officials in local infrastructure projects.

Table 3: Pre-1988 Backgrounds of Well-off Rural Vietnamese Households
(annual per capita income of 1 million or more *dong*)[68]

	North Highlands and Midlands	Red River Delta	North Central Delta	South Central Coast	Central Highlands	South
No. of households in sample	309	281	255	240	149	908
Regular cultivators	35%	57%	34%	65%	66%	74%
Coop. officials	31%	23%	28%	21%	23%	18%
Armed/militia forces	25%	11%	28%	5%	4%	2%
State employees	8%	9%	10%	7%	7%	6%

Source: Nguyen van Tiem et al., *Giau Ngheo trong Nong Thon Hien Nay* [Wealth and poverty in the countryside at present] (Hanoi: Nong Nghiep, 1993), pp.100-1, 110-11, 120-1, 130-1, 234-5, 254-5, 264-5.

The increasing corruption mentioned by top Vietnamese leaders is certainly not restricted to urban areas. But there is a distinct impression that due to the poverty of the general population and close monitoring by villagers in tightly knit communities, resources have generally been distributed with relative equity, and that the higher percentages of successful entrepreneurs from the ranks of former cadres in northern and central Vietnam

[68]   Nguyen van Tiem et al. set the 1992 poverty line at 13 kg. of rice per person a month (equivalent to approximately 280,000 *dong* a year), and he and his colleagues consider wealthy any households with an annual per capita income of 1 million *dong* or more. See Nguyen van Tiem et al., *Giau Ngheo trong Nong Thon Hien Nay*, p.13. In contrast, the World Bank set the rural poverty line in 1992-93 at 1.04 million *dong* per person a year! Households that are considered wealthy by Vietnamese standards can be considered merely non-poor by World Bank standards.

predominantly reflect their numerical strengths in these two regions and possibly also their managerial experience. To the extent that power generates wealth, we can hypothesize that this is more the case at the higher levels of the bureaucracy than at the level of village administration.[69]

We suggest that in northern Vietnam, the self-enriching activities of rural cadres were constrained in comparison to China by the lesser success of rural industrialization and commercial development, the greater poverty of the population, as well as by a more assertive rural populace located in tightly-knit and highly endogamous communities.[70] Many Vietnamese farmers were willing to challenge policies and practices that benefitted a more prosperous minority, as attested by the widespread switch in the early 1990s away from auctioning off land parcels in northern villages, notwithstanding national directives to the contrary.

The composite moneyed class is consequently still in an incipient stage of development in rural northern Vietnam. Such a class becomes more clearly visible only when we also consider the urban population. The 1994 salary increase to civil servants and military personnel that brought their official annual incomes to 2-18 million *dong* shifted more than 2 million people and their dependents, considered "middle class" in the urban context, into the same ranks as the wealthy of the countryside. According to government statistics from 1993 to 1994, the ranks of the (largely urban) truly wealthy had grown by 240 per cent during the previous four years.[71] If we add "unofficial" incomes from the exercise of power in the national bureaucracy (thereby benefitting officials privately from foreign investments and aid), the gap seems to be substantially widening between, on the one hand, the urban elite

---

[69]   On the basis of the strong correlation between power and income discovered in sociological studies in Hanoi, Tuong Lai has suggested that power is the primary basis there for urban differentiation in wealth. Tuong Lai, "Nhung Y Tuong Co Ban Rut Ra Tu Bao Cao Tong Ket Cuoc Khao Sat Xa Hoi Hoc ve Phan Tang Xa Hoi o Ha Noi" [Basic points from the final report on the study of social stratification in Hanoi], *Xa Hoi Hoc*, no.45 (1994), pp.3-7.

[70]   In the village of Hoai Thi (pop.762 in 1990), the rate of village endogamy was around 50 per cent for the entire population, while rising to 75 per cent among new marriages in the 1986-90 period. In the village of Son Duong in Vinh Phu province, where Luong has conducted field research, it reached 82 per cent for the three-year period of 1989-91. See also H. V. Luong, "Vietnamese Kinship: Structural Principles and the Socialist Transformation in Twentieth-Century Northern Vietnam", *The Journal of Asian Studies*, vol.48, no.3 (1989), pp.741-56.

[71]   "Doi Moi's Widening Gap between Vietnam's Rich and Poor", *Vietnam Investment Review*, 4-10 April 1994. According to official statistics for north Vietnam, rural GDP per capita stood at 20 per cent of the urban level in 1990. By 1995, it had declined to 14 per cent of the urban GDP per capita because of significantly greater economic growth in the cities. See Dang Tho Xuong et al., *Nong Nghiep Nong Thon,* p.57.

and a minority of well-off households in the market-oriented communities and, on the other hand, the great bulk of the rural population.

Conclusions

We have observed that both China and northern Vietnam experienced relatively egalitarian land distributions when the collectives were split up, but income differentials thereafter have widened to a far greater extent in China than in Vietnam. As seen in these pages, this has been due mainly to three factors: differences in government policies; in intra-village structures and pressures; and in levels of economic development. In China more than Vietnam, the government has pursued policies that favour those households who already have a head start in what we have called a "wager on the strong", while the Vietnamese government's initial feints in that direction have been deflected by counter-pressures from rural Vietnamese communities. Most importantly, the differences in socio-economic differentiation between rural China and northern Vietnam also reflect the fact that China's rural coastal regions and areas near cities have witnessed an ongoing economic boom. A surge in rural industrialization is most responsible for powering this boom, a phenomenon that has not yet occurred in Vietnam.

There is no virtue in poverty. If the smaller income disparities in northern Vietnam are due largely to a lower level of rural development and come at the price of lower overall standards of living, then more decent living standards alongside greater income disparities would provide a far preferable outcome. But such an argument would, we believe, be predicated upon erroneous assumptions. Many scholars in the field of development studies since the 1970s have argued that there is no necessary trade-off between economic progress and relatively equitable distributions in income. Taiwan provides a prime example: its rapid and sustained economic growth was accomplished without any widening — and indeed, with a narrowing over time — of differentiations in income.

As the development of the Vietnamese countryside proceeds, northern Vietnam may or may not follow the pattern of the commercialized districts of rural China. But in light of Vietnamese government policy and the internal structures of Vietnamese villages, income disparities in rural northern Vietnam are likely to be more muted in the short and medium terms, both within villages and across regions, than is being witnessed today in China. (In the longer run, however, the de facto privatization of land in Vietnam may possibly contribute to greater socio-economic differentiation there.) In both countries, the degree of socio-economic stratification that gets set in place during this period of rapid economic transition away from agrarian socialism will determine the nature of society for decades to come, and in this single important respect rural northern Vietnam may hold better prospects than the Chinese countryside.

SEVEN

Political Change in China and Vietnam: Coping with the Consequences of Economic Reform

Barrett L. McCormick[*]

My purpose is to compare and assess the political prospects of the Chinese and Vietnamese states. I will argue that economic reform has profoundly changed both societies such that their "traditional" Leninist institutions are increasingly less effective tools for building popular legitimacy or managing society. My argument is that Leninist institutions work best in societies where citizens have limited access to information and alternative perspectives, and where political authorities control residence and employment. Moreover, they only work as effective tools for a limited range of ends, such as mobilizing societies to fight wars or to wage political campaigns. At present, however, in China and Vietnam economic reforms have changed both the state's goals and the social and economic environment in ways that make Leninist institutions increasingly irrelevant. In both countries, citizens are increasingly sceptical of and alienated from these institutions. Leaders in both states are broadly aware of this problem and have tried to strengthen their elected parliaments and legal systems so as to create new forms of legitimacy. But these projects have been hampered by leaders' reluctance to risk "chaos" by accelerating the decline of the existing institutions (which are after all the basis of their power). Rapid economic growth and improving standards of living provide leaders in both states with some degree of latitude, and they may yet succeed in refashioning more stable institutions. But it is also possible that the core institutions in both

[*] I am grateful to the East-West Center and the Research School of Pacific and Asian Studies at the Australian National University for their generous support and to the Graduate School at Marquette University for additional assistance. I am also indebted to Anita Chan, Ben Kerkvliet, Jon Unger, William Turley, David Marr and Edward Friedman, whose careful reading of earlier drafts of this chapter has been of invaluable assistance.

countries will continue to decay, leaving politics increasingly corrupt and coercive.

It is best to begin, however, with a major qualification to this institutional argument. Comparative Communism — a field of study that must now move from political science to history — offers a general confirmation of the power of institutional analysis. While most of the sub-fields of comparative politics have been framed by "area studies" and hence loosely based on the assumption that connected histories or a common culture would result in similar politics, Comparative Communism was based on the assumption that similar institutions would result in similar politics.[1] Broadly speaking, the institutional assumption worked. Similar institutions did engender significantly similar results in very different societies. There were, however, also some very important differences in outcomes — not least the collapse of Communist parties in some countries and their persistence in others — that suggest limits to institutional arguments. Fundamental differences between China and Vietnam, such as different sizes, different histories and different choices made by their leaders, have had a deep and persistent impact on the political systems in each of these countries and leave Vietnam with better prospects for an incremental transformation of its existing institutions.

The most obvious and perhaps most important difference between China and Vietnam is that Vietnam — with less than 4 per cent of China's land area and less than 7 per cent of China's population — is much smaller. An extended discussion of the implications of size is beyond the scope of this chapter,[2] but, in general, China's larger size implies greater diversity, more complex relations between the centre and localities, a more complex administrative structure, and a stronger bargaining position in international politics. Such gigantism, however, makes the Chinese state more unwieldy than Vietnam's.

There are also critical differences in the histories of these two Leninist states. While China and Vietnam each had both wars and political campaigns, painful political campaigns were more prevalent in China, while Vietnam won wars. Although the Vietnamese Communist Party has much to regret, including not least the means by which the south was incorporated into the socialist state and certain economic blunders of the 1980s, today it enjoys somewhat greater legitimacy and security than its Chinese counterpart.

Finally, Mao and Ho Chi Minh left different legacies. Leading scholars have compared elite politics under Mao to an imperial court.[3] His campaigns

---

[1]   Another "area" not clearly based on common histories and culture is "advanced industrial societies".

[2]   For a discussion of this, see Richard E. Feinberg, John Echeverri-Gent and Friedemann Müller, *Economic Reform in Three Giants: U.S. Foreign Policy and the USSR, China, and India* (New Brunswick: Transaction Books, 1990).

[3]   See, for example, Frederick C. Teiwes, *Politics at Mao's Court: Gao Gang and Party Factionalism in the Early 1950s* (Armonk: M. E. Sharpe, 1991).

and purges impeded collegiality and undermined institutions. In Ho Chi Minh's Vietnam, the same group governed from the 1950s on into the 1980s. None of his colleagues met the tragic fate of Liu Shaoqi or Lin Biao. As Melanie Beresford writes: "More than any other socialist state, then, Vietnam has an institutionalized system for transferring power from one generation to the next".[4]

In sum, while China and Vietnam have similar institutions, they have been used in different ways for different purposes and in different contexts. This makes the considerable similarities in the two countries' present circumstances all the more remarkable, but it also strongly suggests limits to institutional arguments.

Leninist States

Even so, similar institutions have created similar problems for both states. Both the Vietnamese and Chinese Communist Parties established Leninist states built upon a distinctive common constellation of institutions. Economic reform not only undermines and incapacitates these institutions, but also mandates the development of new and different sorts of state capacities.

Michael Mann's distinction between two forms of state power, despotic power and infrastructural power, can be used to extend and refine the question of the capacity of states. Mann defines despotic power as "the range of actions which the elite is empowered to undertake without routine, institutionalized negotiation with civil society groups", and infrastructural power as "the capacity of the state actually to penetrate civil society, and to implement logistically political decisions throughout the realm".[5] Despotic power, then, speaks of the "autonomy of the state" and the ability of state powerholders to act unilaterally and arbitrarily and to deploy coercion and, ultimately, violence to further their interests and enforce their will. Infrastructural power calls attention, instead, to the state's ability to establish matrices of institutions that penetrate society. The development of infrastructural power has been the critical factor in the growth of the power of modern states. While on any given day leaders who use despotic power may appear more powerful than those whose power is rooted in institutions, the power of despots may not have the staying power of institutions.

Leninist states deployed relatively high levels of both despotic and infrastructural power. Most modern states are born out of violence, Leninist states no less than others. The Chinese and Vietnamese states were both installed by armies that won civil wars, although foreign forces were more important in Vietnam's wars than China's. Both regimes' victories were

---

4   Melanie Beresford, *Vietnam: Politics, Economics and Society* (London: Pinter Publishers, 1988), p.88.

5   Michael Mann, "The Autonomous Power of the State: Its Origins, Mechanisms and Results", in John A. Hall (ed.), *States in History* (London: Basil Blackwell, 1987), p.113.

followed by the forceful reallocation of wealth and property, although there was considerably more violence in China's land reforms and political campaigns than in Vietnam's. Police and prisons remained a pervasive threat in both states.

Leninist states, however, were quite different from states such as Idi Amin's in Uganda, where violence was the primary foundation of power. China and Vietnam both represented themselves as leaders of titanic struggles: the Vietnamese state waging decades of patriotic war and the Chinese state organizing countless mass campaigns against class enemies and various other targets. Both states were extremely successful in mobilizing societies in pursuit of these ends. This was not just a matter of proclaiming popular goals, but required appropriate institutions. China and Vietnam mustered an array of institutions that penetrated society relatively more thoroughly than in many other states. The critical institutions included the household registration system which restricted geographical mobility and in particular kept peasants in the countryside;[6] the employment system that turned enterprises into highly organized political and social units as well as economic units;[7] and the network of neighbourhood police stations and their auxiliary committees[8] that kept close watch on local residents, and, along with employers, kept files on their political activities. These institutions made it possible for the state to keep almost all of their citizens under close surveillance almost all of the time and created powerful incentives for conforming to directives from higher-level authorities. Indeed, Leninist states made a serious attempt to capture the whole of society within the "crystalline structures of the state", to use Rudolf Bahro's memorable phrase.[9]

However, these institutions were only effective because of the supportive context in which they operated. For example, the urban household registration system was supported by a grain distribution system that made access to state-rationed grain — which could only be obtained with a proper registration — a practical necessity. Similarly, the closely supervised urban labour markets ensured that anyone without proper household registration was likely to be unemployed. Employers' success in maintaining political conformity detracted from economic efficiency and hence required an environment in which the state granted subsidies and controlled prices to guarantee the economic viability of economically inefficient enterprises. An enterprise's exclusive

---

6   For an excellent account of the household registration system, see Tiejun Cheng and Mark Selden, "The Origins and Social Consequences of China's Hukou System", *The China Quarterly*, no.139 (September 1994), pp.644-68.

7   See Andrew G. Walder, *Communist Neo-Traditionalism: Work and Authority in Chinese Industry* (Berkeley: University of California Press, 1986).

8   See Barrett L. McCormick, *Political Reform in Post-Mao China: Democracy and Bureaucracy in a Leninist State* (Berkeley: University of California Press, 1990).

9   Rudolf Bahro, *The Alternative in Eastern Europe* (London: New Left Books, 1978), p.38.

access to housing and other consumer goods was essential to recruiting political activists and to gaining workers' acquiescence to political study. The lack of a labour market also contributed to workers' willingness to collaborate with the authorities in their work units. Neighbourhood surveillance, in turn, worked best in the context of a closed society in which finding another residence was difficult, and in which critical reports passed along to employers or other authorities could create unpredictable difficulties.

In short, most people's lives were lived within the bounds of state institutions, and these institutions granted leaders and managers considerable influence over individual behaviour. As Andrew Walder has explained, state-owned enterprises brought economic, social and political functions under one roof;[10] and though less well funded, rural communes and village governments took on a similar range of functions. In both countries, the state's ownership of the means of production, its control over the distribution of credit and access to raw materials, its authority to establish prices and set production quotas, and its ability to regulate access to consumer goods ranging from luxuries to the necessities of daily life offered managers and supervisors considerable authority over many levels and spheres of social life. This organized quality of so much of social life was linked to the state's collectivist ideology, whose millenarian goals in turn correlated both with political campaigns and with an economic life that largely consisted of the quest to meet production quotas. The institutions of the planned economy were embedded in and served a system of power that had serious defects but nonetheless possessed some measure of coherence.

One key component of this environment was the maintenance of a public discourse that excluded discussion of alternatives to the official ideology. Michael Schoenhals has outlined the mechanism of censorship in China in some detail, explaining how individual phrases or formulations are approved for official use, and the system by which articles are approved for publication.[11] Bui Tin, former editor of an important Vietnamese newspaper, explains that this process turns writing into an organized institutional activity.[12]

Whether or not they sincerely believed in what they were doing, ordinary citizens played an active role in producing this discourse. Virtually all citizens participated in grassroots political institutions such as political study groups organized in workplaces and neighbourhoods, where they were required to reiterate the gist of official texts. At times all Chinese were even required to participate in practices such as "criticism-self-criticism" which were designed to provide a deep scrutiny of each individual's thinking.

---

[10]   Walder, *Communist Neo-Traditionalism*.

[11]   Michael Schoenhals, *Doing Things with Words in Chinese Politics* (Berkeley: Institute of East Asian Studies, 1992).

[12]   Bui Tin, *Following Ho Chi Minh* (London: Hurst, 1995), especially p.56.

Both China and Vietnam — and other Leninist states — used their control of the media to propagate a chiliastic message. This was most apparent in China during the Mao years when citizens were told — and many believed — that political campaigns such as the Great Leap Forward and Cultural Revolution were leading the way toward the realization of utopian futures. They were encouraged to accept fantastic beliefs such as that "studying" quotations from Mao could take the place of medical science. Ho Chi Minh and the Vietnamese Communist Party avoided such extremes. Nonetheless, Ho and his followers were not simply pragmatic nationalists, but upheld all of the baggage of official Marxism-Leninism. As David Marr has observed, "they believed that without an ideology of radical change, nationalism as the sole goal was a dead end".[13] In other words, both Vietnamese and Chinese Communists believed that historical progress — itself a problematic symbol — was only possible with adherence to a state ideology and that all those who rejected this ideology were doomed to failure and defeat. They believed that their ideology would not only solve practical problems such as ameliorating poverty and providing peace and security, but would eventually lead to a utopian future.

The Vietnamese and Chinese Leninist states demonstrate important similarities in contrast to some other Leninist states. Although secret police were utilized by the state, they were in no way as important as in the Soviet Union and Eastern Europe, where the weakness of grassroots political organization made the secret police essential. The mobilization and supervisory functions that were assigned to separate organizations such as secret police and censors in the Soviet Union and Eastern Europe were more effectively managed by grassroots organizations in China and Vietnam. The result was that it has been much harder to separate society from the state in those two countries, which in turn provided the state institutions and the official ideology with a more secure foundation.

Yet in both China and Vietnam the economic reforms require abandoning the ideology. This is embarrassing of itself but also inevitably leads to calls for examining the historical record of deeds committed in the name of this ideology and for "reversing the verdicts", in China's political argot, of those penalized earlier. Vietnamese leaders have much to account for, but Chinese leaders have considerably more. There has been considerable progress toward reversing the verdicts of the Cultural Revolution, but there are still potentially reversible verdicts, such as accounting for the tens of millions of people who died in the Great Leap Forward, or for the decision to use military force against unarmed demonstrators in June 1989.

---

13   David Marr, *Vietnamese Tradition on Trial, 1920-45* (Berkeley: University of California Press, 1981), p.320. For a useful consideration of Vietnamese nationalism, see Thaveeporn Vasavakul, "Vietnam: The Changing Models of Legitimation", in Muthiah Alagappa (ed.), *Political Legitimacy in Southeast Asia: The Quest for Moral Economy* (Stanford: Stanford University Press, 1995), pp.257-89.

The Impact of Economic Reform on Institutions

The key strengths of traditional Leninist institutions — their ability to supervise and mobilize — are not particularly relevant to the tasks of economic reform; indeed, these institutions become obstacles to some aspects of reform. By the 1980s, the command economies that they had created were not competitive in the world economy. The Leninist ideology and its institutions and economic strategy were based on the premise that participation in the capitalist world market was equivalent to surrendering to imperialism. By the 1980s, though, it had become apparent to the leaders of both states that while command economies were falling behind, some East and Southeast Asian states had been able to turn the world market to their dramatic advantage.

In both Vietnam and China, entry into the world economy has shifted power away from central authorities and toward diffuse groups of more autonomous actors. Both countries' primary comparative advantage lies in supplying cheap labour to foreign investors. Neither China nor Vietnam has yet succeeded in using foreign investment or access to foreign markets to transform state-owned enterprises into institutions like Japan's neo-*zaibatsu* or Korea's *chaebol* — models which themselves now seem dated. Instead, foreign investors require a flexibility found only at lower levels and in smaller organizations. Decentralization has been the hallmark of economic reform, and this has not only meant dismantling the mechanisms of the planned economy such as central control of prices and materials, but has also had implications as far-reaching as depriving the central government of badly needed revenues.

The decentralization required to make economies more competitive unleashed dynamic forces that leaders have not been able to control. At the outset neither country's reformers had a clear sense of where or how far their reforms should proceed, and they faced considerable opposition, not least from lower-level leaders who were reluctant to give up administrative control of economic assets and opportunities. Reform proceeded in small increments and was often based on "experiments" conducted by lower-level authorities. Chinese reform leaders encouraged those at the lower levels to be "bold" and take risks, essentially instructing them to defy both existing regulations and conservative officials to institute profitable new practices. So many people were disillusioned with the collective economy, and the potential rewards were so great, that there was never a shortage of willing experimenters. Particularly in the Chinese countryside, farmers leaped at the chance to escape the collective economy, and by means ranging from secrecy and bribery to shrewd manipulation of state and market prices or open defiance they pushed reforms forward much faster and farther than even the reformers had intended.[14] In Vietnam, resistance from southern peasants had made

---

[14] See Kate Zhou, *How the Farmers Changed China: Power of the People* (Boulder: Westview Press, 1996); and Daniel Kelliher, *Peasant Power in China: The Era of Rural*

collectivization difficult to implement; and in the north, as Benedict Kerkvliet suggests, "thousands upon thousands of individual acts of insubordination and evasion" constituted a form of debate and bargaining through which "peasant households who opposed or disliked collectivization have had their way".[15] In both countries, the reforms weakened institutions that had previously kept farmers and urban residents alike in check, and in so doing committed the nation to a process of reform that went far beyond anyone's initial expectations.

In both countries, reformers have built support for the reform program among lower-level officials by turning the right to reform into a lucrative privilege. This process is most apparent in China where, in Susan Shirk's term, reform was accomplished with "particularistic contracting" that "applied different rules to each enterprise and locality", which gave officials at every level opportunities to earn political support from subordinates in exchange for granting them generous contract terms".[16] Vietnam witnessed similar procedures.

The importance of elite support for reform can hardly be over-estimated. In Soviet successor states such as the Ukraine and Belarus where local officials have resisted reforms, the consequences have been disastrous. "Particularistic contracting" made brilliant use of existing hierarchies and patrimonial relationships to build a constituency for ever more economic reforms. But there have also been a series of unintended consequences. Applying different rules to different localities and enterprises runs counter to proclaimed legal norms and, indeed, gives the impression that those who succeed have done so because of the special privileges they have been allotted by higher levels, rather than because of their hard work or good ideas. In other words, the "particularism" in particularistic contracting taints the process of reform with the appearance of corruption and the popular perception that power is being transformed into money.

In both countries, the success of reform has in turn undermined traditional political institutions. The remaining state-owned enterprises have been forced to begin to give more priority to economics and less to politics. "Reds" have generally had to give way to "experts". Many of the benefits formerly provided by state-owned enterprises, such as subsidies for housing and medical insurance, have diminished or are simply no longer available. Indeed, many Chinese state-owned enterprises cannot even afford to pay workers all of their wages or retirees their pension, and some have been forced to lay off employees who had thought they held secure positions. In this atmosphere it is difficult to motivate workers to participate in Party-sponsored political

---

Reform, 1979-1989 (New Haven: Yale University Press, 1992).

[15] Benedict J. Tria Kerkvliet, "Village-State Relations in Vietnam: The Effect of Everyday Politics", *Journal of Asian Studies*, vol.54, no.2 (May 1995), pp.396-418.

[16] Susan L. Shirk, *The Political Logic of Economic Reform in China* (Berkeley: University of California Press, 1993), p.16.

activity. Former "transmission belts" such as the official trade unions have had to become increasingly solicitous of their members' interests to retain their attention.

Seen from the vantage point of ordinary Vietnamese and Chinese citizens, the growth of the market has reduced dependency on the state. Those workers who remain in state-owned enterprises can no longer rest assured that political conformity will guarantee prosperity or even security. Goods that were once in scarce supply and rationed through political channels are now readily available in competitive markets. The emergence of labour markets has offered workers and peasants a means to escape the once rigourous restrictions against moving or even changing employers. In China especially, because industrialization has spread far more rapidly than in Vietnam, vast numbers of rural people have flowed to the cities, where the new residents have lived at the margins of state organization. In times past, those who displeased their superiors were likely to remain trapped in dead-end jobs, but now those who go into business for themselves or find work with a private firm or foreign-funded enterprise may well make more money than those who remain behind.

The Impact of Economic Reform on Public Discourse

It is not strictly true that China and Vietnam have chosen to conduct economic reform but not political reform, while Gorbachev chose to tackle political reform first. When challenged on this, Gorbachev replied that he had had no choice but to reform the political system as a means of undermining opposition to economic reform.[17] Chinese and Vietnamese leaders, too, have had to significantly change their political systems to build broader-based support for their reform programs. To be sure, the Communist Parties of China and Vietnam remain ruling parties. They have not conceded as much autonomy to social groups as in reforms in Russia and Eastern Europe. But the reforms have significantly weakened the state's control over society. Groups such as farmers, workers, entrepreneurs, foreign investors and even intellectuals have more autonomy and a greater chance of being heard than ever before in the history of these regimes. At the same time, as observed, relations between central and local officials have been profoundly transformed.

In this environment, economic reform presents enormous challenges for ideology in both countries. For one thing, both states have had to strip the official idea of "socialism" of much of its content, gradually reaching a point where "socialism" means little more than a single-party system and economic growth. In a back-handed way, both Parties' credibility has been improved by giving up aspects of their ideology that few people believed in anyway.

17 Marshall Goldman, *Lost Opportunity: Why Economic Reforms in Russia Have Not Worked* (New York: W. W. Norton & Company, 1994).

Nonetheless, these changes have far-reaching and dynamic implications.[18] Ideas such as the importance of egalitarianism, the benefits of economic planning, and the evil character of market economies, have been discredited. Ideas once condemned as befitting only dangerous enemies have been approved. Conceding the benefits of a market economy and consigning the realization of communism to a very remote possibility means forgoing one of the main justifications for a powerful and autonomous state. Granting legitimacy to private economic endeavours means tacitly countenancing a partial withdrawal of official political controls. Declaring participation in the international economy to be an appropriate means to promote national development makes it more difficult to justify suppressing information about other countries or restricting contact with foreigners. Exculpatory mechanisms such as quoting Mao's endorsement of pragmatic "practice" to claim that the new ideas are actually truer to the core of the socialist ideology than the old ideas, or claiming that old goals must be delayed while China endures a long "preliminary stage of socialism", cannot conceal the abrupt discontinuity between the old line and the new, particularly when the old line was imposed with such great force and cost. Each Communist Party has acknowledged that a great portion of its thinking over much of its history has been tragically wrong.

The institutions that formerly created incentives for citizens to participate in the production of official ideology have been undermined. The decline of ideology and its increasing irrelevance to the conduct of affairs has demoralized both ideologues and their organizations. With material well-being now much more closely linked to economic rationality than political correctness, the networks that were once able to mobilize vast hierarchies of political study have become increasingly passive. Many of the cultural institutes that used to produce state-approved art and literature have had their funding cut. Formerly prestigious and powerful theoretical institutes have had to define new roles or else face difficult times. Party schools in China and Vietnam have hosted seminars in Western economic theory and corporate management techniques. One Chinese journal that formerly stood as a bastion of conservative orthodoxy resorted to publishing pictures of scantily clad women to regain market share.[19]

As the Party's grip on the public sphere has weakened, market forces have established a new public sphere that is usually apolitical, but sometimes includes contentious messages. One commentator writing about Vietnam

---

18   For the best account of this for China, see Feng Chen, *Economic Transition and Political Legitimacy in Post-Mao China: Ideology and Reform* (Albany: SUNY Press, 1995). For an analysis of Vietnam that is highly critical of these changes, see Gabriel Kolko, *Vietnam: Anatomy of Peace* (London: Routledge, 1997).

19   Jianying Zha, *China Pop: How Soap Operas, Tabloids, and Bestsellers are Transforming a Culture* (New York: New Press, 1995), reports on this transformation of the *China Culture Gazette* [*Zhongguo wenhua bao*] in 1993's first weekend edition (Zha, p.105).

noted, in words that apply equally to China, that "The abolition of state subsidies, greater and greater advertising resources, and the end of monotheism have also expanded the spaces for freedom of the press, even if it is often content to use these spaces for sensationalism or personal gain".[20] China and Vietnam now have a popular mass culture driven by market forces. Both countries now have large numbers of private booksellers, many of whom operate informally and are thus difficult to regulate. In Vietnam, for example, popular novels are now published in runs of 100,000 to 200,000.[21] One correspondent reported that photocopies of illegal texts disguised to look like schoolbooks are sold under the counter in Hanoi and Saigon.[22] In China, private book vendors have access to shadowy networks that distribute books not approved by the authorities. Pornography, some of it pirated from foreign sources, may well be the most important commodity in this market, but these networks also supply politically sensitive works and even banned books — which fetch vendors and distributors high prices. While formerly dominant purveyors of political orthodoxy have fallen on hard times, the overall number of journals and newspapers has dramatically increased. By 1990 there were more than twice as many newspapers in China as in 1978 and more than six times as many periodicals.[23] In the music industry, Hong Kong-based firms are increasingly important in production and distribution.[24] The movie directors Zhang Yimou and Chen Kaige have used foreign funding to produce films that have been banned by the Chinese authorities, only to receive international acclaim. Jia Pinguo's novel, *Feidu* (Defunct Capital) — which was widely criticized for an abundance of gratuitous sex and nihilism — had a legitimate press run of 700,000 and sold another two million pirated copies within four months before it was officially banned (which served more to raise its price than remove it from circulation), making it China's all-time best-selling novel.[25]

One important result of the new public discourse is that the gap between private belief and official ideology has become more apparent. It would be

20 Nguyen Ngoc Giao, "The Media and the Emergence of a 'Civil Society'", unpublished paper presented at the Vietnam Update 1994 Conference, 10-11 November 1994, Australian National University, Canberra.

21 Ibid.

22 Henry Kamm, *Dragon Ascending: Vietnam and the Vietnamese* (New York: Arcade Publishing, 1996), p.160.

23 Alan Liu, "Communications and Development in Post-Mao Mainland China", *Issues and Studies*, vol.27, no.12 (December 1991), p.75.

24 Jianying Zha, *China Pop*. See especially ch.7, "Islanders", pp.165-200. For an intriguing discussion of contemporary Chinese music, see Andrew F. Jones, *Like a Knife: Ideology and Genre in Contemporary Chinese Popular Music* (Ithaca: Cornell East Asia Program, 1992).

25 For an interview with Jia and an account of the *Feidu* phenomena, see Jianying Zha, *China Pop*.

incorrect, I think, to say that the present-day cynicism in either country is a result of reform. Rather, the old system served to keep doubters isolated and their views hidden, whereas in private conversations today people feel free to express openly critical views. Writing about Vietnam but using words equally applicable to China, David Marr has observed that:

> if one mentions the words "ideology" or "politics" to university students, they are likely to laugh cynically and say that their only goal is to make money. If pressed, some will describe themselves as "pragmatists". Some still possess sufficient faith in the socialist morality taught them in secondary school to use it as a harsh mirror against which to judge their elders.[26]

The Party itself is not oblivious to this development.[27]

The increasing visibility of this gap suggests a parallel with the situation in Eastern Europe in the decade prior to 1989. There, too, the implausibility of the official ideology became an open secret. Ordinary people came to perceive the official public discourse to be lies, and dissidents such as Václav Havel discovered that the "power of the powerless" was to tell the truth in public.[28] It could well be that, akin to the former East European governments, both the Chinese and Vietnamese governments will discover that transparent lies can only be perpetuated through cynical repression — the only alternative being a series of ideological concessions that might well end with the government's acknowledgement of its own illegitimacy.

Both Parties have attempted to compensate for the collapse of traditional ideology by turning to developmental and nationalist themes. Rapid economic growth, rising standards of living, and supportive rhetoric by other East Asian leaders such as Singapore's Lee Kuan Yew and Malaysia's Mohamad Mahathir regarding Asian values and the decline of the West lend credibility to these nationalistic developmental claims. As noted above, Vietnamese history perhaps leaves the Vietnamese government with stronger nationalist credentials than the PRC, but current circumstances give the Chinese government more international leverage for making such claims.

Developmental ideology pressures governments to maintain consistently high rates of growth. Unlike liberal democratic ideologies which emphasize procedures over substance, or orthodox Marxism-Leninism which defined itself as successful for having transformed the nature of countries' polities and economies, developmental ideologies establish concrete standards of economic performance to which regimes can be held accountable. While recent rates of growth may make this seem an acceptable risk, the recent crisis of the South Korean and various Southeast Asian economies demonstrates just

---

26   David G. Marr, *Vietnam Strives to Catch Up* (New York: Asia Society, 1995), p.19.

27   Gareth Porter, *Vietnam: The Politics of Bureaucratic Socialism* (Ithaca: Cornell University Press, 1993), p.71.

28   Václav Havel, *Václav Havel or Living in Truth* (London: Faber and Faber, 1986).

how quickly things can change. Nor is there any guarantee that developmental ideology will prove a station on the way to democracy.

Moreover, the current version of developmentalism is inextricably linked with gaining personal wealth, and many Vietnamese and Chinese have ambiguous evaluations of this. The Chinese writer Wang Shuo has produced a series of fictional works that celebrate narcissistic hoodlums who seek to make money by means fair or foul, and that satirize any pretence to ideals, including those of both the Party and ostensibly high-minded intellectuals.[29] Wang's works have been enthusiastically received, helping him to amass the private wealth that he openly seeks. While the turn toward such private concerns is a step toward political passivity, it is also a form of flaunting one's withdrawal from conformity to official politics. Moreover, and perhaps more importantly, the widespread perception that officials are at best no different from anyone else and at worst particularly greedy is deeply discrediting. The Vietnamese writer, Duong Thu Huong, who calls herself a dissident, says:

> For Vietnamese now the essential interest is money. The money motivation explains everything. They feel that if you have money you can satisfy all your desires. The Party officials and the leaders are not sufficiently cultivated to refuse money, nor to consider that money may not be the only motivation. There are cadres who are poor, but that is because they occupy positions that they can't turn to profit.[30]

These ostensibly Marxist-Leninist states may well prove difficult environments for developmental ideologies. While the use of political power to gain personal wealth might be acceptable in many states, the remnants of socialist ideology make this more problematic in China and Vietnam. Remnants of traditional Leninist discourse are useful to those constituencies whose interests are hurt by economic reform. Workers, for example, can readily cite time-honoured slogans to discredit economic reform. In short, the government focus on "getting rich" may not prove a successful ideology. Wang Shuo's characters may be fashionable, but few people really want to live in a hoodlum society. The general perception that both states' cadres are getting rich by nefarious means can easily be condemned both publicly and privately by drawing on the state's ostensible commitment to socialist values. The increasingly obvious gap between official ideals and reality engenders a threat to political stability.

Law and Legitimacy

Leaders in both Parties are concerned with the political impact of economic reform and have adopted various strategies to resist political decay. Using "old

---

29   On this, see Geremie Barmé, "Wang Shuo and Liumang ('Hooligan') Culture", *Australian Journal of Chinese Affairs*, no.28 (July 1992), pp.23-64.

30   Cited in Kamm, *Dragon Ascending*, p.143.

tactics in new conditions", both Parties have attempted to mount various campaigns against such perceived evils as "spiritual pollution", "peaceful evolution" and corruption, and they have deployed familiar strategies such as study groups for cadres, political sessions for ordinary citizens, orchestrated media campaigns, propaganda lauding model cadres and dedicated model workers, and occasional show trials. However, in the new conditions created by economic reform these tactics have largely been unsuccessful. Ordinary citizens have been able to remain passive in the face of such efforts and, as noted above, are often scornful.

Sensing the limits of traditional Leninist institutions and tactics, both Communist Parties have sought an alternative by strengthening laws and democratic procedures. This attempt is fraught with ambiguity. Official definitions of democracy still emphasize collective goals and view the socialist brand of democracy as having little in common with "bourgeois" democracy. Yet even the official characterization of democracy recognizes the importance of legality: that only elected governments are legitimate, and that government leaders are answerable to the people's elected representatives.[31]

The political reforms associated with "strengthening socialist democracy" have focussed on parliamentary institutions and elections. China's constitution, for example, declares that people's congresses, China's name for parliaments, are to be the "highest organ of political power" at each level of government. Vietnam's constitution similarly guarantees that the National Assembly "is the highest organ of state power".[32] In 1995, the head of the National People's Congress, Qiao Shi (who has subsequently retired), called for the People's Congress to become a "real power body", and he spoke on numerous occasions about the importance of extending and strengthening people's congresses' supervision of administrative organs.[33]

Both countries have reformed election procedures for parliamentary elections. China promulgated a new election law in 1979 which mandated open nominations, secret ballots, more than one candidate, and direct elections to county-level people's congresses in rural as well as urban areas (with deputies to provincial people's congresses and the National People's Congress

---

[31] At the same time, some leaders — and even more intellectuals — have promoted definitions of democracy that emphasize the need for a greater span of individual rights and political competition. For an account of the struggle for democracy in China, see Merle Goldman, *Sowing the Seeds of Democracy in China: Political Reform in the Deng Xiaoping Era* (Cambridge, Mass.: Harvard University Press, 1994).

[32] For some examples and analysis of pro-reform rhetoric from Vietnamese leaders, see Carlyle A. Thayer, "Political Reform in Vietnam: Dôi Mói and the Emergence of Civil Society", in Robert F. Miller (ed.), *The Development of Civil Society in Communist Systems* (St. Leonards: Allen and Unwin, 1992), pp.110-29, 172-7.

[33] "Qiao Shi — People's Congress to Become a 'Real Power Body'", Xinhua, 5 January 1995. Translated in BBC Monitoring Service: Asia-Pacific, 10 January 1995. For a general account of the reasoning behind democratic reforms in China, see McCormick, *Political Reform in Post-Mao China*.

to be indirectly elected). When first introduced, these laws generated considerable enthusiasm and resulted in hotly contested elections in at least a few locales, most notably at Beijing University.[34] Local Party leaders quickly regained control of the process, however, and with only a few exceptions subsequent elections were routine and predictable. As in the former governments of the Soviet Union and Eastern Europe, appropriate ratios of men and women, of intellectuals, workers, and peasants, of Party members, "satellite party" members and non-party members are worked out in advance and in turn elected.[35]

Vietnamese elections may be marginally more competitive than China's. In particular, deputies to Vietnam's National Assembly are directly elected by ordinary voters. In one of the most conspicuous and unusual contests, an incumbent was defeated despite being endorsed by Vietnam's Party Central Committee. In contrast, deputies to China's National People's Congress are indirectly elected by provincial people's congresses which are in turn elected by county people's congresses.[36]

In many respects, however, the conduct of elections in the two countries is similar. Vietnam has the same quota system for various social groups. Campaigns are apt to consist of little more than publicly posting short biographies of the candidates and brief speeches with little substantive content. In China, where I have conducted interviews among voters, deputies and officials to local people's congresses, many voters lamented that they lacked even the most basic information about candidates, while deputies reported having little time to meet with constituents or, for that matter, to attend to official duties.[37] While many respondents expressed support for people's congresses in principle, there is little evidence that existing elections provide a meaningful link between voters and candidates in either country.

While elections in both countries tend to be predictable, the parliaments themselves have been somewhat livelier. In late 1986, the Vietnamese National Assembly took the government to task for failing to control inflation, and in 1988 it criticized the government for demanding delivery of rice from provinces struck by famine;[38] in 1989, the Assembly had to extend its session for several days before deputies could reach agreement on a draft for the new

[34] Andrew J. Nathan, *Chinese Democracy: An Investigation into the Nature and Meaning of "Democracy" in China Today* (New York: Alfred A. Knopf, 1985), especially pp.193-223.

[35] Barrett L. McCormick, "China's Leninist Parliament and Public Sphere: A Comparative Analysis", in Barrett L. McCormick and Jonathan Unger (eds), *China After Socialism: In the Footsteps of Eastern Europe or East Asia?* (Armonk: M. E. Sharpe, 1996), pp.7-28.

[36] For an account of elections in Vietnam, see Carlyle A. Thayer, "Political Reform in Vietnam", *Current Affairs Bulletin* (Sydney), vol.70, no.1 (June 1993) pp.22-6.

[37] I was in China for three months each in 1989, 1990 and 1991 conducting interviews on local people's congresses.

[38] Porter, *Vietnam*, pp.75-6.

constitution;[39] and, in 1997, the National Assembly rejected the Prime Minister's choice for the Governor of the Central State Bank, on account of the many problems in the central bank's operations.[40] Assembly sessions have been broadcast live, so its activities are known beyond the confines of the political elite. In China's National People's Congress, it is now relatively common for 20 to 30 per cent of the deputies to vote against an unpopular candidate or legislative proposal, and especially in provincial and county congresses candidates nominated for high office by the Party are occasionally rejected. At the 1995 meeting of the National People's Congress, two of Li Peng's nominees for cabinet-level office received only lukewarm endorsements. Deputies have also required significant revisions in Li Peng's work reports. Various legislative proposals have been hotly debated, including the bankruptcy law. The law on martial law that was passed in the 1996 session was modified by deputies to restrict its application somewhat. In both China and Vietnam deputies regularly question ranking officials and sometimes ask difficult questions.[41]

Citizens in both countries are increasingly likely to take their complaints to parliamentarians. Some of the Chinese deputies whom I interviewed were well-intended activists who acquired justly deserved reputations for helping citizens to resolve bureaucratic tangles. But Chinese respondents were nearly unanimous in their belief that an appeal to a people's congress was a last resort similar to appealing to a newspaper, an avenue that most would only take when more effective channels such as direct appeals to the officials in question had failed.

The results of the parliamentary reforms are ambiguous. On the one hand, the two countries' parliaments have made important symbolic points. Government officials must at least appear to be elected and must make regular reports on their work to the people's elected representatives, who in turn go through the motions of discussing, amending and criticizing. Over time these rituals have acquired increasing weight. Deputies, leaders and staff members in the assemblies and people's congresses have every incentive to work to further strengthen their own institutions, a goal which is endorsed after all by official ideology. It is possible that over time incremental reforms will continue to gradually increase the influence of these legislative bodies, and it is also possible that a crisis may make them suddenly seem more important — as in 1989 when deputies to China's National People's Congress unsuccessfully attempted to convene a special session in the hope of impeaching the hard-line government.[42] Most would agree, though, that at

---

[39]   Thayer, "Political Reform in Vietnam".

[40]   Reuters News Service, 30 September 1997.

[41]   The best source for China's National People's Congress is Kevin J. O'Brien, *Reform Without Liberalization: China's National People's Congress and the Politics of Institutional Change* (Cambridge: Cambridge University Press, 1990).

[42]   For an account of this incident, see Richard Baum, *Burying Mao: Chinese Politics in the*

present the electoral and parliamentary practices in both countries fall far short of the ideals stipulated in either constitutions or rhetoric. Simply put, Communist Party leadership limits parliamentary prerogatives. In China, for example, while people's congresses no longer contain official Party committees, in most cases the congress agendas are approved by a Party committee prior to convening a session. Ironically, while parliamentary government is intended as a more effective means of governing a more open society, the very openness of contemporary Chinese and Vietnamese society means that higher standards must be met before people will be persuaded that parliaments are effective.

Both countries are also officially committed to the development of legal systems. As John Gillespie observes, "Evidence suggests that the relationship between a flourishing market and stable and predictable legal rights is well understood in Vietnam by lawmakers in central ministries and senior leaders of the Communist Party of Vietnam".[43] William Alford thinks that Chinese leaders have also publicly committed themselves to attaining high standards of legality.[44] Toward this end, both countries' parliaments have passed a prodigious number of new laws, but China is significantly ahead in terms of the sheer volume of legislation.[45] Legal reform got a later start in Vietnam, but according to one scholar who has investigated reforms in both China and Vietnam, is moving at a faster pace and in some ways is more advanced.[46]

While legal statutes offer the appearance of impartiality and modernity, thus far in China the legal system is more a system of "rule by law", that affords authorities a means of selectively declaring and enforcing their will, than an autonomous system of "rule of law". In Vietnam the official terminology specifically proclaims "state rule *by* law", not *of* law.[47] But even the standards of "rule by law" are frequently compromised. In both China and

Age of Deng Xiaoping (Princeton: Princeton University Press, 1994), pp.268-9.

43   John Gillespie, "Private Commercial Rights in Vietnam: A Comparative Analysis", *Stanford Journal of International Law*, vol.30, no.2 (Summer 1994), p.325.

44   William P. Alford, "Double-edged Swords Cut Both Ways: Law and Legitimacy in the People's Republic of China", *Daedalus*, vol.122, no.2 (Spring 1993), pp.45-69.

45   China's new Administrative Procedures Law is particularly important in that it gives ordinary citizens the right to sue the government in cases of malpractice. This law has had an impact: 27,000 suits had been filed between the time the law came into effect in 1990 and the end of 1993. Of these, 20 per cent resulted in rulings against government agencies, and in another 10 per cent government rulings were changed to meet requests. China now has more lawyers than in 1949. "Xinhua Says a Third of Citizens' Lawsuits Against Authorities Have Won", Xinhua News Agency, 12 July 1994, reprinted in BBC Monitoring Service: Asia-Pacific, 16 July 1994; and "China Records Increase In Lawsuits Against State", Reuter News Service, 17 November 1994.

46   Mark Sidel, "The Re-emergence of Legal Discourse in Vietnam", *International and Comparative Law Quarterly,* vol.443, no.1 (January 1994), pp.163-73.

47   David Marr, *Vietnam Strives to Catch Up* (New York: Asia Society, 1995), p.13.

Vietnam, government agencies are liable to resist any unfavourable rulings or to be indifferent to judicial authority.[48]

Both countries are, nonetheless, symbolically committed to law and parliamentary democracy, but have yet to establish institutions that meet their expressed ideals. Kevin O'Brien has put forward the important argument that as Chinese leaders accept parliaments as a normal part of the political system, they can be seen as becoming "embedded" in the political system even if they lack autonomy from other institutions such as the Party. Clearly, both laws and parliaments have become "embedded" in both China and Vietnam. At the very least, allowing parliaments to select leaders and making leaders accountable to parliaments has important symbolic value, as do legal rituals. Moreover, there is some substantive content in these rituals. Parliaments do encourage raising issues that might not otherwise be raised, and laws, even if routinely violated, may nonetheless discourage officials from committing flagrant abuses. "Embeddedness" is a much lower standard than autonomy, though, and there is no guarantee that autonomy will follow in the foreseeable future. In the meantime, both countries' judicial and legislative institutions fall far short of the ideals expressed by leaders and constitutions. Few people in either country believe that parliamentary elections truly express popular sentiments or that elected deputies have much say in political affairs. The Party officialdom's reluctance to give up power and privileges poses the primary obstacle to genuinely competitive elections, or parliaments' assuming the status assigned by constitutions, or the rule of law. It is one more example of a gap between official ideals and reality that becomes more apparent as economic reform transforms society.

Corruption and Violence

To develop a general sense of the state of political institutions in China and Vietnam, we can draw on Samuel Huntington's argument that violence and corruption tend to occur when social demands cannot be satisfied through existing institutional channels.[49] The problems discussed above, such as the gap between ordinary people's opinions and what can be expressed in public

---

48   See Anthony Dicks, "Compartmentalized Law and Judicial Restraint: An Inductive View of Some Jurisdictional Barriers to Reform", *The China Quarterly*, no.141 (March 1995), pp.65-81. Sidel notes similar problems in Vietnam. See "The Re-emergence of Legal Discourse". Another Western analyst wrote about Vietnam that "This year, however, has seen the nature of risk shift from that associated with a partial legal vacuum to the multiple risks associated with laws that contradict other laws, laws that are enacted but not enforced, and laws that pass measures in apparent contradiction to the policy of Vietnam to create conditions that are favourable for foreign investment". *Australian Financial Review*, 10 May 1995, cited in David W. P. Elliott, "Vietnam Faces the Future", *Current History*, vol.94, no.596 (December 1995), pp.412-9.

49   Samuel P. Huntington, *Political Order in Changing Societies* (New Haven: Yale University Press, 1968).

media, weak legal systems and parliamentary institutions, and the limits placed on representative institutions, are not merely theoretical problems but have a direct impact on everyday lives. They mean that problems are difficult to resolve through institutional channels and increase the probability of violence and corruption.

In both China and Vietnam, leaders have emphatically declared that the present level of corruption constitutes a serious threat to political stability. In China, Jiang Zemin has warned that "if we do not fight this hard battle [against corruption] with resolution, the Party and state are indeed in danger of collapse".[50] Vietnam's Prime Minister is only a little less sanguine:

> The state of corruption plus incapabilities, red tape and domineering behaviour, and the lack of a sense of discipline among numerous officials in various state machines at all levels and branches ... have ... jeopardized the renovation process and brought discredit to the Party's leadership.[51]

Corruption is notoriously difficult to measure, but there is considerable evidence that it is a very serious problem in both China and Vietnam. Various surveys of international businesspeople report China to be among the two or three most corrupt countries in Asia.[52] Gaining a licence or permit is apt to require a bribe. Managers of state-owned enterprises may require bribes before signing a contract. The state is unable to protect the assets of state-owned enterprises from parasitic managers. Smugglers handle everything from drugs and guns to rice. Police investigations can be compromised. Taxes are assessed arbitrarily. Local governments establish inspection stations along highways and extort fees from trucks and travellers. Persistent allegations indicate that Chinese naval units commandeer freighters in coastal waters. By most accounts, corruption in Vietnam is also a pressing problem, but not as serious as in China. By one estimate corruption in Vietnam adds 5 to 15 per cent to the costs of projects involving foreign partners.[53] According to official

---

50 See "Jiang Zemin Tells Party Cadres — 'If the Economy Fails, We Will Collapse'", Xinhua Domestic Service, 5 March, 1994, trans. in BBC Monitoring Service: Asia-Pacific, 9 March 1994.

51 Cited in Allan E. Goodman, "Vietnam in 1994: With Peace at Hand", *Asian Survey*, vol.30, no.1 (January 1995), pp.92-9.

52 "Hard Graft in Asia", *The Economist*, 27 May 1995, p.61. See also "A Global Gauge of Greased Palms", *New York Times*, 10 August 1995, p.E3; and Peter Norman, "New Zealand 'Least Corrupt' Country", *Financial Times*, 3 June 1996, p.5. Nicholas D. Kristof and Sheryl WuDunn write: "A survey of 3,300 people in 1992 found that those questioned spent an average of 118 *yuan*, or several weeks' income, on 'gifts' each year for people from whom they sought assistance. Nationwide that amounts to about $20 billion a year". This figure, though, would not appear to include money or resources diverted from state coffers, which seems to me the most prevalent form of corruption. See *China Wakes: The Struggle for the Soul of a Rising Power* (New York: Times Books, 1994), p.187.

53 Elliott, "Vietnam Faces the Future", p.413.

accounts, smuggling is among the more serious problems, with one estimate that over half the consumer goods coming into Ho Chi Minh City are smuggled.[54]

China is also becoming an increasingly violent country. The regime's show of force in 1989 brought an end to massive urban demonstrations, but there have been widespread demonstrations in rural areas and a rising tide of labour disputes in urban areas. While information is sketchy, the rural incidents appear to have been sparked by practices such as paying for peasant harvests with IOU's and a heavy burden of arbitrary fees and taxes. These practices are most common in poorer inland areas lacking successful collective enterprises. The spectre of rural unrest has galvanized the central authorities, who have responded with regulations and laws intended to curb these practices, but arbitrary taxes and fees remain a pressing problem. Vietnam has also had rural disturbances. One report, for example, states that in Thanh Hoa province there have been over 120 incidents of "major or even fierce struggles".[55] In 1997, thousands of peasants demonstrated for months in various locations in neighbouring Thai Binh province.[56] In both these cases, peasants seem to have been motivated by extreme taxes and abusive officials, but other recent reports of smaller scale unrest involve land disputes and religious autonomy.[57]

Chinese workers are also increasingly restive. In 1993, the number of labour disputes taken to arbitration was exceptionally high, but the 19,000 disputes taken to arbitration in 1994 was another 50 per cent above that.[58] Beijing alone saw over 300 labour disputes in the first quarter of 1995, which was again 50 per cent more than during the first quarter of 1994.[59] Strikes continued through 1996 and 1997 with, for example, an estimated 100,000

---

[54] George Irvin, "Vietnam: Assessing the Achievements of *Doi Moi*", *Journal of Development Studies,* vol.31, no.5 (June 1995), pp.725-51.

[55] Benedict J. Tria Kerkvliet, "Politics of Society in Vietnam in the Mid 1990s", in *idem* (ed.), *Dilemmas of Development: Vietnam Update 1994* (Canberra: Department of Political and Social Change, Australian National University, 1995), p.20.

[56] "Large-scale Protests Across Thai Binh Province", Free Vietnam Alliance Press Release, 24 July 1997 (http://www.fva.org/0897/story2.htm).

[57] See, for example, "Violent Suppression of Religious Protests in Dong Nai Province", *Free Vietnam Alliance*, Paris, 10 November 1997 (http://www.fva.org/1197/story11.htm).

[58] Of these, 45 per cent were in state-owned firms, and only 15 per cent were in firms with foreign participation. "China Sees Sharp Rise in Labour Disputes", Reuters News Service, 10 May 1995.

[59] "Beijing Labour Disputes Soar in First Half of Year", Reuters News Service, 31 May 1995. See also Lo Ping and Li Tzu-ching, "The Enemy's Presence Is Discovered in 17 Provinces and 33 Cities", *Zhengming*, no.200 (1 June 1994), pp. 9-10, trans. in BBC Monitoring Service, Summary of World Broadcasts, 6 June 1994.

laid-off workers demonstrating in Mianyang, Sichuan, in July 1997.[60] Plans announced in the fall of 1997 which called for privatizing large numbers of state enterprises are widely expected to lead to escalating tensions. There has also been an increasing number of strikes in Vietnam. According to official figures, there were 24 significant strikes in 1994, 48 in 1995, and 35 in the first eight months of 1996,[61] and at least 38 strikes during the first six months of 1997.[62]

To their credit, Chinese authorities have tried to deal with these problems through legislation. A law on agriculture was passed in the summer of 1993 that gave peasants the right to refuse to pay improperly authorized fees, and the system of arbitration mentioned above was instituted under a new labour law. However, these laws have been incompletely implemented. Although farmers and workers are apt to cite such laws to resist the abuses of grassroots authorities, the results often are uncertain and sometimes violent.[63]

While modest violence has emerged from below, both states have had conspicuous recourse to violence as a means of controlling society. The violence used to suppress the 1989 Chinese democracy movement is the single most important example, but subsequently many dissidents have been harassed, beaten, and detained in ways that flagrantly violate Chinese laws. In Vietnam a similar crackdown has been underway in recent years. Henry Kamm summarizes the situation in Vietnam as follows:

> The secret police controls the lives of ordinary citizens through a fine-meshed network of spy-on-your-neighbour informers that reaches down to every village hut and cubicle apartment in cities and towns. Vietnamese suspected of holding independent views are entitled to far closer observation and occasional summonses for "informal chats" with police or Party officials, and the very few who have voiced unpopular opinions are subjected to imprisonment, threats, loss of job, undisguised surveillance, ostracism, and other forms of open intimidation.[64]

---

[60] Agence France Presse reported that the authorities' attempts to suppress these demonstrations led to 100 injuries and 80 arrests. See "Latest Development on Workers' Demonstrations in Mianyang, Sichuan", in *China News Digest,* 20 July 1997.

[61] "Labour Conditions in Vietnam: Recent History and Future Direction", The Free Vietnam Alliance, Paris, 1 October 1996 (http://www.fva.org/ document/vn_labor.htm).

[62] Diem H. Do, "The Current Condition of Vietnam", Congressional Human Rights Caucus Briefing on Vietnam Washington, DC, 30 September 1997 (http://www.fva.org/ 1097/story3.htm).

[63] Kevin O'Brien has labelled this "policy-based resistance". See Kevin J. O'Brien, "Implementing Political Reform in China's Villages", *Australian Journal of Chinese Affairs,* no.32 (July 1994), pp.33-60.

[64] Kamm, *Dragon Ascending,* p.46.

Notably, the secret police in Eastern Europe were able to maintain similar networks of informers long after these regimes had lost legitimacy.[65] The events of 1989 point to an important difference between China and Vietnam, however. The nationwide scale of the demonstrations illustrated a level of popular dissatisfaction in Chinese society that may not exist in Vietnam. The Chinese government's use of violence in 1989 did gain more time for further reforms, but at the cost of yet more alienation. The Chinese government's fear of being called to account for this and so many previous incidents may explain its reluctance to tolerate autonomous organizations as these could conceivably articulate such demands. The Vietnamese leadership's ability to avoid such a violent confrontation between state and society means that an incremental evolution toward a more open society is more feasible — yet the current situation in Vietnam suggests that the Party is not inclined to take advantage of this opportunity.

It does not appear that an organized opposition is likely to threaten either state at any time in the near future. Instead, the coercive arms of both states have been able to suppress organized opposition. Nonetheless, the changing nature of society requires both states to develop new institutions and new strategies for governing. A state-centric analysis that understands politics primarily in terms of the state's policies and institutions will very likely overlook the most important and most dynamic elements in these nation's politics.

Conclusion

Both China and Vietnam face an urgent political dilemma. In both countries economic reform has created societies that are less dependent on the state than at any time since the establishment of Leninist states. Markets have offered citizens access to goods that were once regulated by the state, as well as alternative sources of employment and considerable mobility. The growth of market economies provides a foundation for citizens to spend their lives in pursuit of private ends. Markets have also produced new channels for public discourse, thereby changing its content. The new public discourse does not at present stand in opposition to the state, but it makes Party ideology appear increasingly irrelevant to most citizens. As yet there are no organizations like Poland's Solidarity waiting in the wings to storm the political stage, but no one can yet see the end of this process.

In the context of an increasingly autonomous society, the institutions that used to maintain the state are losing ground. Party committees, neighbourhood committees, state-owned enterprises, mass organizations, censors, ideological institutes, political study, household registration, and all such institutions of political and social control are in decline. The society they used to manage no

---

[65] For a fine account of relations among secret police, informants and their victims in Eastern Europe, see Tina Rosenberg, *The Haunted Land: Facing Europe's Ghosts after Communism* (New York: Random House, 1995).

longer exists. Nor have the Chinese and Vietnamese states been entirely successful in their attempts to create new political institutions that might be more effective in the new social context. Economic reform has not been based on careful planning and the way has not been cleared by new institutions like central banks, tax departments and economic regulators. Instead, reform has been conducted in an *ad hoc* manner that creates more corruption than institutions. Parliamentary and legal institutions have made enormous progress, but in practice have accomplished far less than official rhetoric would claim. By default, violence and corruption are becoming increasingly conspicuous in both societies.

Rapid economic growth is not enough to create a stable politics. To the contrary, history is replete with examples of political instability ruining once brilliant economic prospects. Economic growth does create the potential for a new politics based on nationalism and developmentalism. The economic forces currently working in China and Vietnam have clearly captured the energy and enthusiasm of great numbers of citizens. However, new institutions are required to guide and direct this energy and enthusiasm. Parliamentary and legal reforms have not yet demonstrated the capacity to do this. The widespread perception that state power mainly serves to protect the interests of parasitic officials presents a clear and present danger. The perception that official ideology is a lie creates the possibility of living in Václav Havel's truth. If these states cannot reverse the present decline of infrastructural power, they will be increasingly vulnerable to political violence and instability, especially if economic growth falters.

It could be that despite the similar institutional setting Vietnam has a greater chance of success than China. For the various reasons observed earlier, the Vietnamese Party is better positioned to implement incremental reforms. The Vietnamese Party's more recent victory in 1975 affords it more ongoing prestige than the Chinese Party's victory in 1949. Moreover, the Vietnamese victory over foreign forces is readily portrayed in terms more nationalist than socialist. The Chinese Communist Party, on the other hand, has bequeathed itself a terrible legacy with the Great Leap Forward and the Cultural Revolution. These struggles for an ephemeral Communist utopia severely undermined its claim to nationalist credentials. Moreover, the Chinese leadership is now further burdened with the legacy of the Beijing Massacre of 1989 that will complicate the process of reaching an accommodation with society. Finally, China's larger size and markets permit Chinese leaders more freedom to plot an aggressively nationalist foreign policy as a means of overcoming their domestic vulnerabilities. For all of these reasons I suspect that the Vietnamese state may be better able to adapt to social change with inclusive and adaptive strategies, while China's leaders may be tempted toward more repressive and authoritarian strategies. Nevertheless, the fundamental dilemmas these two states face are much the same.

EIGHT

Chinese and Vietnamese Youth in the 1990s

David Marr and Stanley Rosen

To a considerable extent, the perspectives of the Chinese and Vietnamese youth of today are a product of the surge in both countries towards a market economy, and the simultaneous opening to diverse foreign influences. Their parents came of age in completely different circumstances — the Cultural Revolution in China and the Anti-American War in Vietnam — and the parents' educations and occupations were much more directly tied to or influenced by opportunities provided by the state.[1] Not surprisingly, a yawning generational gap makes it difficult for older people and youth to communicate. Parents are troubled by youthful passions for foreign music, clothing fashions and consumer products. Communist Party leaders in both countries persistently exhort youth to remember their roots and to eschew "poisonous" alien culture.

In making comparisons between the youth in China and Vietnam, we need to ask whether the youth culture of one nation influences the other. There is no evidence that Chinese young people today pay any particular attention to developments in Vietnam. On the other hand, Vietnamese young people do watch Chinese television programs, listen to Chinese popular music and read translations of Chinese *kung-fu* (martial arts) stories, although the vast majority of these influences originate in Hong Kong and Taiwan, not the PRC. With regard to government actions, Beijing officials may listen with interest as visiting Vietnamese delegations describe problems and prospects *vis-à-vis* the younger generation, but they do not appear to have borrowed any policies from their small neighbour to the south. By contrast, Hanoi officials not only pay close attention to Beijing's efforts to manage young people but even

---

[1]   Discussions in these pages about Vietnam prior to 1975 refer to the north unless otherwise noted.

sometimes imitate China's efforts — for example, in recent campaigns against "social evils" and "cultural poisons".

This Chapter will focus on the circumstances and attitudes of the young people of the two countries and the two governments' efforts to influence them through the state's policies toward entertainment, education and employment.

Party and State Management of Youth

Long before Communist Party rule, Vietnamese and Chinese leaders regarded the proper socialization of young people as a legitimate concern of the state. Confucianism offers abundant counselling on how to prepare young people to serve the state as well as the family. In addition to that tradition, the Communist Party leaders of both countries have drawn on Soviet theory and practice when formulating programs aimed at socializing young people.[2]

Even before taking state power, the Parties in both countries established "mass" organizations for workers, women and other sectors of society — and, for young people, a Communist Youth League (the name in Vietnam was later changed to the Ho Chi Minh Communist Youth League). The core function of these leagues was to serve as a transmission belt between the Party and activist youth and to recruit, indoctrinate and test prospective members of the Party. In the early years, league membership in both countries was hotly contested, because the leagues served as channels for upward mobility. League members competed to show their support of Party policy and their worthiness by their enthusiastic advocacy of regime goals. In both Vietnam and China, the Youth League permeated the school system and had branches in state enterprises, government bureaus, the military and the mass media.

Over the decades, young people's enthusiasm for the leagues has ebbed and flowed. But since the late 1980s, the general mood of young people for these official organizations has largely been one of indifference. Membership is no longer nearly as competitive as before, and indeed is available to almost anyone who wants to join. With true believers now very rare among the youth of China and Vietnam, and reward structures no longer a state monopoly, political activism in support of regime value is perfunctory at best.

In an effort to render the official youth organizations more appealing, the Communist Party officials in Vietnam have been recently creating alternative organizations. In late 1995, for example, a Ho Chi Minh City Student Union was inaugurated to attract new members at campuses where the Youth League had not been successful. One purpose is to allow students a conduit to voice their concerns, another is to assuage the suspicions of overseas counterparts about the "Communist" in the League's name. According to one participant, the Student Union drew spiritual sustenance from the heroic Saigon student

---

2   On Soviet theories of socialization, see George Avis (ed.), *The Making of a Soviet Citizen: Character Formation and Civic Training in Soviet Education* (London: Croom Helm, 1987).

movement of the early 1970s and has been able to represent student "political interests", two developments that were probably not initially the intentions of Communist Party leaders.[3] In China, students are allowed to form associations (*shetuan*) covering such areas as academic discourse, hobbies, culture and media. Not forgetting the events of 1989, when students created their own autonomous student unions to replace the discredited official transmission belts, Party and Youth League authorities continue to monitor such associations, in part by providing money, personnel and campus space, but also by regulating and periodically evaluating each group's activities.

In both countries, government leaders have been attempting to reach out to the youth through new avenues, with new content. Following the "Beijing spring" of 1989, the Chinese Communist Party realized that it had to rebuild its legitimacy and to develop a new policy that would have some appeal to young people.[4] Recouping its standing in the public eye has also been a concern of the Vietnamese Communist Party since the near total collapse of the nation's economy in the late 1970s and early 1980s. In this regard, a priority for the Parties in both countries has been to raise the standard of living and permit a wider variety of economic and entrepreneurial activities. But they have also been pursuing other tacks, including allowing citizens a much more varied cultural life. In both China and Vietnam, evening entertainment has been enhanced with the rapid increase in the number of discos and karaoke bars and the importation of popular foreign movies such as "The Fugitive", "True Lies", "Forrest Gump" and "The Bridges of Madison County". A virtual revolution in consumer goods was spearheaded by the increasing flow of cosmetics, toiletries and similar commodities from Western multinational corporations. This appeal to what might be called the soft underbelly of youth — and what Mao would have called "sugar-coated bullets" — can perhaps best be seen in the field of popular music. In place of the pounding rock music of rebellion that was so important a part of the 1989 student movement, the sentimental love songs from Hong Kong and Taiwan favoured by state agencies have become dominant.[5]

In particular, in both countries television has become an important medium used by the Communist Party to influence the values and preferences of the population, especially children and teenagers, replacing older mobilization campaign techniques. Yet the overtly political television programs — for example, the endless news shots of meetings where dour cadres address deadpan audiences — are generally ignored by viewers.

---

3   Tu Quy Nhan, writing in *Tuoi Tre Chu Nhat* [Sunday youth], 3 September 1995. A national student association has been established too, but its general secretary, Dr Nguyen Quoc Anh, talks about "training young intellectuals for the country", not student political interests. *Nhan Dan* [People], 8 January 1996, p.3.

4   Some of the material in this section is drawn from Stanley Rosen, "China Since Tiananmen Square", *The World and I* (April 1996), pp.36-42.

5   *New York Times*, 9 January 1995, pp.B 1, 4.

Government campaigns to improve transportation and traffic discipline, to prohibit all use of firecrackers, and to eradicate "social evils" receive extensive coverage on television and radio alike, yet these only hold people's attention for a week or two. But officials have increasingly encouraged TV production teams to experiment with local content dramas, and in Vietnam new documentaries and educational shows. These are often viewed attentively, and the quality of presentation is steadily improving. Thus, a cleverly-designed Vietnamese documentary on family planning, aired in February 1996, had grandparents, parents and children glued to the set, responding to each cue. A weekly science program attracts younger members of the family. But most popular shows are of a considerably different genre. One of the most popular recently among the younger set in Vietnam was a re-run of the 1960s "Batman" series, complete with Vietnamese language interpretation over the feisty English dialogue, although the irony and double-entendres in the original were lost in translation.[6]

Television in China, according to large-scale national surveys, is far more important than the schools as a socializing agent.[7] Chinese officialdom, as in Vietnam, has tried to turn this pervasive communication technology to its advantage by encouraging certain programs and messages while discouraging if not forbidding others. An example is the government's concerted offensive at various times during the 1980s and 1990s against the moral corrosion said to be caused by the influx of "colonial culture". This is an expression used to criticize everything from the movies of Zhang Yimou and Chen Kaige, which are said to win their international prizes in the West by presenting an unflattering portrait of a backward China, to Western names for Chinese business enterprises, products and even local districts ("China's Wall Street", "the Paris of the East", and so forth).[8] Restrictions, for example, have been placed on the number of non-mainland programs that can be shown in prime time.

Through television and other media, China's regime has also openly embraced the virtues of traditional culture, even claiming it can play a role in the nation's future rise to great power status. When the economic success of the "four small dragons" in Asia is explained, the "deep influence" of

---

6   Personal observation in Da Nang, January/February 1996.

7   For surveys, see *Shehui wenhua shenghuo yu zhongxue deyu diaocha wenji* [Essays on a survey of social and cultural life and ethics education in middle schools] (Beijing: Renmin Daxue Chubanshe, 1990). More generally, see James Lull, *China Turned On: Television, Reform, and Resistance* (London: Routledge, 1991); and Jianying Zha, *China Pop: How Soap Operas, Tabloids, and Bestsellers are Transforming a Culture* (New York: New Press, 1995).

8   A front-page article in one Chinese magazine complained that 36 per cent of the trademarks of local companies use Western-sounding names, which "could have an adverse effect on children". See *China News Digest*, 28 June 1996.

traditional Chinese culture is noted as a major factor.[9] The new model hero for the era of the socialist market economy is Kong Fansen, and political hagiography makes a virtue of his upbringing in Shandong province, the heartland of Confucianism, and the fact that he was "deeply influenced by the heroes of the past millennia and by the traditional virtues of the Chinese nation".[10]

China's leadership indirectly acknowledged that heavy doses of political dogma are unappealing to most people, especially youths, when it took steps to promote patriotism while de-emphasizing politics. Beginning in the autumn of 1994, for the first time since university entrance examinations were restored in the late 1970s, students applying to study science did not have to take an examination in politics. Many educators expected the exemption to be extended eventually to humanities and social science students.[11] At the same time, however, there has been a sharp increase in "patriotic education", to teach students to be proud of being Chinese and to emphasize the achievements of Chinese culture, the Chinese people and the role of the Communist Party in honouring and furthering these achievements. This is an astute move since so few young people now believe in Marxism-Leninism-Mao Zedong Thought anyway.

In Vietnam, patriotic campaigns among the young have not resurfaced since the brief war with China in 1979. But the government has had other educational and propaganda campaigns in which youth were among the targeted audiences. A significant one, very similar to those in China, concerns an ongoing debate over foreign influences. If one of the key reformist slogans of the late 1980s was "openness", many Vietnamese politicians, like their Chinese counterparts, now argue that restrictions must be enforced on what comes in from overseas. This extends from the rampant smuggling across the Chinese frontier to the content and format of foreign advertising. Even Communist Party members loyal to the reform strategy sometimes wonder if Vietnam is losing its soul to Coca Cola, Madonna and Hollywood. Elderly revolutionaries routinely express worries about today's youth losing their roots (*mat goc*), complaining that young people show little or no interest in the nation's proud history, to the extent that Vietnam's existence may be threatened once again by a national inferiority complex and a tendency to "rent ourselves out to others", rather than self-strengthening.[12] Concerns like

9   U.S. Foreign Broadcast Information Service, *Daily Report: China* [FBIS], no.227, 25 November 1994, pp.33-4; translated from *Renmin ribao* [People's daily], 9 November 1994, p.4.

10   FBIS, no.144, 27 July 1995, pp.13-18; from *Renmin ribao*, 2 June 1995, pp.1, 4.

11   FBIS, no.132, 11 July 1994, pp.27-8; from *The South China Morning Post*, 10 July 1994.

12   Tran Bach Dang, "Vai kinh nghiem ve su xac lap li tuong trong Thanh Nien" [A few experiences with establishing ideals among youth], in Thai Duy Tuyen (ed.), *Tim Hieu Dinh Huong Gia Tri cua Thanh Nien Viet Nam trong Dieu Kien Kinh Te Thi Truong* [Understanding value tendencies of Vietnamese youth in conditions of the market

this have prompted Vietnam's Communist Party in recent years to become more concerned than a couple of decades ago in claiming to defend and preserve authentic Vietnamese tradition and "national culture" (*van hoa dan toc*).

Worries that Vietnamese and Chinese culture may be swamped by foreign influences often overlap public anxiety about the perceived explosion in crime, violence, social vices and cultural depravities. After a decade of hoping that economic development would resolve personal as well as national dilemmas, many people are increasingly disturbed by the psychological, social and cultural by-products. Vietnamese newspapers have published endless stories of children hitting or even killing their parents, pupils striking their teachers, teenage boys gang-raping girls, young burglars killing unarmed occupants of houses, and youth gangs fighting each other on the streets. When young people are caught and interrogated by the police, they often reportedly blame their actions on long hours spent viewing pornographic videos from America and Thailand or violent videos from Hong Kong, Taiwan and America. Other social and cultural deviations perceived as increasing among youths include drunkenness, heroin addiction, sexual harassment, homosexuality (previously never mentioned in the press), gambling, intimidating teachers who give pupils low marks, and cheating on examinations.[13]

In December 1995, Vietnam's Prime Minister issued decrees designed to mobilize the bureaucracy, mass organizations and the public at large to eliminate "social evils" (*te nan xa hoi*) and "poisonous culture" (*van hoa doc hai*). Vietnam's campaign was patterned after a similar one in China that had begun earlier in the year, a good example of Hanoi's Communist leadership paying close attention to developments north of the border and emulating them selectively. Deepest concern among Vietnamese officials and the media was reserved for children and teenagers, who were seen as the sector of society most vulnerable to these evils and poisons. As the campaign developed, attention centred especially on houses of prostitution, massage parlours, karaoke bars, video shops and advertising signs carrying foreign words. A previous decree on the size of foreign wording on billboards and shop signs was dusted off and enforced enthusiastically by police throughout the country, with foreign lettering painted over or covered with paper. Although worries about social vices were widespread among the populace and within the government, politically astute Vietnamese and Chinese also realize that such campaigns are designed by conservatives in the Communist Party to embarrass the proponents of continued rapid economic transformation.

---

economy] (Hanoi: Chuong Trinh Khoa Hoc Cong Nghe Cap Nha Nuoc KX-07 [State-level industrial science program no. KX-07], 1994), pp.84-8. My thanks to Hy Van Luong for making a copy of this government report available to me.

13   Nguyen Manh Hien, writing in *Thanh Nien* [Youth], 26 March 1996; and *Tuoi Tre Chu Nhat*, 28 January 1996.

It is not a foregone conclusion that officials in China and Vietnam can control or significantly influence young people, especially high school and university students. Over the past century, politically stirred-up students have rocked regimes in both countries. China's Communist Party knows this first hand, more so than its Vietnamese counterpart. The Cultural Revolution and the 1989 "Beijing spring" are the most well-documented cases, but there were also student demonstrations in 1985 and 1986, another democracy movement in 1978-81, and criticism of the Party by students and intellectuals during the Hundred Flowers movement of 1957. In Vietnam, students helped to topple the regime of Ngo Dinh Diem in the South in 1963, and undermined the capacity to govern of each subsequent administration during the next decade. In the North, students returning from the Soviet Union and Eastern Europe chafed at tight government restrictions on intellectual discourse, but limited their explicit criticisms to coffee-shop conversations among friends. During the late 1980s relaxation of controls, university students in Hanoi gathered several times to protest about living conditions in dormitories, although they showed no inclination to broaden their list of grievances to include political issues.

Programs to induce youths to align themselves with the regime may end up surprising both countries' leaders. The Chinese government's success in turning youthful anger outward, toward the "foreign", carries with it the risk of not being able to contain and control nationalist sentiment, particularly given the strong current of individualism and rejection of authority found in surveys of groups as diverse as rural young people and graduate students at Beijing University.[14] Thus, in September 1996, as the Diaoyutai islands dispute between Japan and China began to heat up, China's leaders found themselves in an uncomfortable position, having initially encouraged criticism of Japan's actions, and then being compelled to rein in the patriotic impulses which were then unleashed. The fact that student self-mobilization was being coordinated through internet computer messages made the challenge to regime control particularly alarming. The post-Deng regime may well discover the truth of the old Chinese proverb that "when riding a tiger it is difficult to dismount" (*qihu nanxia*).

Surveys suggest that Chinese youth may be thinking of patriotism in ways that do not entirely correspond to what the regime has been angling for. In one telling study in 1994 among 698 youth in Shanghai and surrounding areas, respondents were given a list of 18 values and asked to rank their top four and their bottom four. Patriotism — which had ranked fifth in a similar survey in 1984 — ranked second in 1994. Among workers, peasants and science students it was ranked first. Only a relatively low ranking by liberal arts

---

14   For example, Li Yagang, "Dangqian nongcun qingnian sixiang guannian xianzhuang" [Ideological concepts of village youth today], *Qingnian yanjiu* [Research on youth], no.9, September 1994, pp.37-40; and Liu Dehuan and Yang Liwei, "Gaige kaifang dui daxuesheng jiazhi guannian de yingxiang" [The influence of reform and opening up on the values of university students], *Qingnian yanjiu*, no.1, January 1992, pp.1-8, 14.

students prevented patriotism from replacing "self-respect" as the most valued concept. A more detailed analysis reveals, however, that present-day patriotism is not what it was during the Maoist era, when youths would go where they were needed within the country. When asked in the early 1990s to evaluate the statement "Defending the Nation is Every Person's Sacred Duty", 85 per cent of respondents still generally concurred, but when asked to make other personal sacrifices for the benefit of the country, the response tended to be considerably less enthusiastic.[15] Most peasant youths, for instance, are only concerned about politics if it directly impinges on their own lives or the livelihood of their families. Hence, only 10 per cent in a recent survey conducted in a county in Shanxi province agreed with the famous motto of the Maoist period, that one should be a "rust-free screw" in the great machine of the state, and serve the nation as needed.[16]

Attitudes among Vietnamese youth similarly show signs of departing from what the authorities might desire. A large 1993 survey asked young Vietnamese to comment on national current affairs (see Table 1).

Table 1:   Political Awareness and Attitudes of Youth

Statement	University students	All youth
Renovation [reform] is necessary	85.6%	86.3%
Need to expand cooperation with other countries	83.9	72.4
Need to renovate even more strongly	51.6	63.7
Economic policy is appropriate but many limitations/restrictions remain	62.2	48.5
East European situation influences Vietnam	48.4	48.5
Our country is gradually developing well	48.1	41.1
Don't believe renovation will win out	8.5	10.6
Don't pay attention to politics	13.8	7.6

Source: Thai Duy Tuyen (ed.), *Tim Hieu Dinh Huong Gia Tri cua Thanh Nien Viet Nam*, p.165.

Most youths responded in a politically correct manner. But one in ten respondents dared to question the ultimate victory of the state's "renovation"

---

15   Huang Jiangang, "An Investigation of the Moral Condition of Beijing University Students", *Qingnian yanjiu*, no.4, April 1993, pp.1-6.

16   Li Yagang, "Ideological Concepts of Village Youth".

184   DAVID MARR and STANLEY ROSEN

policy, perhaps because they expected a conservative backlash at some point in the future. "Don't pay attention to politics" may be a deliberate departure from public Communist Party policy, in which all citizens are instructed to perform their civic duties. Students take this non-political stance far more often than youth in general, because of cynicism or economic pragmatism.

The national high school and university system, which the Communist Party still regards as a prime vehicle for promulgating suitable political and social values, may engender public discontent, at least in Vietnam. In Da Nang in 1995, Youth League members formally complained to their principal after their high school teacher wrote "socialism" on the blackboard and then crossed it out vigorously with her chalk. When she refused to retract her action, the principal is said to have gone before the class to state that her argument might be correct, but that she was wrong to express it in the classroom. Within a day, students throughout the city had heard of this episode, and many of them expressed sympathy for the teacher.[17]

Education

Young Vietnamese and Chinese live in cultures where education retains tremendous prestige. Tradition has bequeathed many young men and women a respect for teachers second only to their fathers, a near reverence for the written word, and the assumption that those among them who memorize large quantities of facts, achieve top marks, and receive diplomas will be honoured with high social status. If a child shows the right mental equipment at an early age, even poor rural families will go to great lengths to provide conditions whereby he (or she, since the 1950s) may sail over the various examination hurdles.

Even amidst the death, destruction, social dislocation and psychological trauma of thirty years of war in Vietnam, youths there could still be seen attending literacy classes or mastering calculus. Young men and women in the north studied because it was patriotic, integral to the revolution and vital to Vietnam's future, not merely because their families or the authorities told them to do so, or because they thought it would bring personal rewards.

In China, too, during the Maoist period, authorities implored youngsters to study in order to serve the country, and opportunities for formal education expanded. Chinese schools were expected to produce students who were "both red and expert", who would become academically or technically proficient in their fields of study while openly demonstrating their political commitment to the revolutionary goals articulated by the Chinese Communist Party.[18] But, in

---

[17]   Discussion with university student, Da Nang, 21 February 1996. So far as we could tell, the teacher was not fired.

[18]   There is an extensive secondary literature on Chinese education from 1949 to 1976, and on student strategies to maximize their success in such a politicized and uncertain environment. See, inter alia, Theodore Chen Hsi-en, *Chinese Education Since 1949: Academic and Revolutionary Models* (New York: Pergamon, 1981); Susan Shirk,

practice, both countries went through periods during the 1950s-1970s in which achievement was measured more in terms of Communist Party credentials and commitment to the revolution than technical skills.

In the 1980s, the governments in both Vietnam and China took measures to reduce the "political" function of education and to increase education's capacity to serve the new imperatives to modernize, industrialize and catch up with the fast growing economies of their Asian neighbours and the "developed" world. At the same time, both governments have moved away from trying to provide free or low cost education, shifting more of the costs to families.

Both Vietnam and China's education policies have explicitly sanctioned the creation of an essentially bifurcated educational system, with a small "elite" sector to train the first-class scientists and engineers necessary to meet the ambitious targets of the modernization program alongside a "mass" sector that is expected to provide basic educational skills, with the possibility of additional vocational training. The elite education sector in China has been heavily financed by the central government, and also receives funding from such organizations as the World Bank; the mass sector has been greatly dependent on local government, collective and individual funding. The elite sector is becoming more and more hierarchically structured; the mass sector is becoming more and more "open" and diverse.[19] For Chinese youth, this bifurcated, hierarchical system offers differential rewards. For those who make it into the elite sector, upward mobility has even included the opportunity to study abroad; for those who don't, it often means an education only to the end of junior high school. Notably, too, fewer advance into tertiary studies than in much of the Third World. Only about 3 per cent of 18 to 22-year-olds in China receive a tertiary education.

Vietnam has even lower figures. As of 1993 a mere 2 per cent of young men and women aged 18-24 were involved in any kind of tertiary studies. At the same time, Vietnamese authorities have, as in China, been giving more emphasis to some universities and colleges than to others as it revamps the country's tertiary educational system. After years of war and neglect, the infrastructure for higher education in the country during the early 1980s was rudimentary for most fields of study and professional training. Since the early 1990s, the government has re-emphasized the necessity for longer-term human resource development to underpin macro-economic reforms and foreign

---

Competitive Comrades (Berkeley: University of California Press, 1982); Jonathan Unger, *Education Under Mao* (New York: Columbia University Press, 1982); and Stanley Rosen, *Red Guard Factionalism and the Cultural Revolution in Guangzhou* (Boulder: Westview Press, 1982). For a recent book on debates from the turn of the century to 1979, see Suzanne Pepper, *Radicalism and Education Reform in 20th-Century China* (Cambridge: Cambridge University Press, 1996).

19   Stanley Rosen, "Recentralization, Decentralization, and Rationalization: Deng Xiaoping's Bifurcated Educational Policy", *Modern China*, vol.11, no.3 (July 1985), pp.301-46.

investment, but the press has no difficulty in pointing out glaring weaknesses in implementation.

In May 1985, the Chinese Communist Party's Central Committee adopted a major decision on education reform, highlighted by a provision to introduce nine years of compulsory education. The decision, which became law in 1986, required the most developed areas of the country (encompassing about a quarter of the population) to have nine years of compulsory schooling by 1990. Regions with "medium-level development" (containing about half of the population) were required to meet this goal by about 1995. Economically backward areas (the remaining quarter) were to be given state support and were simply told to do their best.[20] Vietnam's constitution declared the state's responsibility to enforce and pay for compulsory education for all children, until the clause was watered down to a simple social aspiration in the 1992 revised text.

Enrolment trends are worrying to many observers, including both parents and government officials. In Vietnam, for a few years following the end of the war, primary school enrolments expanded throughout the country and students poured into secondary schools and universities in the north, reflecting pent-up demand and the search for new career opportunities. By 1977-78, however, primary-school enrolments began to decline ominously as families reluctantly put their children to work in the fields to make ends meet, or village administrators found it impossible to finance more than a few hours per day per pupil of the most rudimentary instruction. Throughout the 1980s, the resources devoted to education dropped steadily as a proportion of the Vietnamese government's overall budget. Teachers' incomes fell far behind the inflation rate, forcing them to devote ever more time and energy to supplementary jobs, aggravating the widening malaise in education. By 1989, only 60 per cent of primary school children were reported as completing 5th grade. The numbers of young people attending secondary and tertiary schools continued to drop, despite population growth in those age categories.

From the early 1990s, the proportion of Vietnam's state budget devoted to education started to increase again, along with enrolments. Nevertheless, in 1993, only 36 per cent of children aged 11-14 went to school, and senior high school and tertiary enrolments continued to fall. In 1993, only 11 per cent of Vietnamese children aged 15-17 were in school.[21]

China's national-level enrolment figures, if taken at face value, suggest that enrolments there are much higher. According to the official figures for

---

20   The document is translated in FBIS, no.104, 30 May 1985, pp.K 3-4. For a discussion of the various problems in popularizing education, see Suzanne Ogden, *China's Unresolved Issues: Politics, Development and Culture* (3rd ed.) (Englewood Cliffs: Prentice-Hall, 1995), pp.311-48.

21   These figures are ameliorated slightly if one recognizes that some children aged 15-17 were attending lower secondary schools and some aged 11-14 were attending primary schools. World Bank, *Vietnam Poverty Assessment and Strategy* (Washington, DC: World Bank, Country Operations Division, January 1995), p.84.

1996, 98 per cent of primary school age students entered their classrooms at the beginning of the year, and the retention rate reached 88 per cent. About 75 per cent of the relevant age cohort (12-15 years old) are attending junior high school, and 48 per cent of these students reach various forms of senior highschool.[22] But educators in China who have conducted their own surveys are sceptical of such high official enrolment statistics. They have noted in interviews with Rosen that the schools' data are often self-reported, with little independent verification. Indeed, a common theme in popular books and articles published in China is the "crisis" in education, particularly at the primary and secondary level.[23] One area of concern is the number of dropouts. The State Statistical Bureau reported that dropout rates in lower middle school stood at nearly 6 per cent and in primary school at 2 per cent in 1991, yielding a figure in excess of 5 million pupils. While more recent data show some improvement in these figures, it is important to note that in addition to these "official" dropouts, Chinese educators frequently talk about "invisible dropouts", referring to those who may not have officially withdrawn but simply do not come to class or pay any attention while there.[24]

In both China and Vietnam the introduction of a user-pay policy for schooling has been responsible for many youngsters' dropping out of school. Since 1989 in Vietnam, governments have charged tuition fees at all levels of the educational system. Besides these official fees, Chinese and Vietnamese families must also contribute informal fees, which have become more expensive during the 1990s. Parents complain about these extra fees, but they must respond positively if they wish teachers to give their children any attention. Families must also purchase textbooks and uniforms, and, depending on how far from home the school is located, possibly pay for transport, food and lodging. As a result, by 1993 in Vietnam, more than half of the total expenditure on public schools came from households, not the state, a fundamental reversal of patterns during the previous four decades.[25]

The situation is very similar in China. The fees which parents pay often began as charges that local authorities levy on the schools themselves. Surveys typically reveal an array of more than twenty such fees or more. A study of

---

[22] *Introduction to Education in China* (bilingual edition) (Beijing: State Education Commission, 1996), p.7.

[23] For example, see Wu Wen and Luo Daming, *Chenzhong de chibang: Zhongguo jiaoyu yousilu* (Chengdu: Sichuan Renmin Chubanshe, 1994). Chapters 5-10 of this book are translated under the book's title in English, in Gerard A. Postiglione (ed.), "Heavy Laden Wings: Sad Contemplations on China's Education (I) and (II)", *Chinese Education and Society*, vol.28, nos 1 and 2 (January-February and March-April 1995). Also see Wei Feng (ed.), *Zhongguo zhishijie dazhendang* [The great tremors in China's intellectual circles] (Beijing: Zhongguo Shehui Chubanshe, 1993). Chapters 4-7 on education have been translated in *Chinese Education and Society*, vol.29, no.6 (November-December 1996).

[24] Postiglione, "Heavy Laden Wings (I)", pp.13-14.

[25] World Bank, *Vietnam Poverty Assessment and Strategy*, pp.86-7, 92-4.

five provinces conducted by the State Education Commission found that on average each school was assessed 10,000 *yuan* to support a variety of projects and activities, ranging from training the local militia to donating money to the Three Gorges Dam project; the schools could only survive by passing the costs on to the students.[26] A trade union study of 200 parents with children at 108 primary and middle schools in Chongqing, one of China's largest cities, found that the average cost of miscellaneous fees for primary students at the beginning of the autumn term in 1994 was 96 *yuan*; for junior high students it was 155 *yuan*; and for senior high students it was 257 *yuan*. Once the year began, additional fees were required, in one school topping 400 *yuan* per year.[27] At such rates, school fees might well consume 15 per cent or more of an average urban household's expenditures.

The combination of official and informal fees charged to students in Vietnam has led to a situation in which the line between public and private schooling has faded or vanished entirely. Well-off families in Ho Chi Minh City or Hanoi try first to place their children in one of several elite public schools, paying whatever is necessary on the side. If this is not feasible, they place them in private schools (formally designated *dan lap*, or "established by the people"), at prices that range from 100,000 to 340,000 *dong* per month, the latter representing almost double Vietnam's average monthly per capita income.[28] Among poorer families, the inability to pay for textbooks, uniforms and transport is often cited as the main reason their children cannot advance to secondary level. Although the press occasionally carries local proposals to exempt the poor from certain school costs, the central government appears disinclined to follow that path. Children of war invalids and war dead (on the DRV side of the conflict) do receive dispensations, but those eligible decline with each passing year.

In this fee-paying environment, educational attainment is increasingly linked to income. A Vietnamese family in the poorest quintile of the population would have to use its entire non-food budget in order to send one child to upper secondary school. Understandably, few made it that far in 1993, and extremely few to tertiary institutions. More than half the children in the richest quintile of households went to lower secondary school; seven per cent continued on to colleges and universities. Per capita state spending itself heavily favours the secondary and post-secondary students over primary

---

26   Chen Youshu,"Zhongxiaoxue wenti shoufei de jiben leixing ji duice" [The basic types of questionable fees collected by primary and middle schools and countermeasures to deal with them], *Neibu wengao* [Internal draft documents], no.11, 1994, pp.16-22.

27   Ran Er, "Luan shoufei: luan zai he chu, luan you he lai?" [Reckless fee collection: is it reckless in where it comes from or in where it goes?], *Beijing qingnian bao* [Beijing youth news], 22 February 1995, p.3.

28   Kim Dung, "Tro Dan Lap hoc ra sao?" [How are private school pupils doing?], *Nhan Dan*, 31 January 1996. Teachers at these private schools receive 1-2.5 million *dong* per month, substantially above salaries at public schools.

school pupils. According to World Bank calculations, "subsidizing one better off student in post secondary education costs 30 poor students who could be enroled in primary school".[29]

Table 2:   Enrolments as a Proportion of Relevant Age Group, by Quintile in Vietnam, 1993

Education level	Poorest quintile	II	III	IV	Richest quintile
Primary	67.7	77.3	80.7	84.7	86.2
Lower secondary	18.6	25.7	36.3	44.2	56.0
Upper secondary	1.9	3.0	6.9	12.8	27.6
Post secondary	0.0	0.4	1.0	1.0	7.0

Source: World Bank, *Vietnam Poverty Assessment and Strategy*, p.84.

Current trends in China similarly exhibit increasing differentiation and disparities at every level of education. This in turn has had an effect on the increasing influence of money to ensure educational success. Private schools have been growing at a rapid rate since 1992, although not to the extent one finds in Vietnam. In 1994, Xinhua News Agency reported there were more than 40,000 private schools in China, including 16,990 kindergartens, 4,030 primary schools, 851 middle schools, and 800 colleges and universities. While representing less than four per cent of the 960,653 schools across the country, such growth suggests that the state monopoly over education has begun to recede. Private schools range from extraordinarily expensive elite institutions in booming Guangdong province, at which the *nouveaux riches* conspicuously compete in showing off their wealth, to rural primary schools which charge less than the state schools. Not surprisingly, press reports have focused on the most outrageously expensive schools.[30] At the kindergarten and primary

---

29   World Bank, *Vietnam Poverty Assessment and Strategy*, p.88. Also see pp.86-7, 92-4.

30   Xinhua News Release, no.1305, 17 June 1994, as cited in Julia Kwong et al., "Private Schools in China (II)", *Chinese Education and Society*, vol.29, no.5 (September-October 1996), p.3. For additional information, see Jing Lin (ed.), "Private Schools in China", *Chinese Education and Society*, vol.29, no.2 (March-April 1996); and Jing Lin (ed.), "Private Schools in China (III)", *Chinese Education*, vol.30, no.1 (January-February 1997). For a broad overview, including the resurgence of private schooling in post-Mao China, see Peng Deng, *Private Education in Modern China* (Westport: Praeger, 1997).

school levels, such schools offer more individual care and service than do public schools and, for busy parents, can provide boarding facilities for their children during the week.

Beginning in the 1980s, tertiary educational institutions in both Vietnam and China have, similar to the lower levels of schooling, been charging fees, ending a system in which higher education was virtually free to qualified students. In China, fees in public higher education date from the early 1980s when national institutions set up for-fee branch campuses in major cities. In 1985, the state started encouraging "commissioned training", under which enterprises paid the full cost for students they planned to hire upon graduation. By 1993, 40 per cent of the total students enrolled were such "commissioned-training" students.[31] In 1986, universities were permitted for the first time to enrol a limited number of self-paying students. Like the commissioned-training students, their scores on the national unified entrance examination could be slightly below those of regularly admitted students. The numbers of such students admitted climbed from 3 per cent in 1986 to 15 per cent in 1992 to 25 per cent by 1993. When universities in 1992 were given the right to decide their own fee structure, some immediately raised fees for popular subjects such as business and finance. In 1993 the state issued a major policy document stating that higher education should gradually move from a system under which the government guaranteed education and employment to one in which students were held responsible for both.

Prior to the late 1980s, as in China, the state in Vietnam attempted to guarantee higher education to qualified students and assure them of jobs when they graduated. Since then the government has introduced tuition charges for higher education. A Vietnamese university student in 1993 paid an average of 65,000 *dong* per month, including books and travel as well as the assorted fees, an amount equal to about half of a university lecturer's basic salary.[32] Many students who qualify for admission are unable to attend because they cannot afford it. Some students hold jobs and study at the same time, working part-time as salespeople, café waiters, bicycle lot attendants or cyclo drivers.[33] Aware that many young men and women in the countryside are disadvantaged compared to urban youth, Vietnam's Communist Party has been creating university scholarships for rural and ethnic minority youth. But officials admit that much more financial assistance is needed and that rural youths admitted to tertiary study suffer a higher than average dropout rate.

---

[31]   This discussion draws heavily on Huiping Wu and Ruth Hayhoe, "Fee-Paying Public Universities and Private Institutions", *China News Analysis*, no.1534 (1 May 1995). For more detail on changing patterns in the financing of higher education, see *China: Higher Education Reform* (Washington, DC: The World Bank, 1997), especially ch.4.

[32]   World Bank, *Vietnam Poverty Assessment and Strategy*, pp.92-3.

[33]   Nguyen Huu Thai, "Sinh Vien va Thanh Pho ve dem" [Students in the city at night], *Sai Gon Gai Phong* [Liberated Saigon], 8 October 1995.

The cost in the mid-1990s for a Chinese family to maintain a student at university for a year amounted to about 3,400 *yuan*, counting tuition and living expenses.[34] While urban families could perhaps manage that, given the one-child policy and both parents working, many rural families cannot. One avenue for such students is to apply to specialized, fully government-subsidized institutions, which offer what have become unfashionable majors and have difficulty recruiting qualified students: in agriculture, forestry, mining and teachers' training. Another possibility has been opened by the universities themselves, which have begun redistributing a liberal percentage of the fees they receive in the form of scholarships.[35] Unlike Vietnam, few students work part-time, although this may change with the new tuition policies.

The fashionable majors in China are computer studies, international trade, finance and foreign languages. In Vietnam, 34 per cent of young men and women surveyed in five locations across the country in 1993 wanted to study a foreign language, 18 per cent wanted to study computers/informatics, and 17 per cent wished to study economic management.[36] Saigon students have summarized their preference in the following slogan: "First English, second Informatics, third Economics, fourth Law".[37] Other popular subjects include accounting, commerce and tourism.

Students must be wary of institutions that promise far more than they can deliver. In the buccaneer capitalist environment in Vietnam of the 1990s, academic administrators frequently make extravagant claims for their courses.[38] Teachers also vary dramatically in quality. A significant number were recipients of "friendship degrees" from the former Soviet Union, were poorly equipped when they came home and have had little opportunity to retrain in the past decade or more. The Ministry of Education and Training, which asserts responsibility for accrediting institutions, courses, teachers and degrees, is so far behind the frenetic pace as to be almost irrelevant. A Communist Party member and holder of a doctoral degree asks rhetorically: "Is this situation primarily the result of commercialization of schooling, of such negative phenomena as buying degrees and selling grade points or underrating ethical and political education, which is so widespread today?"[39]

---

[34] Huiping Wu and Ruth Hayhoe, "Fee-Paying Public Universities".

[35] ibid., pp.1-5.

[36] Thai Duy Tuyen (ed.), *Tim Hieu Dinh Huong Gia Tri cua Thanh Nien Viet Nam,* p.32. The 34 per cent figure for foreign languages appears low, given the general enthusiasm for English language study. However, rural and poor respondents may have rated their chances of finding a suitable course and teacher too small to mention.

[37] *Sai Gon Giai Phong,* 29 October 1995.

[38] The classified pages of several newspapers in Saigon and Hanoi are replete with hyperbole-laden education advertisements, some of the most questionable involving foreign institutions.

[39] Nguyen Quoc Anh, "Ve Van De Dao Tao Tri Thuc Tre cho Dat Nuoc" [On the question

China has seen less disruption in tertiary education. Some new entrepreneurial universities have sprung up, and some traditionally illustrious departments experienced difficulty in the early 1990s recruiting students in, for example, literature, philosophy and history. Administrators at the prestigious universities soon adjusted to new market imperatives, however, setting up departments of management, business and foreign trade, often with outside help from Taiwan, Hong Kong or the overseas Chinese, and proceeded to attract many of the best students.

Some Vietnamese at provincial universities in cities like Da Nang and Hue and Hai Phong are indignant about shoddy educational practices. A higher proportion of students come to provincial universities explicitly to secure a diploma and enhanced employment potential, as distinct from enjoying the social, intellectual, and cultural environment that their urban counterparts want. They are more prone to get angry over administrative bungling and teachers who behave more like petty entrepreneurs than moral exemplars. They want to believe official promises of a bright future as a result of educational achievement, but there is also a feeling of being trapped at low-grade institutions, of missing out on the secrets of success, and hence being consigned to a lifetime of mediocrity at some local bureau or enterprise.[40] Given some particularly flagrant cases of institutional mismanagement or insensitivity, this sort of frustration could boil over. Provincial universities in China also are beset by this diploma-mill atmosphere, but given past repressions, students are less likely to take to the streets.

Work

Economic reforms in Vietnam and China have significantly altered where and how people find employment. For the previous generation, particularly in urban areas, the state had a big say in who would be trained and educated, where one worked, and where one lived. Options and opportunities outside this state-dominated system were few. Now, however, employment possibilities are more diverse.[41] Many young people still hope to work in the state sector of the economy, but most do not count on the state to find work for

---

of training young intellectuals for the country], *Nhan Dan*, 8 January 1996.

40   Phuoc Tien, "Lam sao de nuoc di ra be lai quay ve nguon" [How to let the water go out to the sea but then return to its source], *Quang Nam-Da Nang Cuoi Tuan*, 7 January 1996, p.4. The title alludes to the problem of students needing exposure to international-quality learning, but then returning to home localities.

41   On recent changes in China, see the ten translated articles in Jianliang Wang and Xiaolu Hu (eds), "The Chinese Job Assignment System for Graduates of Higher Education (I)", *Chinese Education and Society*, vol.27, no.3 (May-June 1994). For educational strategies adopted in different localities by parents for the future employment success of their children, see Stanley Rosen, "Education and Economic Reform", in Christopher Hudson (ed.), *The China Handbook* (Chicago: Fitzroy Dearborn Publishers, 1997), pp.250-61.

them. The obvious "plus" in this new environment is that people have greater scope to exercise their own initiative.

With this freedom, however, comes the responsibility for finding work on one's own. This worries many young people. A large Vietnamese government survey of youth values in 1993 left no doubt that occupation and work problems concern young people ahead of everything else.[42] Higher education, although an asset and sometimes essential for landing one of the better jobs in today's market economy, does not guarantee satisfactory employment. Many Chinese and Vietnamese university graduates spend years looking for work pertinent to their training and still may not find it. According to a 1995 survey of graduates from nineteen Hanoi tertiary institutions, 32 per cent of the class of 1991 were either unemployed or working in temporary positions unrelated to their schooling. Among those interviewed in detail, an engineering graduate from the Polytechnic University was reluctantly marketing soft drinks, while his girlfriend who had graduated from Hanoi University's Faculty of Letters was a nanny for three children. Other female graduates had decided that the only way to "solve the employment problem" was to get married.[43] Employment agencies for intellectuals have cropped up recently, but placement rates are not impressive. Yet the higher rates of youth unemployment in Vietnam compared to China can be largely explained by the lower number of Vietnamese entering the state sector, rather than the overall levels of economic activity. As the pressures increase on Chinese state-owned enterprises to "rationalize" operations, to include lay-offs or hiring freezes, life for young workers and new school graduates will become more uncertain.

In China, male graduates experience less difficulty finding suitable employment than their Vietnamese counterparts. However, university-educated Chinese women can encounter serious problems, and their plight appears to be getting worse, with more and more hiring units openly stating that they do not want women graduates. The growing bias in China against hiring educated women is not reflected in Vietnam, although Vietnamese women still face discrimination in certain job categories and in promotion.

The generation of young people in Vietnam believes that money, more than state initiative, education, personal experience, willpower or social connections, is essential to finding a good job.[44] One needs money in order to study, to purchase work equipment, to be apprenticed, to set up a shop or market stall, to obtain licences, and to pay off assorted intermediaries. To get funds, many young people borrow from outside the family, usually at

---

[42]   Thai Duy Tuyen (ed.), *Tim Hieu Dinh Huong Gia Tri cua Thanh Nien Viet Nam*, p.164.

[43]   Que Dinh Nguyen, in *Thanh Nien*, 16 January 1996, p.49. This article also makes veiled references to unemployed university graduates who have become members of groups that prey on "the places that created them", or who use their intelligence "in the service of disreputable goals".

[44]   Thai Duy Tuyen (ed.), *Tim Hieu Dinh Huong Gia Tri cua Thanh Nien Viet Nam*, p.167.

exorbitant interest rates carrying the threat of Mafia-style retaliation if not repaid in full.

Another important factor in finding employment is geography. Increasingly, Chinese and Vietnamese people move around in search of employment prospects. Compared to a decade ago, young people in the 1990s, especially men, are more likely to leave home to find employment elsewhere. The common pattern is from rural to urban, and in China this often means from interior rural areas to coastal metropolitan areas, attracting job-seekers at both ends of the educational spectrum, ranging from students with graduate degrees to the "floating population" of 80-100 million migrant workers from the countryside. But people also transfer from one urban area to another with greater job opportunities. For this reason, many educated young Vietnamese from Hanoi have moved to Ho Chi Minh City, where 65 per cent of skilled workers are employed in non-production or service enterprises.[45] In China, a survey in 1993 of 548 Masters students at eight universities in the inland city of Wuhan found that 68 per cent wanted to find work in the open economic zones on the coast, while another 21 per cent wanted to work in Beijing.[46] Their three most important criteria in choosing jobs were, in descending order, "level of income", the district's "prospects for development", and "availability of opportunities".

Rural youth have been far less particular, with many simply hoping to find any urban employment, even short-term casual jobs.[47] In many Vietnamese and Chinese cities curbside labour markets have sprung up, where young men from rural areas stand waiting for someone to hire them. Other rural youth come to cities armed with introductions to workers or labour recruiters from the same home district, who help them find rudimentary lodging, the occasional job, and a sense of community amidst an otherwise alien, hostile environment.[48] A survey conducted by the Chinese Youth and Juvenile Research Centre found that 22 per cent of rural youth leave the countryside for the entire year to seek work, another 29 per cent are gone for about half a year, around 20 per cent leave for three months, and only 38 per cent remain at home for the entire year.[49] A study in eleven Chinese provinces

45   Vietnam News Agency, 27 December 1997.

46   Wu Xianghan, "A Study on the Current Job Selection Preferences of Postgraduate Students", *Qingnian yanjiu*, no.11, November 1993, pp.9-15, translated in Stanley Rosen (ed.), "University Enrolment, the Teaching Profession, and Job Selection", *Chinese Education and Society*, vol.28, no.5 (September-October 1995), pp.69-84.

47   To stem the migration to Vietnam's cities, the World Bank and UNDP have advised more autonomy for local government, higher priority to rural infrastructure, and improved access to credit and secondary education in the countryside. *The Economist*, 4 March 1995, p.38.

48   Li Tana, *Peasants on the Move: Rural-Urban Migration in the Hanoi Region* (Singapore: ISEAS, 1996.)

49   *Ming bao*, 21 March 1994, p.9, cited in Ju Wenzhong, "Nongcun qingnian zai

estimated that 72 per cent of the 64.5 million peasants who left their villages to seek work in 1993 were below the age of 35.[50] Vietnamese rural youth who present themselves at new urban industrial zones are quite often turned away for lack of requisite skills. The government aims to train at least one million workers each year until 2000, yet admits it needs to reorganize job promotion centres and vocational schools first.[51]

The work the rural Chinese youth find is often referred to in the press as hard, dirty, tiring and dangerous, and is concentrated in the construction, textile, mining and machinery sectors. Their Vietnamese male counterparts also often end up doing the most menial and backbreaking work in construction and manufacturing. Many others are cyclo drivers, vendors, rubbish collectors and porters. Women work in the urban footwear and textile industries, wash clothes and are petty traders, maids and hostesses in cafes and bars. Life for these young labourers, especially the men, is rough and ready, with earnings often spent quickly on carousing or in repaying loans and favours. Nevertheless, these new urban workers in China and Vietnam manage to send money home to their families still in the countryside.

In the new market environment, several professions preferred in the past are not favoured now. Government organizations are no longer among the most attractive sectors of the job market for most Chinese and Vietnamese youth. In Vietnam, teaching, medicine and engineering, which not long ago enjoyed stable state salaries and benefits, heavily subsidized housing and lifetime job security, have been traumatized by the government's economic reform program. For example, in Ho Chi Minh City in 1995, more than 500 qualified physicians were listed as unemployed, even though Vietnam as a whole possesses only 4-5 doctors per 10,000 people. While waiting for better times, some of these doctors have taken jobs as hotel receptionists, taxi drivers, shop assistants or waiters.[52] The need for dedicated young professionals is extreme in large parts of the Vietnamese countryside, yet few villages can afford to pay for them, and many professionals fear being stuck far from the urban centres.

In China, market demand for engineers is enough to soak up most young graduates. Doctors also readily find employment, although, like Vietnam, vast areas of the countryside continue to lack adequate medical facilities. The teaching profession has substantial problems, despite barrages of state propaganda about China's tradition of revering the teacher-pupil relationship,

---

chengzhenzhong de jiuye zhuangkuang yu wenti" [The employment situation and related questions concerning rural youth in cities and towns", *Qingnian yanjiu*, no.5, May 1995, p.1.

50   Ju Wenzhong, p.2. The results of these two studies are sufficiently different to warrant comment. Perhaps the second study refers to persons who leave for the whole year. Or the statistics may be flawed.

51   Vietnam News Agency, 25 December 1997.

52   *Thanh Nien*, 23 January 1996, p.10.

and despite the continuation of tuition wavers for students who train to be teachers. At Beijing Normal University, the country's top teacher-training institution, about 50 per cent of the graduates are able to avoid becoming teachers. In outlying regions, because teacher training is often the only subject being offered to any advanced level, many students embark on the course knowing full well that if they graduate high in the class they will be head-hunted by local business enterprises.

The professions that many Chinese and Vietnamese youth in the 1990s prefer are those that have benefitted from their country's "opening" to the world. According to survey findings, the favoured occupations among young Chinese involve interacting with outsiders and using "entrepreneurial" skills, and the favoured localities are the coastal cities, which have felt the greatest impact from the outside world. Nearly 50 per cent of the Masters students surveyed in 1993 wanted to work in private, foreign-owned or joint-capital enterprises; 17 per cent preferred universities and research institutes; while only 9 per cent wanted jobs in government organizations, and 5 per cent state-owned enterprises. The most important criteria for choosing a work unit were, in descending order, "prospects for personal advancement", "income", "a unit's growth prospects", and "material benefits". In Vietnam, university graduates understand that the best opportunities for getting rich in Vietnam today are in real estate, tourism, trade and employment by foreign enterprises. English-language competence is the common denominator (just as French was for aspiring intellectuals in the early twentieth century).

Ideals and Identity

The ideals of Chinese and Vietnamese young people since the late 1980s are less clear-cut, less altruistic and more self-centred than those of previous post-revolution generations. Both governments appear to have willingly sacrificed many of their former socialist ideals and offered citizens an opportunity to make money and enjoy life in return for their acceptance of the political *status quo*. They have had many takers. The get-rich-quick mentality is widespread. Public opinion polls in China show that one of the most popular slogans among youth today — taken from the popular TV mini-series "Stories from the Editorial Office" (*Bianjibu de gushi*) — is "Money isn't everything, but without money you can't do anything". A poll at South China Agricultural University in Guangzhou discovered that 70 per cent of the students felt that "seeking a better tomorrow was not as good as living a happier life today".[53] When elderly political leaders urge selfless service to the nation, youth in both China and Vietnam smile politely and perhaps respond that personal advancement is the surest, most satisfying way to contribute to society at large. In both Vietnam and China, the slogan "wealthy citizens, strong

---

[53]   Lin Zhongnian, "New Changes in Ideological Trends among Guangdong University Students in the New Era", *Qingnian tansuo* [Youth exploration], no.2, 1995, p.18.

country" (*dan giau nuoc manh* in Vietnamese; *fu qiang* in Chinese) represents tacit official recognition of this popular attitude.

Such thinking among young people contributes to a yawning generation gap, making it difficult for older people and youth to communicate. The most serious gap in China is between the second generation after the revolution — those now middle-aged who grew up in the seventeen years before the Cultural Revolution — and the fourth generation — those said to be "favoured by God" (*tian zhi jiaozi*) because of the opportunities available to them during the reform period. The fourth generation calls the second generation "the gray or gloomy generation" (*huise de yidai*) because they are overly cautious, fearful of breaking political and social taboos, and "completely worn out" (*pibei bukan*). In its turn, the second generation criticizes the fourth generation for having no sense of mission or of responsibility, for being too much like Western youths of the 1960s.[54]

Vietnam also has its generational differences. The principal divide is between those who came of age during the anti-American war, who are now in their forties or early fifties, versus those who have come of age during the past 5-10 years of dramatic economic and social change. The older generation, like their Chinese counterparts, recall nostalgically the sense of purpose and group solidarity of their generation when they were teenagers, and demand respect for the sacrifices they endured. On the other hand, most younger Vietnamese are tired of war stories, convinced that these have little relevance to present conditions, and eager to look to the future. Just as in China, if the older generation of Vietnamese possessed a coherent normative message to communicate to youth it might make a difference, but the Marxist-Leninist ideology which dominated Vietnam until the mid-1980s and China until the late 1970s is now believed by only a handful of elderly revolutionaries.

A vital question in the 1990s may not be how often the younger generations in China and Vietnam agree or disagree with the specific opinions of their elders, but whether or not they ought to be able to make up their own minds and act accordingly. Some young people deliberately defy their elders on matters ranging from dress to the choice of occupation. A much smaller group tries to expand the limits of political and cultural discourse, often in quiet alliance with alienated intellectuals from earlier generations. But few are "rebels", and for the most part the younger generation cannot be considered at odds with, or a disappointment to, their elders. In neither China nor Vietnam are the young people totally preoccupied with self-aggrandizement or unconcerned with group achievement. Most importantly, they generally continue to accept family discipline on vital questions of education, vocation and major financial obligations. They are acutely aware of how much their elders expect from them and, compared to young people in the West, show much less inclination to confront or shock their elders directly.

---

[54]   Zhang Yongjie and Cheng Yuanzhong, *Di sidai ren* [The fourth generation] (Hong Kong: Zhonghua Shuji, 1989).

Young Chinese and Vietnamese still exhibit loyalty to childhood friends, classmates and work mates, and they consider themselves patriotic, committed to a national identity, prepared to fight if attacked from outside. They believe in a proud "national culture", although how exactly to define and uphold this is subject to lively discussion in both countries. In Vietnam, the Communist Party slogan "Industrialization and Modernization" is widely endorsed by young people, revealing how profoundly the modernity agenda propounded in the first decades of this century continues to motivate yet another generation. In China, the "Four Modernizations" slogan may have become a cliché, even the butt of some pointed humour, yet Chinese youths identify strongly with a revitalized, wealthy and powerful country that deserves its rightful place in the hierarchy of nations.

Today, although many young Vietnamese and Chinese are cynical about constant official calls to commit themselves to idealistic pursuits, that does not mean they reject ideas of social justice, democracy, altruism or self-sacrifice in a worthy cause. Surveys have shown that Chinese university students, to take one important and extensively studied group of youth, overwhelmingly acknowledge the importance of ideals even while a majority say that they are unclear what these ideals should be.

The attitudes of Chinese youth, particularly toward foreign things and ideas, have repeatedly undergone far more radical shifts since the 1960s than is the case among Vietnamese youth. The tendency of Chinese youth to embrace or reject outside influences *in toto* is perhaps best reflected by a comparison between the 1988 television documentary "River Elegy" and the more recent *cause célèbre*, a book titled *The China that Can Say No: Political and Sentimental Options in the Post Cold War Era*.[55] Each elicited similar passions, albeit from the opposite end of the political spectrum. What the documentary praised is condemned by the book, and vice versa. The documentary, viewed by millions across the country, attacked major icons of Chinese civilization, including the Great Wall, the image of the dragon, and the Yellow River.[56] The message was that China's stunted development

---

[55]   Song Qiang, Zhang Zangzang, Qiao Bian and two anonymous authors, *Zhongguo keyi shuo bu* (Beijing: Zhonghua Gongshang Lianhe Chubanshe, 1996). Written in three weeks, this book sold more than 100,000 copies in one month, making the authors celebrities in China and attracting considerable attention abroad. See Jasper Becker, "Writers Who Can't Stop Criticizing", *The South China Morning Post*, 3 August 1996, p.16.

[56]   There are a number of English translations of, and commentaries on, *River Elegy*. The most comprehensive is Su Xiaokang and Wang Luxiang, *Deathsong of the River: A Reader's Guide to the Chinese TV Series Heshang*, edited and translated by Richard W. Bodman and Pin P. Wan (Ithaca: Cornell East Asia Series, 1991). See Stanley Rosen and Gary Zou (eds), *Chinese Sociology and Anthropology*, vol.24, nos 2 and 3 and vol.25, no.1 (Winter 1991-92, Spring 1992 and Fall 1992) for a translation of the documentary film and commentaries from mainland China, Hong Kong and Taiwan. For an insider view of the background to the production of *River Elegy*, see Chen Fong-ching and Jin

stemmed primarily from the country's cultural insularity, the fear of losing "Chinese identity", and the concomitant lack of openness to Western ideas. Chinese civilization, it seemed to say, could only advance by following a Western model of development. Almost a decade later the five young Chinese authors of *The China that Can Say No* expressed some dissatisfaction with their own government, but make a forceful, nationalistic polemic in defence of Chinese achievements and express an often bitter anger towards the United States, Great Britain and Japan. One may question whether the book is representative of the feelings of post-Tiananmen youth (some reviewers label the authors opportunistic). Nevertheless, recent opinion surveys in China suggest a strong rise in patriotic values and a concomitant distrust of America and the West in general.

In the mid and late 1980s, Chinese students on college campuses often distrusted their own government and its media so thoroughly that they would appeal to visiting foreign scholars to tell them the "truth" about Chinese foreign relations. The Voice Of America and BBC were considered highly reliable sources. Seven years later the United States and more generally the concept of democracy no longer have such a favourable image. To a considerable degree, the regime appears to have been successful in its "competition" with the West to win the hearts and minds of Chinese youth. In one extensive survey, Chinese urban youth were asked to choose: (1) the country you like best; (2) the country you like least; (3) the country you believe is most friendly to China; and (4) the country you believe is most unfriendly to China.[57] On all four questions, the United States ranked among the top three choices. Moreover, on another question, 74 per cent stated that the United States is the foreign country with the greatest influence on China. Although the United States was third (12 per cent) among the countries most liked, following only China itself (46 per cent) and Singapore (14 per cent), it was a clear first among the countries most disliked (39 per cent), well ahead of Japan, Vietnam and Russia, which were the next three choices. Only 4 per cent considered the United States the country most friendly to China,[58] while 72 per cent considered it the most unfriendly. North Korea was considered most friendly by a whopping 68 per cent, followed by Japan at 8 per cent. Even some youths who listed the United States as their favourite country felt it was the most unfriendly toward China.[59]

Guantao, *From Youthful Manuscripts to River Elegy: The Chinese Popular Cultural Movement and Political Transformation 1979-1989* (Hong Kong: The Chinese University Press, 1997).

[57] The survey, conducted by the Chinese Youth Research Centre and the Chinese Youth Development Foundation, was serialized in the China Youth Daily. Several of those articles from *Zhongguo qingnian bao* [China youth news], 22 and 24 July and 4 August 1995, have been translated in FBIS, no.184, 22 September 1995, pp.18-23.

[58] Following the United States as most unfriendly were Japan, Vietnam and Great Britain.

[59] *Beijing qingnian bao*, 9 January 1995, p.A 4.

A subsequent survey in six provinces and municipalities found that 90 per cent of those polled believed that the United States exhibits a hegemonist attitude toward China; 96 per cent of university students held this view. Ninety-four per cent saw the United States as "unfriendly" to China on the Taiwan issue, 91 per cent believed that the United States erects obstacles to China's entry into GATT/WTO, and 84 per cent considered US criticisms of China's human rights situation malicious. University students were more critical of the United States than were young workers. At the same time, the poll found that Chinese youths regard highly some aspects of American society and culture, including the country's wealth, work efficiency, competitive spirit and respect for the professions. Nearly 54 per cent agreed that American democracy is a "wealthy people's democracy" and 81 per cent believed that the United States is promoting "bogus democracy" and pursuing "true hegemonism and expansionism" in the world.[60]

Vietnam has had no comparable surveys about attitudes toward foreign countries, and there is no other evidence that youths there are particularly concerned with identifying which foreign nation is a potential enemy, which nation is most friendly, and so forth. The Vietnamese government itself has not waged any concerted campaigns on such matters since the 1970s. But Vietnamese youth are concerned, as young people in the country often have been, about what it means to be Vietnamese. Such angst grows from a love-hate relationship with China, which goes deep into the country's history, and a multitude of other influences from Southeast Asia and the West, while at the same time there exists a deep-felt need to be unique and to stand proud amidst all the cultures of the region, if not the world.

In 1995, one of Vietnam's most popular newspapers, *Tuoi Tre*, invited readers to contribute to a forum on "Youth protecting and developing national culture". The forum livened up with a letter from a Faculty of Tourism student, proud of his Mekong delta roots, but insistent that his generation's objective in life should be to assimilate "everything modern [communications, technology, industry, and so on] with the ultimate objective of actualizing a Vietnam today that can be conveyed to generations after us". Then came a letter from a rural youth who had failed his university entrance exams for lack of money to prepare properly, yet retained an ambition to help out his family and village, if necessary as an urban day labourer. He mocked the tourism student's preoccupation with defining what was "outmoded", "truly modern", and "falsely modern". One writer suggested that Vietnam had long ago proven itself able to resolve cultural contradictions, between "land and water, state and family, ruler and subject, spirit and flesh, the living and the dead, Confucianism, Taoism, Christianity and Buddhism". Another argued that today's company managers are faithful to national culture if they pay their workers well, market good products, and do not ally with foreigners to

---

60   FBIS, no.105, 17 May 1996, p.A 10, translating from *Ming bao* [Hong Kong], 17 May 1996. The survey was conducted by the Chinese Youth Research Centre.

appropriate the country's natural resources and hoard profits. A division emerged between those writers who insisted on defining and preserving a set of agreed Vietnamese cultural practices and values, versus those who argued that today's challenges required large-scale adaptation of new things and abandonment of some outmoded ones.[61]

As in most cultures, it is easier for Vietnamese to declare what is unacceptable than to define a specific set of values and practices endorsed by the community at large. Thus, the majority of Vietnamese probably consider Western rock music offensive or incapable of assimilation, yet there is no consensus on what constitutes popular Vietnamese music today. On Valentine's Day, trendy young men in Saigon and Dalat present gifts to young women, and a big music bash takes place at the Ho Chi Minh City Youth Culture Palace. Other Vietnamese consider this yet another case of crass Westernization and consumerism. Female professionals come under regular criticism for neglecting home duties. For example, a young female physician was condemned as a "Westernized daughter-in-law" when she filed for separation after being struck by her husband in an argument over her coming home late from foreign language class rather than attending to the needs of his family.[62]

In China, a shared goal among those embracing and rejecting foreign influences is to create a China that is rich and powerful. As inheritors of one of the world's great civilizations, their country a permanent member in the UN Security Council and the earth's most populous country, many Chinese youth foresee their nation as the leading international power of the twenty-first century. Vietnamese youth have no such pretensions, although they are proud of their forebears who defeated French, American and Chinese aggressors in turn, and they are eager to see their country catch up with states like Thailand, Malaysia and South Korea. Vietnamese of all ages mock the Chinese tendency to be overbearing or condescending, especially when it comes to people like themselves who live on the periphery of the Middle Kingdom. At a deeper level, Vietnamese are far more accustomed to foreigners coming and going, more prepared to see themselves in relative terms, not as *sui generis*.

Today's youth in the two countries are also different because the huge influx of "foreign things" arrived six or seven years earlier in China than in Vietnam. Chinese youth had their love affair with Western popular culture in the late 1980s, but since then have been exercising a greater degree of discrimination. Indeed, if *The China That Can Say No* is representative, a powerful backlash is underway. In an interview with a foreign reporter, one of the book's authors spoke of America as possessing a "Doomsday culture" without any philosophical underpinning, and he warned that advanced US technology, spread by means of computers and Hollywood film imagery, was

---

61   *Tuoi Tre*, 16 and 23 September 1995; 5 and 21 October 1995; 7 November 1995; 16 December 1995; 2 January 1996.

62   *Phu Nu* [Women], 27 January 1996.

being used to compel others to sacrifice their national interests to American designs.[63]

In comparison, Vietnamese youth did not gain wide-open access to Western popular culture until 1992-93 and they are still inclined to follow each new trend with enthusiasm. In early 1996, the Party and government launched a campaign against "social evils" and "degenerate culture", both assumed to be foreign-related, but this soon lost momentum. Nonetheless, along with many of their elders, a few young Vietnamese intellectuals are beginning to emphasize the need to reflect on what is being imported, to discuss the implications, and to exercise more conscious choices over the longer term. Assuming this trend persists, one might even predict a book titled "The Vietnam That Can Say No", condemning Hollywood films but not computers and demanding a reassertion of national values — but within a global context that the Vietnamese would need to learn to exploit creatively, not hope to reshape in their own image.

Conclusions

Our discussion of youth in contemporary China and Vietnam has revealed a number of similarities in attitude, behaviour and social and institutional conditions. In both countries they must similarly make their way amidst the legacies of Confucianism and Leninism, war and revolution, yet they have no direct life experience of these. The generation gap has never been wider in China and Vietnam alike. Some youths listen to hard rock cassette tapes, view the latest Hollywood blockbuster, watch TV soap operas, try to fathom the intricacies of commodity markets, alien managerial practices or quality control procedures, and aspire to a level of creature comforts never dreamed of by their parents.

Rulers in both Beijing and Hanoi consider it quite important to mould the outlooks and manage the behaviour of young people, yet they find this increasingly difficult to accomplish. Especially noticeable is the decline of the Communist Youth Leagues as vehicles for propagating and enforcing regime values. Within the schools, political and moral instruction has faded in significance, the prestige of teachers has declined, and pupil dropout rates have reached alarming proportions. For those families with money, study programs for children can now be implemented with little or no reference to government priorities. Because university degrees are a vital stepping-stone to elite status in both Vietnam and China, the pressure on young people to perform remains intense, although course options are much more varied than before.

When the time comes for young men and women to enter the workforce, the state in China and Vietnam no longer monopolizes employment

---

[63]   Jasper Becker, "Writers Who Can't Stop Criticizing".

opportunities, and it no longer prevents individuals from travelling far from home in search of a job. The surge of rural youth to the cities of both countries has potentially explosive social implications. Meanwhile, Chinese and Vietnamese elders alike complain that today's youths are less altruistic, less obedient and more self-centred than previous generations. Among themselves, however, young people often voice intensely idealistic sentiments that could have unpredictable political consequences.

Yet the differences between the young people of the two countries are perhaps more instructive than the similarities. Young Vietnamese pay regular attention to what is happening in China, Hong Kong and Taiwan, especially when it comes to business, sports and entertainment, but very few young Chinese bother to follow events in Vietnam. Young people's attitudes have undergone far more radical fluctuations in China during the past half century than in Vietnam. Although both countries possess twentieth-century precedents of student political activism, one must go back to the 1960s student movement in South Vietnam for anything comparable to the impact of the student-inspired movement of 1989 on Chinese society.

In Vietnam as well as China, young people often express considerable cultural self-doubt at one moment, followed by equally intense cultural pride or protectiveness at another. Chinese youth, however, take matters of national honour and prestige on the world stage more seriously than do Vietnamese youth, reflecting ancient Middle Kingdom attitudes as well as obvious differences in size and power. On the other hand, when faced with a major foreign threat, the young people of Vietnam have shown a capacity to leap into action, in ways not necessarily agreeable to the authorities.

It appears the Chinese political leadership is more proactive than its Vietnamese counterpart when it comes to trying to influence youth values, to allocate resources to education, or to foster work opportunities for young people. Although neither country's Communist Party has proven particularly successful in promoting its ideology among today's youth, or in enforcing "proper" behavioural standards, the state in China still appears to do more at various levels to influence day-to-day youth activities than is the case in Vietnam. It may also be that young Chinese intellectuals are more inclined to see themselves as part of the existing state system, even when highly critical of specific Party policies, than young Vietnamese intellectuals, who are often busy creating space for themselves on the periphery.

NINE

Vietnamese and Chinese Labour Regimes: On the Road to Divergence

Anita Chan and Irene Nørlund*

At a macro level the Chinese and Vietnamese industrial economies are developing in quite similar ways, with dramatic changes in their labour markets, employment systems and labour regimes. But it will be argued in this Chapter that they are also beginning to diverge along separate routes with regard to labour issues. It will be seen that the Vietnamese government has been more willing to grant trade unions some space to defend workers' interests, whereas the Chinese government has chosen to keep the unions under a tight rein.

Trade Unions Under Pre-Reform Socialism

China's workers are "represented" by the All-China Federation of Trade Unions (ACFTU), and Vietnamese workers by the Vietnam General Confederation of Labour (VGCL). Known as "transmission belts", these bodies served for several decades before the economic reforms as state bureaucracies assigned the contradictory function of representing the interests of both the workers and the Party-state. But in a system where all sectoral interests have been subordinate to the interests of the Party-state, in reality the "belts" could only transmit top-down information and directives. Although they grandly claimed to protect the rights of workers, they were prevented from having a chance to act out this bottom-up function.

* The information in this chapter was accumulated during several field trips to Vietnam and China during the mid-1990s. We are indebted to Vietnamese and Chinese colleagues who provided valuable assistance. The material on Vietnam is based partly on research into the textile industry that was conducted by Irene Nørlund during 1985-1988 and 1994, 1996, and 1997. For China, field research was undertaken from 1994 to 1997 by Anita Chan. Both authors have interviewed an array of Vietnamese and Chinese government, Party and trade union officials, managers and workers. In Australia we are

When the collective ethos was dominant in Vietnam and China, the trade unions' role as transmission belts was not much called into question or challenged by the workers.[1] After all, socialist enterprises belonged to the state, were paternalistic providers, and functioned as residential communities. The trade unions' primary task was to act on behalf of the enterprise in distributing goods to workers, organizing social activities for the community, allocating workers' housing, and looking after other material needs. Their other major task was to mobilize workers to fulfil and over-fulfil production quotas set by the command economy, by periodically whipping up frenzied production campaigns. In Vietnam, the unions had the additional task of supporting the war effort.

Yet another function assigned to the trade union cadres was to serve as ombudsmen and counsellors for employees' work-related and personal family problems. They provided the human touch for bureaucratic institutions. Trade union cadres helped to arrange hospital visits and funerals, facilitated potential marriages, mediated marriage breakdowns, distributed relief funds, and so on. In Vietnam, during the war the trade unions also helped to evacuate the young and old from the war zones[2] and to arrange family visits to the rear.[3] During a time of protracted war, and in a society where people ordinarily live on the margin, this human face of the Party-state as represented by the unions was appreciated by the workers more than most critics of Communist trade unions recognize. Parallels can be found in today's post-communist Russia. With Russian workers' livelihoods threatened, the former official trade union has successfully withstood competition from newly formed unions. Among other reasons, the former official unions have the experience and organizational capacity to help provide a "safety net": "In conditions of acute economic

indebted to a number of trade unionists who shared their observations, contacts and experience in Vietnam. In Denmark thanks are due to the General Worker's Union (SID), which generously arranged for us to interview twenty Vietnamese trade union representatives visiting Denmark in 1995. The authors are also grateful to Jiang Kelin, for his documentary research assistance in poring through Chinese-language and Vietnamese English-language newspapers; the workshop participants and Gerard Greenfield for their comments; and Ben Kerkvliet and Jonathan Unger for their editing. Funding for the field research came from the Australian Research Council and the Nordic Institute for Asian Studies/Council for Development Research, Denmark.

[1]   In the first four decades of Party rule, Chinese workers expressed mass dissatisfaction several times, but at none of these times did they turn to the union for assistance. During the Maoist period the contention was largely over political control rather than control over the labour process. In Vietnam during these same decades, the workers did not challenge the state in the same fashion because the nation's attention was focused on the war.

[2]   Thanks to Melinda Tria Kerkvliet for providing us with this information.

[3]   This information was obtained from a group interview we conducted with twenty trade union officials who were undergoing training in Denmark with the General Worker's Union in June 1995 (henceforth referred to as the 1995 Denmark interview).

crisis, these functions of the traditional unions were valued more and more highly".[4]

All in all, while the functions of the Chinese and Vietnamese trade unions were very similar in the pre-reform period, there were also differences. Before the reform period the ACFTU was weaker than its Vietnamese counterpart *vis-à-vis* their respective Party-states. In China, two attempts by the ACFTU to wrest greater freedom from Party domination failed in 1956-57 and in 1966, inviting harsh retaliation from the Party: beginning in the early 1970s the Chinese Communist Party went so far as to disband the ACFTU.[5] In the early 1980s the Party revived the ACFTU but granted it only limited leeway. At every level of the bureaucratic hierarchy, the trade unions were placed under the grip of the corresponding Party hierarchy.

The situation in Vietnam was quite different, in part because the unions at one time came under two governmental systems. In the north, in spite of the strict discipline demanded of north Vietnamese society during the war, Vietnam's Communist Party was not able to impose an authoritarian bureaucratic structure to the same degree as in China. As Gabriel Kolko has written, "All wars more or less transcend the control of those leading them ... The logic of mass movement inevitably conflicts with all elitist, self-perpetuating parties".[6] Because of the war, the union had stronger ties with its constituency. In Vietnamese workplaces solidarity against a real common national enemy dwarfed management-worker differences. In contrast, China under Mao's rule was short of real enemies, and the authorities had to create "class enemies" and to launch periodical "struggle campaigns". The Chinese workplace was infused with mistrust and animosity which exploded into internecine violence in the mid-1960s during the Cultural Revolution, and degenerated into cynicism and lethargy in the 1970s.[7]

---

4   Boris Kagarlitsky and Renfrey Clarke, "Russia's Trade Union Movement: Bureaucrats and Militants in the Epoch of Capitalist Restoration", *Links*, no.1, April-June 1994, pp.19-28. According to SID labour organizer Sten Pedersen, who has carried out training courses for many Eastern European unions since the collapse of communism in their countries, the former official unions in all these post-Communist countries have outlasted the new alternative unions. Even in Poland the former official union continues to have a much larger membership than Solidarity.

5   Elizabeth Perry, "Labor's Battle for Political Space: The Role of Worker Associations in Contemporary China", in Deborah Davis, Richard Kraus, Barry Naughton and Elizabeth Perry (eds), *Urban Space in Contemporary China: The Potential for Autonomy and Community in Post-Mao China* (Cambridge: University of Cambridge Press, 1995), pp.302-25. Also see Anita Chan, "Revolution or Corporatism? Workers and Trade Unions in Post-Mao China", *Australian Journal of Chinese Affairs*, no.29 (January 1993), pp.31-5.

6   Gabriel Kolko, "Vietnam Since 1975: Winning a War and Losing the Peace", *Journal of Contemporary Asia*, vol.25, no.1 (1995), pp.4, 6.

7   Andrew Walder, *Communist Neo-Traditionalism: Work and Authority in Chinese Industry* (Berkeley: University of California Press, 1986), ch.6.

In southern Vietnam the unions were not part of the state apparatus. Prior to 1975 there was no socialist ethos demanding that workers subjugate their interests to the state. Instead, southern Vietnamese workers and unions sometimes took a confrontational stance against capital and the Saigon government.[8] Strikes were frequent, and labour activists and trade unionists were beaten up, killed or thrown into jail. This militant historical past is not yet a distant memory.

Industrial Reforms and Their Consequences

The economic reforms in both countries have enormously affected the conditions of workers. Given the logic of marketization, it is natural that the shifts in working conditions in China and Vietnam should have charted somewhat similar routes.[9]

In both countries the main macro-economic and enterprise reform programs, in addition to marketization, involve entry into the global economy; raising productivity in the state sector by reforming management practices; forcing enterprises to be responsible for their own gains and losses; reducing excess labour in the state-owned enterprises (SOEs); gradually instituting a contract system in place of life-time employment; introduction of a labour market; reductions in state workers' benefits; a widening of the wage gap; and separation of the Party from administration by vesting the enterprise manager with greater power. On the shopfloor, work discipline has been tightened, and welfare socialism can no longer be taken for granted by the workers.

In China, a process of shrinking the core industrial state-sector workforce has been under way for more than ten years. But the Chinese government could only implement this intermittently in the 1980s for fear of "social instability". During the 1989 Tiananmen protest movement, the workers' message to the government was clear: they should not be sacrificed to the economic reforms.[10] Nevertheless, in the 1990s the government renewed its attempt to rid state enterprises of excess workers. The number of money-losing state enterprises has continued to climb (from about 30 per cent in the 1980s to about 40 per cent by 1995 and 75 per cent in 1996),[11] strengthening

---

8   See Trinh Quang Quy, *The Labour Movement in Vietnam* (publisher unknown, 1970), pp.41, 117-18. We are grateful to Melinda Tria Kerkvliet for drawing our attention to this book.

9   See, for example, David Wurfel, "Doi Moi in Comparative Perspective", in William S. Turley and Mark Selden (eds), *Reinventing Vietnamese Socialism: Doi Moi in Comparative Perspective* (Boulder: Westview Press, 1993), p.47.

10 Andrew G. Walder and Gong Xiaoxia, "Workers in the Tiananmen Protests: The Politics of the Beijing Workers' Autonomous Federation", *Australian Journal of Chinese Affairs*, no.29 (June 1993), pp.1-29.

11 *Japan Economic Newswire*, 27 October 1994; *Zhongguo tongji* [China's statistics], no.1, 1996, p.27; and Reuters, Beijing, 23 June 1997.

the government's determination to press for more bankruptcies;[12] a privatization program was officially announced at the Fifteenth Party Congress in 1997. Since about 20 per cent of the country's 700 million economically active population were employed in state enterprises and urban collectives,[13] any crisis of unemployment affecting these workplaces could potentially have grave political repercussions.

Yet layoffs have increased rapidly. In the 1980s the expanding economy was able to absorb surplus labour from the state sector. But by 1995 the numbers of officially registered unemployed reached 5 million, and the numbers of workers instructed to stay at home on partial or no pay at all had reached 20 million. All told, this amounted to about 18 per cent of the 109 million state-sector employees (out of a total of 148 million urban employees).[14] By 1997 the official unemployed exceeded 10 per cent.[15] In addition, the pensions of 30 million urban retirees were not keeping up with inflation, and some were not receiving any of their pensions at all.[16] The dissatisfied state-enterprise workers and retirees worry the political leadership as potential sources of social instability. Still, without sufficient funds in the state coffer to prop up loss-making state enterprises, the Party declared at the Fifteenth Party Congress in October 1997 that the reforms would be "deepened": that is, far greater numbers of state-enterprise workers will be thrown out of work.

Urban unemployment in Vietnam is even more severe than in China. The Vietnamese government was at first reluctant to restructure the state sector, but when it did so it went about it with determination. Since 1990, half of the state enterprises have been closed down or merged into larger units. The number of state workers declined from 1.4 million in 1985 to just under 1 million in 1992, when it bottomed out.[17] The impact on the state workers who lost their posts was severe. But the overall impact on the country's social fabric has not been as noticeable as in China, given that Vietnam's state industrial sector only employed about 5 per cent of the country's entire labour

---

12   *Japan Economic Newswire*, 27 October 1994.

13   *Zhongguo laodong bao* [China labour news], 13 June 1996.

14   *Gongren ribao* [Workers' daily], 30 November 1995.

15   *Nanfang gongbao* [Southern workers' news], 29 April 1997.

16   *Gongren ribao*, 7 March 1996.

17   Tran Hoang Kim, *Economy of Vietnam: Review and Statistics* (Hanoi: Statistical Publishing House, 1994), p.146. The number for 1992 is a little higher (695,000). See *Statistical Yearbook of Labour, Invalids and Social Affairs 1993* (Hanoi: National Political Publishing House, 1994), p.45. Also see Dang Duc Dam, *Vietnam's Economy 1886-95* (Hanoi: Gioi Publishers, 1995). In Vietnamese statistics the industrial labour force is not divided into urban and rural. However, unlike China, very few of the state enterprises are located outside the cities.

force in 1985.[18] State workers made up 38 per cent of the industrial labour force in 1985, and this declined to 22 per cent in 1994, reflecting the increasing importance of the non-state sector. The figures from 1996 are not entirely comparable with the earlier years. The first large-scale labour market survey indicated that state labour constituted 28 per cent of the industrial labour force, which probably overstated the proportion compared to earlier data.[19]

The problem of urban unemployment was exacerbated by the demobilization of 400,000 to 500,000 soldiers in Vietnam following the Paris agreement on Cambodia, and by the sudden repatriation of half a million workers from post-Communist Eastern Europe in the early 1990s. All told, urban unemployment in Vietnam by 1993 stood at about 10-15 per cent.[20] Thereafter, however, employment started to expand along with the economy. As a consequence, unemployment by 1996 was officially down to 7 per cent of the labour force.[21]

The Vietnamese economy has not been expanding as rapidly as China's, however. In the 1980s it was still recovering from the war, made all the harder by the American-led foreign trade embargo. Vietnam was afflicted by three years of high inflation in 1986-88, and again from mid-1990 to mid-1992.

---

[18]   Only 11-12 per cent of Vietnam's workforce was employed in the industrial sector, of which 30 per cent worked in the central state sector as of 1985. See Melanie Beresford, "The North Vietnamese State-Owned Industrial Sector: Continuity and Change", *The Journal of Communist Studies and Transition Politics*, vol.11, no.1 (March 1995) p.56. By 1993 this had dropped to a little over 10 per cent of the manufacturing labour force. See *Statistical Yearbook of Labour, 1993*, p.45. Also see Irene Nørlund, "The Labour Market in Vietnam: Between State Incorporation and Autonomy", in J. D. Schmidt, Niels Fold and Jacques Hersh (eds), *Social Change in Southeast Asia* (Harlow: Addison Wesley Longman, 1998), pp.155-82.

[19]   *Status of Labour — Employment in Vietnam* (Hanoi: Ministry of Labour, Invalids and Social Affairs, Statistical Publishing House, 1997), Table C3.3.0.01.

[20]   The figure can only be approximate. The 1993 data from the Ministry of Labour showed total unemployment of 8.3 million. In China, the registered unemployment rate is low, only about 3 per cent, but the number of workers who are not paid full wages or have to stay home is large, reaching 18 per cent of SOE workers. The situation in Vietnam is quite similar. Many workers continue to stay in the state enterprises even though they are employed only part-time or are without work. So long as they are not formally laid off they are counted as employed. In some cities this figure is as high as 20 per cent. In recent years, though, there has been a falling unemployment rate. See *Statistical Yearbook, 1995* (Hanoi: General Statistical Office, 1996), p.39; *Vietnam Economic Commentary and Analysis*, no.6, 1994, p.29.

[21]   *Vietnamese News*, 14 May 1996, p.4. According to the Labour Survey of 1996, unemployment decreased considerably from 1994 to 1996, down to 4 per cent. Unemployment declined especially in the newly expanding cities and special economic zones, whereas it increased in other urban areas. *Status of Labour — Employment in Vietnam*, pp.66-7.

Also in the early 1990s, Vietnam simultaneously experienced an economic recession due to the dissolution of the Soviet-bloc Comecon, and the flooding of Vietnam's market with cheaper and better products, either imported or smuggled, from neighbouring countries, especially China.[22] As one important consequence, the textile industry, which employs the second largest number of workers, registered an absolute decline in output, from 115 million pieces in 1989 to 85 million pieces in 1993.[23] Fortunately, once the quality of local products improved with the injection of foreign capital, production has been on the upturn from 1994, with garments becoming a leading export item by 1996.

Problems in China's labour-intensive industries are of a different nature. The challenge facing shoe factories, for example, is not competition from foreign products, but domestic over-production.[24] In the past decade, the number of shoe factories of all types and sizes has proliferated.[25] Factories undercut each other, driving down prices across the entire industry. In these kinds of labour-intensive industries, the easiest way to reduce production costs is to depress wages and/or downsize the labour force. China's state-run enterprises have lost out to the non-state sector in this cut-throat competition because the government puts a cap on the percentage of workers who can be laid off.[26] In addition, being longer-established factories, the state-owned firms tend to be burdened by a large number of retirees who must be supported out of the present enterprise budget. Despite grave financial difficulties, these firms are supposed to pay these pensions, honour medical bills, and pay workers ¥8 (US$1) to stay home when production lines are idle.[27] The state-enterprise workers, especially those in labour-intensive

---

[22] *Vietnamese Investment Review*, 24-30 October 1994, p.18.

[23] Irene Nørlund, "Vietnamese Industry in Transition: Changes in the Textile Sector", in Irene Nørlund, Carolyn L. Gates and Vu Ca Dam (eds), *Vietnam in a Changing World* (Richmond: Curzon Press, 1995), p.138.

[24] This information was gained from six weeks of visits to footwear factories in Shanghai and Beijing in 1995 and 1996. In addition, a series of interviews was conducted with a variety of government officials and trade union cadres whose work is related to the leather goods industry.

[25] No government department has figures on the exact number of footwear factories in the country. Keen competition was felt by almost all of the factories visited. Even those which had been making steady yearly profits up till 1993 saw profits decline. In Vietnam, because of the competition from foreign goods, there is also a sense of "over-production". See Nørlund, "Vietnamese Industry in Transition", p.143.

[26] Information from 1995 fieldwork in Beijing.

[27] More often than not, in the older state enterprises the ratio of retirees to employees can be as high as 1:2. Since under the Chinese system the work unit itself has to support the entire range of welfare of its own staff and workers, this has become a heavy burden on financially troubled firms. The government's recent policy is to replace this system with an entirely new one whereby all welfare services are centralized at the city level, thus

industries, now work mostly at piece-rates and produce as fast as non-state workers,[28] but their firms nevertheless remain in the red due to their social-welfare functions. Gradually, the enterprises are ridding themselves of their older workers and hiring migrants from the countryside, a practice which undermines state workers' employment opportunities and social security.[29]

Not surprisingly, the number of labour conflicts in the state enterprises has been increasing at a rapid rate. These have included large collective protest actions involving up to 200,000 workers. Many of these labour disturbances have occurred in China's central heartland and the north-eastern heavy industrial regions hardest hit by the reforms.[30] One example was the series of large-scale workers' protests which broke out in various cities in Sichuan in 1997.[31] These workers are well organized and aware of their rights. At times their actions are encouraged and in rare cases even led by local trade-union officials. The protests are usually over delinquent pay, involuntary layoffs, enforced early retirement, erosion of benefits, and so on.[32] With more state firms in the red and the government determined to permit bankruptcy, more protests can be expected.

In contrast, the closure of half of the Vietnamese state enterprises in the early 1990s produced no major upheavals among industrial workers. Whatever conflicts occurred in state firms were usually resolved after negotiations between management and labour. A hundred strikes were reported from 1989 to mid-1994,[33] but most of these occurred in the south in 1992-93 in foreign-funded enterprises that do not possess unions.[34] In recent years, foreign sources indicate that 48 strikes took place in 1995; 73 or 90 in 1996 and 36

---

evening out welfare responsibilities among all enterprises. But state enterprises which are in the red lack the funds to participate in the new program, and thus remain trapped in a vicious cycle.

[28] In the textile industry, for instance, state-sector workers have been made to work at very fast rates for long hours. See Zhao Minghua and Theo Nichols, "Management Control of Labour in State-Owned Enterprises: Cases from the Textile Industry", *The China Journal*, no.36 (July 1996), pp.1-21.

[29] Dorothy Solinger, "The Chinese Work Unit and Transient Labor in the Transition from Socialism", *Modern China*, vol.21, no.2 (April 1995), pp.155-85. Our field research in Shanghai in 1995 also indicated that this is an increasing trend.

[30] *China Labour Bulletin* [Hong Kong], no.3, May 1994, pp.8-9.

[31] *Globe and Mail* [Canada], 18 July 1997; *China Labour Bulletin*, no.37, July/August 1997, pp.13-14.

[32] Anita Chan, "The Emerging Patterns of Industrial Relations in China and the Rise of Two New Labour Movements", *China Information*, vol.IX, no.4 (Spring 1995), p.58.

[33] Institute of Labour Science and Social Affairs of the Ministry of Labour, July 1994.

[34] *Vietnamese Investment Review*, 22-29 November 1993; 70 strikes were recorded in 1992-93. Also see "Vietnam Labour Law Fails to Halt Strikes" (Hanoi: Agence France Presse, 9 July 1995); and *Vietnamese Trade Union*, no.3, 1995, pp.27-8.

during the first eight months of 1997. Seventy per cent of the strikes took place in foreign-funded enterprises.[35]

In both countries, in fact, there have been more labour disturbances in factories operated by Taiwanese, Korean and Hong Kong investors than in the state sector. One reason is that Chinese and Vietnamese workers are experiencing very similar work regimes on the shopfloor in these foreign-funded firms. Their managements tend not to abide by safety regulations, and they pay workers few or none of the benefits stipulated by law. They hire and lay off workers as the situation demands, and shut down production lines and send workers home without any pay. They demand exhaustingly long working hours, overtime work without overtime rates and sometimes without any pay at all, and deduct wages as a penalty for violating workplace regulations.[36] They provide poor and dangerous working conditions, no medical insurance or unemployment benefits, and at times subject workers to verbal and physical abuse.[37] Some of the worst factories have even recruited child labour.

According to both Vietnamese and Chinese trade union officials, the most abusive foreign bosses are the Koreans, next worst are the Taiwanese, and then the Hong Kong Chinese.[38] The latter two groups are the major investors in both countries.[39] The harsh work regimes in many of these Asian firms have

---

35   Communication from the Committee for the Defence of Workers' Rights in Vietnam, France and Associated Press, Hanoi, 25 September 1997, referring to a union inspection report in Vietnam.

36   According to a survey carried out by the Guangdong Provincial General Trade Union in 1994, 34.5 per cent of the workers interviewed said there was no extra pay for overtime work; and 32 per cent were paid below the minimum wage (*Yuegang xinxi shibao* [Guangdong-Hong Kong information newspaper], 2 April 1994). A survey in Vietnam revealed that 15 per cent of foreign-funded enterprises paid employees less than the official minimum wage of US$35 per month set for Hanoi and Ho Chi Minh City (*Vietnam Investment Review*, 9-15 January 1995, p.25).

37   For example, for violations of labour laws by Taiwanese and Korean-owned factories that make Nike shoes, see *Lao dong* [Labour], 19 November 1997; for violations by such factories in China, see the Asia Monitor Research Centre report, "Conditions of Workers in the Shoe Industry in China", November 1995. This does not apply in China and Vietnam to some of the large capital-intensive, high-tech enterprises that are owned by Western firms, which operate on a management philosophy that is softer on workers. See Anita Chan, "The Emerging Patterns", esp. pp.45-8.

38   The information on China comes from interviews in 1994 at Beijing's ACFTU headquarters; information on Vietnam came from the Denmark interviews of 1995. Talks with trade unionists from Indonesia and with Australian business consultants lend support to this observation, as does a report in the *Far Eastern Economic Review*, 22 August 1996, p.63.

39   Taiwanese capital began to flow into Vietnam earlier than from other countries. Taiwan was the major investor in Vietnam until 1997, when Singapore became the largest, followed by Taiwan, Hong Kong, Japan and South Korea. The largest investor in the mainland of China is Hong Kong, followed by Taiwan.

led to an increase in disturbances and strikes and have instigated an adversarial pattern of industrial relations. In China, 250,000 strikes were recorded from 1988 to 1994, and most of these took place in such Asian-invested firms. The number of "labour conflicts", a broader category that includes incidents that stop short of strikes, is climbing apace. In 1995 there were some 210,000 officially recorded cases, a 54 per cent leap over 1994, which was again a 51 per cent increase over 1993.[40]

In the mid-1990s, labour disturbances in China and Vietnam began heading in different directions. In China, strikes became not only more frequent but also more confrontational. China's official media has admitted that "the intense conflicts between bosses and workers in foreign ventures that have occurred in recent years are unprecedented, rarely having occurred in state-owned enterprises";[41] and "The problem now is that as soon as there is an incident, the public security police, for their own reasons, send policemen to intervene in labour disputes, thus aggravating industrial relations".[42] Intimidation breeds violence. In one highly publicized case, more than 500 workers besieged and beat up several Taiwanese managers of a concrete factory.[43] In Vietnam this kind of violence and counter-violence has not yet been reported.[44]

---

[40]   *Gongren ribao*, 21 May 1996, p.5.

[41]   *Beijing Review*, vol.38, no.20 (15-21 May 1995), p.18. The reporting on labour disturbances in foreign-funded firms has become more forthright. In the 1980s the Party specifically banned such news from the press (Information from a Shanghai researcher on labour issues).

[42]   *Gongren ribao*, 11 November 1993. Two cases were cited in this article. In one, a manager in a garment factory hired a police officer to be deputy manager with the express purpose of controlling the workers. When the workers could no longer stand the protracted hours of overtime work, several of them launched a protest. The policeman-turned-manager first fired the "trouble-makers", then got his colleagues in the police station to arrest them. They were released after the intervention of the local union. Another case involved a foreign manager who, just before firing a batch of workers, called in the police. As each of the names of the unfortunate workers was called, they were "accompanied" to the gate by a policeman. In another case, when some workers started complaining after being owed wages for 7-8 months, police were sent into the dormitory to beat up the workers' representatives (*Zhuhai laodong bao* [Zhuhai labour news], 24 October 1994). The use of police and private security guards with connections to the police is very prevalent in south China (based on field findings in January 1996). One Taiwanese joint-venture firm in south China employed 100 security guards for only 2,700 workers (*Gongren ribao*, 17 April 1996, p.7).

[43]   *Zhongyang ribao* [Central daily news, Taiwan], 31 March 1995. This case was widely publicized in the Taiwan press as a negative example of how uncontrollably wild PRC workers could become. What is unusual about this incident is that the rebellion was led by the trade union chair of the enterprise. An English translation of this report appears in *Chinese Sociology and Anthropology*, vol.30, no.4 (Summer 1998), pp.83-6.

[44]   *Vietnam: Economic Commentary and Analysis: A Bi-annual Appraisal of the Vietnamese*

New Roles for the Trade Unions

The Chinese authorities, concerned to maintain social stability, early in the reform period foresaw a necessity to give the trade unions more autonomy so that they could serve as a bottom-up transmission belt, especially in foreign-funded enterprises. When Deng Xiaoping came to power in the late 1970s, aware of the implications of the Solidarity movement in Poland, he revived the ACFTU and allowed limited union reforms.[45] This predated the emergence of any domestic capitalism or a foreign-funded sector. The purpose was to provide a pressure valve to alleviate tensions between managers and workers, especially since the managers were soon to be granted more autonomy. To counter-balance this, the Chinese government raised the *nomenklatura* rank of the enterprise-level trade union chair to a level equivalent to a deputy manager.[46] A few years later multi-candidate elections for trade union chair were introduced,[47] though these elections were not, in practice, democratic. These tinkering-at-the-edges reforms have not helped much, however, to sensitize trade union cadres to workers' interests, so long as the union chair is still a member of the *nomenklatura* and is responsible to the Party secretary or manager in each enterprise.

Nonetheless, as the Party-state decentralized authority and power, the ACFTU at all levels continued to press throughout the 1980s for a bigger share of power. In particular, by the mid-1980s, as state workers' job security and welfare provisions experienced initial cutbacks and the first labour disputes erupted in the foreign-funded sector, the national union officialdom felt challenged to react. Taking advantage of the politically liberal period of 1988 and early 1989, the ACFTU passed a document that dropped the hitherto ubiquitous statement about "the union being under the leadership of the Party". Instead, the primary function of the ACFTU was redefined as the "defence of staff, workers' and the masses' legal interests and democratic rights". If realized, this would have meant a more independent ACFTU.[48]

Economy, no.6 (April 1995), p.31. This is confirmed by Nørlund's meetings with Vietnamese trade unionists from both grassroots and leadership levels in 1994 and 1996. Similarly, an Australian trade unionist who visited Vietnam was informed that the police have not been used during labour disputes.

45   On this, see Jeanne Wilson, "The Polish Lesson: China and Poland 1980-1990", *Studies in Comparative Communism*, no.3/4 (Autumn/Winter 1990), pp.259-80.

46   This decision was issued in the 1985 CCP Central Committee Document no.50.

47   This reform was formalized in 1993 in the trade union constitution. *Zhongguo gonghui di shierci chuanguo daibiao dahui wenjian huibian* [Collection of documents of the Chinese Trade Union's 12th congress] (Beijing: Gongren Chubanshe [Workers' Press], 1993), p.44.

48   This document, entitled "Fundamental Ideas on Union Reform", was passed by the ACFTU 6th plenary session of the 10th standing committee on 9 October 1988. (*Zhongguo gonghui zhongyao wenjian xuanbian* [Selections from important Chinese trade union documents] (Beijing: Jixie Gongye Chubanshe [Machine Industry

Internal debates heard arguments that the ACFTU should share power with the government.[49] This assertiveness was soon crushed in the government's backlash against the Tiananmen protest movement of 1989. A month after the June Beijing massacre, Jiang Zemin, the new head of the Communist Party, delivered a speech to the ACFTU that demanded union compliance with Party instructions. He pointedly declared that the union's number one mission was to "carry out its work under Party leadership".[50] The ACFTU quickly relapsed into its former docility.

Efforts to loosen the Vietnamese Party's grip over unions were more successful. The Sixth Trade Union Congress in 1988 was a watershed in this respect. The Congress declared that the objective was to build strong unions with rights to self-governance. The Congress adopted the slogan "renewal, openness and democracy"; and for the first time at a trade union congress, delegates could air spontaneous opinions, rather than simply offer formalistic statements that were orchestrated from above. Nguyen Van Linh, the Secretary General of the Party, announced at the congress that leading trade-union cadres need not be Party members, and urged union cadres to voice their ideas independent of the Party and management (though he cautioned that this did not mean the union was to be completely free from Party control).[51]

Labour Laws and Union Constitutions

To adjust to the rapidly changing labour situation, both countries recognized the necessity to draw up new legislation, and during the drafting process different interests within the government contended to influence the new legal documents' contents.[52] In China the Trade Union Law was passed in 1992;[53] a

---

Publishers], 1990), pp.100-1).

[49]   This information comes from a former trade-union participant of the debate.

[50]   Zhongguo Gongyun Xueyuan [China Labour Movement College] (ed.), *Xin shiqi gonghui gongzuo zhongyao wenjian xuanbian* [Selections of important union documents in the new era], restricted to internal circulation, 1993, pp.271-8.

[51]   "The Sixth Congress of the Vietnamese Trade Unions", *Vietnam Courier*, no.1, 1989, pp.5-7. Nguyen Van Linh's speech is carried in US Foreign Broadcast Information Service, *Daily Report: East Asia*, [hereafter FBIS-EAS], no.203, 1988, pp.61-5. At the Congress, the VFTU officially changed its name to the Vietnam General Confederation of Labour (VGCL), implying a policy of broadening and decentralizing trade union power. Due to the emergence of a "multi-sector economy", the union also decided that it would create separate union branches for the state, collective and private sectors.

[52]   For an excellent account of the passage of Chinese bills, see Murray Scot Tanner, "How a Bill Becomes a Law in China: Stages and Processes in Lawmaking", *The China Quarterly*, no.141 (March 1995), pp.39-64. Also see Kevin O'Brien, "Chinese People's Congresses and Legislative Embeddedness", *Comparative Political Studies*, vol.27, no.1 (1994), pp.80-107.

[53]   *Renmin ribao* [People's daily], 9 April 1992.

new ACFTU Constitution was drawn up in 1993;[54] and a Labour Law was adopted in July 1994.[55] In Vietnam the corresponding years for these developments were 1990, 1993 and 1994. But the parallel sequencing of legislative activities took place independently of each other. The coincidence reflected the emergence of very similar labour issues; it was not that the two countries were necessarily learning from or influencing each other.

The Vietnamese trade union law opens by reiterating, in stereotypical language, that the union is an organization under the leadership of the Party.[56] The Chinese Trade Union Law in contrast has dropped this socialist phraseology.[57] But the substantive details of the law grant Vietnam's VGCL considerably more autonomy from the Party than the ACFTU has ever been permitted. Although both laws try to maintain a state-corporatist structure, it is the Chinese law which ensures its perpetuation in the state-owned firms. Four major differences can be identified.

First, unlike in China, the Vietnamese unions' role is not to include participation in management or carrying out managerial functions. This stipulation was drawn up in accordance with the wishes of the majority of the VGCL delegates and had also been heatedly debated in the 1989 National Assembly.[58] Both countries' unions have the right to draw up collective agreements with management on behalf of the workers, but the more clear-cut division between management and labour in Vietnam is much more likely to lead to an adversarial kind of industrial relations of a type common in the West.

Second, in Vietnam, when a new trade union branch is established it only needs to "inform" the government of its existence (Article 1.2), whereas in China the establishment of a new union branch needs to be "approved" by a higher level union (Article 13). This decentralized right to organize new branches at enterprises in Vietnam implies the possibility that more autonomous trade union branches may emerge.

A third major difference is that Vietnamese trade unions have the right to join international trade union organizations (Article 1.3), to accept donations

---

54   "Constitution of the Trade Unions of the People's Republic of China", in *The Twelfth National Congress of Chinese Trade Unions* (Beijing, 1993), pp.58-78.

55   *Order of the President of the People's Republic of China*, no.28, July 1994 (in English).

56   Article 1 in the Law on the Trade Unions, adopted at the General Assembly of the Socialist Republic of Vietnam, 30 June 1990, in *Hien Phap nuoc Cong hoa Xa hoi Chu nghia Viet Nam 1992* [The Constitution of the Socialist Republic of Vietnam 1992] (in English and Vietnamese). The implication is that the Party will protect the workers, and therefore the role of the unions is to educate workers. See also Gareth Porter, *Vietnam: The Politics of Bureaucratic Socialism* (Ithaca: Cornell University Press, 1993), p.92.

57   *Renmin ribao*, 9 April 1992, p.3.

58   For example, most of the 18 deputies did not endorse the idea that the unions should be responsible for social security management. See FBIS-EAS, no.110, 2 January 1990, p.68.

from international organizations and foreign trade unions (Article 16.2.a), and to keep these as union assets (Article 17). The Chinese law is silent on such rights, although in practice, Chinese trade unions are forbidden by the Party to join international organizations. Any contact with foreign unions can only be of an informal and formalistic nature.

Fourth is an important difference in union finances. In Vietnam a union official's salary is paid out of union funds (Article 15.3), and the source of union finances includes membership fees as well as allocations from state revenue (Article 16.2.a.b.). This means that although the umbilical cord between the VGCL and the state has not been completely severed, at least some workplace union officials are not on the management payroll, as they generally used to be.[59] The Chinese law perpetuates the dependence of the enterprise-level union officials on management by stipulating that 2 per cent of the enterprises' payroll (including foreign-funded factories) should be budgeted to the union (Article 36.2).[60]

In sum, both laws have granted a bigger role to their respective trade unions in that unions are to represent workers in labour disputes. But the Vietnamese union is allowed a bigger supervisory role than the Chinese union: the former is empowered to "check on" (*kiem tra*) the implementation of the labour contract, recruitment, dismissal, wages, bonuses, labour protection, social insurance and the like, whereas the Chinese union is to "assist" (*xiezhu*) the management in these functions (Article 26). On balance, the Vietnamese Party is willing to devolve more power to the unions.

In 1993 both national unions passed new constitutions.[61] The Chinese trade union structure remains basically unchanged. There is to be little autonomy at the grassroots level, and all union branches in theory are to be subject to the dual leadership of both the industrial unions and the local trade union federation (Article 10). China has 18 industrial unions, but historically these industrial unions have had few functions, and with decentralization of the economy they have been further weakened. In practice, the enterprise union branches today are controlled in each locality by the officials of the

---

[59]   However, because trade union funds in some Vietnamese state factories have been insufficient to pay the salaries of the workplace union cadres, part of the trade union chairs' salary still derives from the enterprise (field data). A Shanghai General Trade Union delegation's report on its visit to Vietnam also noted that many of the state enterprises' workplace unions continue to be financed by the enterprise. (*Shanghai gongyun* [Shanghai labour movement], no.10, 1995, pp.41-2.

[60]   Notably, in many Taiwanese, Hong Kong and Korean-funded enterprises, managers today either adamantly refuse to pay, or pay only on the condition that they control the appointment of the union chair. This information is based on interviews in 1996 in Shanghai and Shenzhen.

[61]   Vietnam General Federation of Labour, *Constitution of the Vietnamese Trade Unions* (Hanoi, November 1993). For China, see "Constitution of the Trade Unions of the People's Republic of China", pp.58-78.

local union federations which, in turn, are under tight local Party leadership. Much as in the past, the entire ACFTU structure has little space to manoeuvre.

The Vietnamese Trade Union Constitution, in contrast, lays out a new organizational structure that is geared to help lower levels of the trade union organization to gain greater autonomy. The constitution downplays the direct leadership role of the Party.[62] The trade union organizations in local areas will be allowed to set up occupational trade unions (Article 14). This means that in the private sector, workers from different enterprises sharing the same occupation or trade can join an occupational trade union.

Beyond unions at the enterprise level, Vietnam will allow industrial and professional unions. These will be "placed under the *direct guidance* (our italics) of the respective national industrial and professional unions in matters concerning the industry and profession" (Article 20.a), but only "under the *direction* (our italics) of the local confederation of labour in matters related to socio-economic problems". Of greater significance is Article 22.1 which states: "the national industrial and professional unions are organized on the basis of the particular traits of their respective industries and professions and *they are not necessarily arranged in accordance with the administrative organization of the State*" (our emphasis). In other words, at all levels of the VGCL structure, there will be a dual command system: the hitherto existing local unions in the state sector which continue to be tied to the local government and Party and, alongside these, industrial and professional unions linked with grassroots occupational unions in the non-state sector, representing interests that may be different from those of the state and the localities' governments. To ensure the viability of the industrial and professional unions, the VGCL should "entrust" them with a certain initial sum of money and property, and thenceforth they will be financially independent (Article 23.5). Ultimately, though, the VGCL still has the power to "decide on the founding or disbanding of" all the confederations and industrial and professional unions (Article 26). If this new trade union structure is to develop, it will mean that the new occupational, industrial and professional unions will be able to gain a fair degree of autonomy from the local Party and government.

In both countries there were heated debates over the drafts of the new Labour Laws.[63] By the time the laws were passed in 1994 (they both went into

---

62 *Constitution of the Vietnamese Trade Unions*, Introduction, p.4.

63 *Bo Luat Lao dong cua Nuoc Cong hoa Xa hoi Chu nghia Viet Nam*, Labour Code of the Socialist Republic of Vietnam, adopted by the National Assembly of the Socialist Republic of Vietnam, 23 July 1994 (National Political Publishing House, 1994). There is an English version translated and published by Phillips Fox, Melbourne, 1994: *Labour Law of the People's Republic of China*, adopted at the 8th National People's Congress, 5 July 1994 (*Jingji ribao* [Economics daily], 6 July 1994, p.2). Thanks go to David Peetz for giving us an English version that he obtained in 1995 from the Chinese government (publisher and date missing). For a detailed analysis of the Chinese Labour Law, see

effect on January 1, 1995), China's had gone through forty drafts,[64] and Vietnam's thirty.[65] In China, to maintain the facade of consensus, differences in opinion over the drafts occurred behind closed doors.[66] In Vietnam, there was a lot more transparency. Headlines like "National Assembly Debates Labour Code",[67] "Controversial Labour Law goes to Parliament",[68] and "Labour Law Provokes Mixed Response"[69] appeared in the government-sponsored journal *Vietnam Investment Review*.

Arguments over the drafts did break out at the VGCL congress. One faction that wanted to transform the trade unions into genuine workers' organizations argued that managers should not remain members of the trade union. Another faction wanted to maintain Party and state dominance over the union. These and other debates went on for months. A full copy of the draft was published in magazines and discussed at the factory level, although not formally on the shop floor.

Both countries' labour laws represent compromises between the unions and other interests. One of the VGCL's most important victories was that, despite persistent objections from other bureaucracies, trade unions were to be set up in enterprises of all ownership types — and fast, within six months after the law took effect (Article 153). Other controversial issues that the VGCL championed concerned the unionization of foreign-funded enterprises, the maximum number of working hours and working days, minimum wages, maternity leave and overtime pay.[70]

David Peetz, "China's New Labour Law: Forging Collective Bargaining from the Rusting Iron Rice Bowl", in Lo Chi Kin, Suzanne Pepper and Tsui Kai Yuen (eds), *China Reviews 1995* (Hong Kong: The Chinese University Press, 1995), pp.14.1-14.17.

[64] Anita Chan, "The Emerging Patterns", p.54.

[65] Interview with the preparatory commission of the Vietnamese Labour Code by Irene Nørlund in Hanoi, July 1994.

[66] The evidence for heated behind-the-door debates derives from two interviews in Beijing in 1994: one with an ACFTU official and one with an official of the Ministry of Labour, both of whom were involved in committees responsible for drafting the Labour Law. Further evidence comes from a meeting held by Beijing's Labour Movement Institute that same year at which Anita Chan was able to observe the union's internal discussion of the draft. The ACFTU's position was definitely pro-labour.

[67] *Vietnam Investment Review*, 3-9 January 1994.

[68] *Vietnam Investment Review*, 30 May-5 June 1994.

[69] *Vietnam Investment Review*, 2-8 May 1994.

[70] Tu Le, "The Labour Code in the Life of Workers: Interview with Pham Gia Thieu", *Vietnamese Trade Union*, no.4, 1994, p.7; Eva Hansson, *Trade Unions and Doi Moi: The Changing Role of Trade Unions in the Era of Economic Liberalization in Vietnam* (Stockholm: Department of Political Science, University of Stockholm, Fall 1994), p.22; Nguyen Tri Dung, "Minimum Working Age Fixed at 15", *Vietnam Investment Review*, 6-12 June 1994; Lan Thanh, "National Assembly Debates Labour Code", *Vietnam Investment Review*, 3-9 January 1994, p.21.

In China, the ACFTU won a debate over how to define a labourer, an issue of central importance because local governments and the Ministry of Agriculture were attempting to deny the status of "labourers" to over a 100 million former peasants who were employed in rural industries, thereby excluding them from the protection of the Labour Law.[71] The ACFTU also won a compromise on the maximum number of regular working hours per week. The ACFTU advocated 40 hours, while other interests within the People's Congress pressed for 48 hours; the compromise was 44 hours. A second dispute was over the maximum number of hours of overtime per month: the argument focused on 24 hours versus 48 hours, and the compromise was 36 hours. In practice, in the years since then the 44-hour work week and the legal maximum of 36 hours of overtime have been regularly violated in the foreign-funded enterprises, and increasingly so in state enterprises as well, as they have been placed under more intense competition from the challenge of cheap migrant labour employed in the non-state sector. But at least the law is in the books, and in the large core state-run enterprises it is largely observed.

One significant similarity between the two countries' laws is the absence of any reference to the Communist Party. Also, both governments, having recognized the necessity that their trade unions should play a bigger role, accept a tripartite structure for industrial relations: of labour, employers and the state.[72] The trade unions' role of protecting workers' labour rights is affirmed. Both laws grant the unions a right to collective bargaining on behalf of the workers, both laws establish the necessity for management to pay minimum wages and to sign labour contracts with workers, both laws recognize the emergence of labour disputes, and both delineate the role of the unions in labour conciliation and arbitration committees.

On close comparison, the Vietnamese law's 198 articles (China's has 107) are more detailed and, if enforced, would more effectively protect labour rights. For example, the Chinese section on collective agreements contains only three brief articles. Collective agreements are mentioned as an option (the word used is "may" (*keyi*); and any draft contract is to be "submitted to the congress of the staff and workers ... for discussion and adoption" (Article 33), leaving vague what happens when a firm has no such congress. The Vietnamese law's section on collective agreements, in contrast, consists of 11 articles with numerous sub-clauses. For instance, the right of the union to

---

71 Anita Chan, " The Emerging Patterns", p.54.

72 Tu Le, "The Labour Code in the Life of Workers", notes that the ILO had given advice in relation to the formulation of the labour law in Vietnam. Also see *Vietnam: Employment and the New Labour Law* (Canberra: Department of Foreign Affairs and Trade [Australia], Southeast Asia section, Vietnam/Laos section, October 1994), p.3. In China, the ILO office in Beijing has been actively promoting the tripartite concept in China. (This information is based on interviews with the ILO Beijing director in 1994 and on ILO documents on China.)

negotiate collectively on behalf of the workers is guaranteed in Article 46.1: "Each Party shall have the right to request the signing of a collective agreement". "A collective agreement shall only be signed if the negotiated content ... is approved by more than 50 per cent of the members of the labour collective" (Article 25.3); and once signed it "shall be made known to all employees of the enterprise ..." (Article 49.1); "each Party shall have the right to request amendments ..." (Article 50); and representatives "shall be entitled to payment of salary during the time of negotiation ..." (Article 43). The Vietnamese law is precise in specifying that an employer's specific non-compliance is a breach of the law.

In the Vietnamese labour law, numerous articles also specifically prohibit employers from exploiting workers' labour. For example, where disciplinary fines are taken from workers' salaries, it is stipulated that "the aggregate amount deducted must not exceed 30 per cent of the monthly wage"; with regard to workers on probation, the wage of the employee "must be at least 70 per cent of the normal wage for the job" and the trial period should not exceed sixty days ..." (Article 32);[73] the workplace's internal labour regulations "must not be contrary to labour legislation ..." (Article 82.1); and prior to proclaiming any labour regulations, "the employer must consult the executive committee of the trade union of the enterprise" (Article 82.2). None of the above specifics exist in the Chinese law. Yet in China these are precisely the kinds of practices that managers have used to extract from their workforce harder work for less pay.

But the biggest difference between the two laws is that after intense debate,[74] Vietnamese law-makers granted workers a right to strike (Article 7.4, 173). The Chinese labour law, by omission, effectively places the issue of strikes in a state of limbo: neither legalizing nor criminalizing it.

Diverging Labour Regimes

The above comparison of the two countries' laws and constitutions suggests that the Vietnamese Communist Party is more willing to relax its hold on the labour unions than is the Chinese Communist Party. But organizational inertia, the ideological legacies of socialism and the two governments' present eagerness to maintain labour peace and to attract foreign capital make for a large gap between what is written on paper and the reality of what gets implemented. In this section we shall argue that while the situation with regard to labour in both countries continues to share "socialist" characteristics, there are definite signs of divergence as well.

---

[73]   The Chinese law does not have an article on wage deductions, but China's "Provisional Regulation on the Payment of Wages" sets the maximum deductions at 20 per cent of the monthly wage (issued by China's Ministry of Labour, December 1994).

[74]   *Vietnam Investment Review*, 25 April-1 May 1994.

In the state enterprises, a collectivist ethos and corporatist structure sometimes persists, and the similarities continue. The line of demarcation between management and labour in practice remains blurred in the state factories of both countries. In Vietnam, the workplace union has representation on the "council of four interests" (*bo tu* — management, Party, trade union and youth league) in which it seems to be able to play a role in wage determination and distribution of profits and in approving management decisions.[75] Similarly, in Chinese state enterprises, wage policies are supposed to need the approval of the staff and workers' representative council. But since a large number of the so-called representatives are members of the managerial staff, including the managers, a system of checks and balances does not exist.[76] The organizational structure in Chinese state enterprises is heavily weighted against the workers. In contrast, the presence of a trade union does make a difference at a Vietnamese workplace. Our fieldwork findings reveal that the Party branches are more likely to follow recommendations from the trade union.

In the foreign-funded sector, the governments and their trade unions in both China and Vietnam regard the escalation of industrial conflict as a pressing problem. With the promulgation of the labour laws, both perceive that maintaining labour peace in this sector will entail setting up union branches in such firms. But to quickly set up large numbers of workplace unions is an impossible task, especially in China where the number runs into the tens of thousands.

Unionization figures for China's foreign-run firms are, at best, approximations.[77] After the labour law was put in place, to fulfil new enrolment quotas local union officials were dispatched to foreign-run factories to seek approval from management to set up a union branch. More often than not the union chair who emerged came from within the managerial staff and in

---

75   Do Muoi's address to the congress of the VGCL, 3 November 1993 (FBIS-EAS, 12 November 1993). This was confirmed during visits to several enterprises in March 1996 and from September to December 1996.

76   The power relations of these institutions in the state enterprises are delineated in the Enterprise Law that was passed in 1988 (*Renmin ribao*, 16 April 1988, p.2). Our comments on how this relationship is working out in the state firms are based on field observations and conversations with trade union officials in 1995. A similar trend was noted by You Ji during his field research in 1992: see "Dismantling Party/State Controls in China's State Enterprises", PhD dissertation, Australian National University, 1993, pp.40-153.

77   An interview with an ACFTU official in charge of organizational matters in 1994 provided a figure of 20-30 per cent, and the official thought that was an under-estimate. In mid-1994 a report provided a figure of 12 per cent of 170,000 foreign-funded firms as unionized. See *Beijing Review*, vol.37, no.28 (11-17 July 1994), p.7. But in mid-1995, a year later, a report stated that 10 per cent of the 100,000 foreign firms that were in operation (out of 200,000 that were registered) had unions. *Beijing Review*, vol.38, no.20 (15-21 May 1995), p.19.

some cases was none other than the enterprise's manager.[78] The national press held up as a model of success the Shekou Industrial Zone trade union, which had begun its expansion into the foreign-funded sector several years earlier and was the first to attain a unionization rate of 99 per cent. Yet a 1993 Guangdong province trade-union report gives the following figures: of the 250 trade union chairs at the foreign-funded factories in Shekou, 13 per cent simultaneously held top managerial positions; another 44 per cent were factory department managers; and the remaining 47 per cent were lower-level managerial cadres, production line supervisors, or ordinary workers.[79] New unions set up in this manner are at best ineffective; at worst they have become a management tool to control workers. In the Shanghai region these management-controlled union branches have been mushrooming in recent years.[80]

Although the number of foreign-funded enterprises in Vietnam only stood at 1,400 in 1996, unionizing them all within six months was no easy task either. Between mid-1994 and 1996 the unionization rate at such firms increased from 15 per cent[81] to 20 per cent.[82] In the new economic zones such as Tan Thuan near Ho Chi Minh City, as in China, there is also the problem that the newly-established workplace unions are dominated by the management. The zone's deputy manager is simultaneously the head of the zone's trade union. Under such a personnel set-up, the 14 unionized foreign enterprises out of 34 in the zone are likely to be management-dominated.

A notable difference between Vietnam and China lies in the emergence of spontaneous labour groups called "labour associations" and "occupational unions", due to Vietnamese workers' demands in the foreign-funded and other

---

78   This was the scenario in the notorious case of the Zhili Toy Factory which caught fire; 84 workers who had been locked in behind barred windows burned to death. Yi Fu, "Feixushang de pingdiao: Shenzhen '11.19' teda huozai shigu jishi yu fanzi" [Pondering at the ruins: reflections and records of the Shenzhen November 19th fire disaster], *Zhongguo gongren* [Chinese worker], no.5, 1994, pp.4-8; also no.6, 1994, pp.8-11.

79   This is from a document we obtained that was circulated by the Guangdong Province Trade Union Research Department, dated June 1993.

80   Information based on 1995 fieldwork in Shanghai. For details on how new trade unions are being set up, see Anita Chan, "Labor Relations in Foreign-funded Ventures", in Gregory O'Leary (ed.), *Adjusting to Capitalism: Chinese Workers and Their State* (Armonk: M. E. Sharpe, 1987), pp.122-50. There are rare cases in China, though, where a new union is formed through workers' demands. One oft-quoted case is the Japanese-owned Garden Hotel in Shanghai. The new trade union and its chair emerged from a spontaneous industrial dispute, and were recognized by the Shanghai General Federation of Trade Unions. The new chairperson, taking his responsibility seriously, resigned from his middle-ranking managerial staff position so as to devote himself full-time to union work. Reportedly, genuine collective bargaining has been taking place regularly at this hotel. *Shanghai gongyun*, no.11, 1994, pp.19-21.

81   *Vietnam Investment Review*, 18-24 July 1994, p.12.

82   *Far Eastern Economic Review*, 25 January 1996, p.22.

sectors. This is particularly the case in Ho Chi Minh City, which has a history of adversarial industrial relations, as noted earlier in the chapter.[83] Taxi drivers in Ho Chi Minh City, after participating in industrial actions and strikes, set up their own union in 1996.[84] By 1996, 492 labour associations totalling 21,800 members[85] had been organized by cyclo drivers, cooks, market porters and the like in the non-state sector.[86] Thus far even the official trade unions are not clear about the status of these labour associations. The VGCL gives them moral support but no money.

Meanwhile, the 17 Vietnamese occupation-based unions (known as "industrial unions" in both Vietnam and China) have gained more autonomy and their number has increased to 24.[87] One of these new occupation-based unions is the Public Sector Union, which was organized with technical assistance from the Australian Public Sector Union.[88] All told, by 1996 these occupation-based unions had 467,000 members, co-existing with the 2.6 million trade union members.[89] In 1997, to further strengthen the occupation-based unions, the unions of five industries (light industry, engineering and metallurgy, chemical, geology and energy) were amalgamated into one large union, the National Union of Industrial Workers. The vice-president of this new union views it as markedly different from the Chinese system of unions. Having spent eighteen months in Shanghai in the early 1990s, he observes that in Vietnam there will be an increasing balance of strength between the occupation-based unions and the locality unions, whereas in China the occupation-based unions only exist in name.[90] There are also plans to create a new union federation to incorporate all of the small unions and organizations of the non-state sector.[91]

---

[83]   This is based on Irene Nørlund's field observations in 1996.

[84]   *Lao dong* [Labour], no.27/96 (3 March 1996); no.33/96 (17 March 1996). A year later the taxi drivers' union merged with other unions under the Ho Chi Minh City Federation of Labour.

[85]   Information from the VGCL based on March 1996 field research by Nørlund.

[86]   See Gerard Greenfield, "Strikes in Vietnam: Between Discipline and Dignity", *Asian Labour Update*, August-October 1995, pp.25-7. Greenfield also notes the emergence of labour associations, but the figure he cites is higher — 700 labour associations by mid-1993.

[87]   Also see Gareth Porter, *Vietnam: The Politics of Bureaucratic Socialism*, p.92.

[88]   Based on interviews in 1994 with the national secretary and a member of the staff of the Australian Public Sector Union who went to Vietnam for the program. Also see an article written by a representative of the Trades and Labour Council of Western Australia in *Vietnamese Trade Union*, no.1, 1995, pp.19-20.

[89]   Information from the VGCL, March 1996.

[90]   Based on Chan's interview in Hanoi with the vice-president of this new union in January 1998.

[91]   *Vietnamese Trade Union*, no.4, 1997, p.8.

If the occupation-based unions are allowed to build up their strength, they may be in a better position to negotiate with the state and employers' associations on behalf of workers in their particular industry or profession. With time the occupation-based union structure might replace the previous enterprise-based union structure where union strength was fragmented and absorbed by the management, the Party, and government. As yet there are no signs of this happening in China.[92]

In China, by contrast, people working in the same profession have not been allowed to form any kind of organization. For example, when taxi drivers in the southern cities of Shenzhen (1994), Guangzhou (1995) and Zhuhai (1996) took to the streets and agitated to set up their own unions, the local authorities resisted. In Zhuhai several of the strike leaders were arrested and sentenced to prison.[93] When a group of migrant workers wrote a letter to the Guangdong Provincial General Trade Union asking for its support for them to set up a "migrant workers' trade union", the union's reply in the local newspaper was that to set up such a union would contravene the trade union law. It advised that the workers could establish a union within the workplace, but not under the name of a "migrant workers' union".[94] Any workers who dare to set up any organizations that smack of autonomous proto-trade unions are likely to be arrested and charged with sedition.[95] Nor is there any sign within the ACFTU structure of industrial unions' gaining any strength. Overarching general unions based on locality under the rein of local Communist Party committees continue to dominate the structure.

The growing divergence in the development of the unions in the two countries is seen, too, in the VGCL's gradual integration into the international labour movement. Within the VGCL, the Vietnamese industrial unions began to join the international union federations once their right to do so was guaranteed by the trade union law.[96] Once the Party allowed the VGCL more autonomy, moreover, the latter actively sought technical and financial

---

92   This observation was made by the director of the ILO office in Beijing in 1995. Also, in 1995 a high-level official of the Shanghai General Trade Union told us that the time was not yet ripe to discuss strengthening of the industrial unions in China. See Gordon White, Jude Howell and Shang Xiaoyuan, *In Search of Civil Society: Market Reform and Social Change in Contemporary China* (Oxford: Clarendon Press, 1996), p.60.

93   *China Labour Bulletin*, no.2, April 1994, pp.17-19; no.15, June 1995, pp.7-8; no.24, March 1996, p.4.

94   *Nanyang gongbao* [Southeast Asian workers' news], 4 April 1996.

95   In November 1996 two young people were formally prosecuted for sedition after been jailed for two years without trial for organizing a "Migrant Workers' Federation" and "Migrant Workers' Friendship Club" (*China Labour Bulletin*, press release, 12 November 1996).

96   Information based on a telephone conversation in May 1996 with the international officer of the Australian Council of Trade Unions, who thought this a significant development that was unimaginable three years back.

assistance from unions around the world. For example, in the late 1980s the VGCL sought contact with the Australian Council of Trade Unions, which then sent a delegation to Vietnam in 1990. Since then various Australian trade unions have built up ties with the VGCL that go beyond the formalistic "friendship" level. The Vietnamese Communist Party and the VGCL have no qualms either in sending staff to Italy and Denmark for training in what the Chinese would call "bourgeois" trade-union organizational techniques. This kind of receptivity to foreign penetration is unimaginable in China today (even though the government is keen to expand China's penetration by foreign capital and by foreign business-management schools). The ACFTU's isolation has been aggravated by the Tiananmen events of 1989. International union sympathy and financial support has gone in exile to Han Dongfang, who headed the Beijing Autonomous Worker's Federation during the 1989 movement. At the yearly International Labor Organization (ILO) convention in Geneva, ACFTU delegates are put on the defensive when Han Dongfang takes to the floor. The ACFTU is losing out on exposure to international labour issues and assistance, which is precisely what is becoming quite useful in helping to build up the VGCL.

Greater union autonomy from the Vietnamese Communist Party is reflected in Vietnamese media reports that show the VGCL holding different positions from the government: for example, "The VGCL is negotiating to put pressure on the government and on joint ventures with foreign investment"; "Nguyen Van Tu, the VGCL chair, called the current [minimum wage] rate of US$35 unfair";[97] and the *Lao dong* [Labour] newspaper reported that Nguyen Van Tu's demand "could be rebuffed by the government because of its concern for the country's competitiveness".[98] This kind of reporting is tantamount to admitting that the state's interest does not coincide with workers' interests, and that these might even sometimes be in conflict. In China the ACFTU similarly wrestled with the government over workers' wages, arguing for wage indexation at a time of rapid inflation.[99] But these failed attempts were carried out behind the scenes. Deprived of publicity, the ACFTU finds it more difficult to improve its image among workers. It is not without reason that *Lao dong* is today one of Vietnam's most popular newspapers, whereas China's *Workers' Daily* is not sold at newstands because few people are interested in buying it.

---

[97] The VGCL fought over several years to raise the minimum wage from US$35 to US$50 a month in Ho Chi Minh City, but without success. *Vietnam Investment Review*, 23-29 May 1994, p.5. Finally, in 1996, it was increased to US$50 a month.

[98] *Vietnam Investment Review*, 21-27 November 1994, p.6.

[99] This information was based on an interview with an ACFTU official in Beijing in 1992.

Conclusion

In spite of starting from a very similar base, the VGCL has succeeded in gaining somewhat greater autonomy from the Party and government than has its Chinese counterpart. It cannot be said that the VGCL is independent, but at least it has begun to develop a two-way "transmission belt". There are signs that the Vietnamese government is genuinely interested in establishing a more clear-cut demarcation between management and trade unions. The ACFTU, in contrast, remains essentially a belt for one-way top-down traffic.

We have traced the historical reasons that have contributed to this difference. Because of Vietnam's wars, the Vietnamese Communist Party's control was never as far-reaching as the Chinese Party's. Although Vietnam introduced economic reforms later than China, once it had commenced the VGCL was quickly able to manoeuvre for increased space to defend workers' interests. The difference in attitude between the two nations' Parties toward their respective trade unions has been crucial. Field observations indicate that the VCP is more supportive of the trade unions than of foreign management.

Once the VGCL was allowed the space to act more independently, a sequence of events helped to consolidate its position. As seen, the VGCL was able openly to debate the drafts of the trade-union and labour laws, and these contained several important rights: to organize, to strike, to change its internal structure, to join the international labour community, and so on. Of critical importance is permission to initiate new non-government-sponsored labour groups and an organizational structure for the official unions that shifts the initiative increasingly toward sectoral industrial unions rather than unions based on locality. The ongoing public debate between the VGCL and the government over the issue of a minimum wage may well be a prelude to future peak-level collective bargaining. The right to strike is a big step forward, although it is undermined by lengthy, cumbersome strike procedural rules that effectively rendered all of the strikes that broke out in 1995 technically illegal. To gain further space to protect labour rights, Vietnamese workers and the VGCL will have to continue to fight for better pro-labour industrial arbitration and strike procedures and to press for serious enforcement of the labour laws.

Two reports illustrate well our conclusion that the two countries' labour regimes are following diverging paths. In 1996, after public outcry in Vietnam over a spate of media reports about Korean and Taiwanese managers' physical maltreatment of workers, *Lao dong*, the VGCL's official paper, took to task a Taiwanese supervisor who had been known to beat workers. In defence of his violent management style, the supervisor was quoted as saying, "before coming to Vietnam he had spent six years working in China where he claimed it was normal to beat workers".[100] The second report, published in *Shanghai*

---

[100]   Transcript of Australian Broadcast Corporation radio program, "Report from Asia", 31 August 1996. Another example is the VGCL's willingness to work with foreign NGOs to help expose Taiwanese and Korean managers' mistreatment of Vietnamese workers. (Based on a series of email communications in 1996 and 1997 with Thuyen Nguyen of

gongyun [Shanghai labour movement], was written by the head of the International Liaison Department of the Shanghai General Trade Union, after visiting Vietnam in mid-1995. In the article he betrayed unmistakable envy. Look at the circumstances of the Vietnamese trade unions, he wrote. Their law guarantees the right to strike; the VGCL's newspaper, *Lao dong*, can use front-page headlines to criticize the government and individual officials; the Vietnamese Party informs the VGCL of all major policies; the Party supports the VGCL in its work; when the trade union and the government have contradictions, the Party usually sides with the trade union; the government consults with the VGCL prior to adjusting prices; and, above all, trade union chairs at enterprises receive their pay and duty assignments from the upper levels of the trade union (rather than the enterprise). That is why "to a large extent they dare to speak up and work on behalf of the workers".[101]

He and the rest of the Chinese delegation may have been too starry-eyed, and the VGCL may have gone to great lengths to impress them, but as fellow trade unionists from the same Communist stock, their sensitivity to the differences cannot easily be dismissed. At least some Chinese trade unionists look enviously toward the Vietnamese for inspiration.

---

the New-York based Vietnam Labor Watch.)

[101]   Zhao Shunzhang, "Impressions of the Vietnamese Trade Union: Observations by the Shanghai Federation Delegation", *Shanghai gongyun*, no.10, 1995, pp.41-2.

INDEX